I0764129

LEAVES FROM THE DIARY

OF AN

ARMY SURGEON;

OR,

INCIDENTS OF FIELD CAMP, AND HOSPITAL LIFE.

BY THOMAS T. ELLIS, M. D.,

LATE POST-SURGEON AT NEW YORK, AND ACTING MEDICAL DIRECTOR AT WHITEHOUSE, VA.

" Literature itself must languish, where thoughts are not renewed by vigorous and varied action."

MADAME DE STAEL.

NEW YORK:
PUBLISHED BY JOHN BRADBURN,
SUCCESSOR TO M. DOOLADY,)
49 WALKER-STREET.
1863.

Entered according to Act of Congress, in the year 1863,

By JOHN BRADBURN,

In the Clerk's Office of the District Court of the United States for the Southern District of New York.

RENNIE, SHEA & LINDSAY
Stereotypers and Electrotypers,
81, 83 & 85 Centre-street,
New York.

R. CRAIGHEAD, Printer,
83 Centre-Street, N. Y.

22 West
Apri

My dear Doctor
I have receive
note of this morning, and
to learn that you are abo
the result of your observa
recent campaigns of the Arm
I am very much obliged fo
compliment you pay me in
dedicate your work to me.
you that it will afford m
pleasure to have you do so
Hoping to have the satisfacti
the work at an early day
I am very tr
Geo

Thos T Ellis M.D.
New York.

Dedicated, by Permission,

TO

MAJOR-GENERAL GEORGE B. M'CLELLAN,

UNITED STATES ARMY,

AS A TOKEN OF ADMIRATION AND RESPECT FOR HIS SKILL AS A GENERAL,

HIS BRAVERY AS A SOLDIER,

HIS COURTESY AS A SUPERIOR OFFICER,

HIS HONOR AS A GENTLEMAN,

HIS CHRISTIAN SYMPATHY FOR THE WOUNDED SOLDIERS OF THE ARMY OF THE POTOMAC, AND

HIS KINDNESS AS A MAN,

BY THE AUTHOR.

PREFACE.

IN submitting to the reading public the following pages, it is but proper to inform them why the author has written these "Leaves from the Diary of an Army Surgeon," or on what grounds he lays claim to their perusal of this narrative of incidents of the war.

In the autumn of 1861, when recruiting was at its zenith, and the City Hall Park was white with the tents of recruiting officers and its streets resonant with sound of fife and drum, repeated and daily representations were made to the then Governor of the State, by commanding officers of regiments, of the incompetency and total want of knowledge of the military and professional duties, by the surgeons who had been appointed to the various regiments already sent to the seat of war; these complaints became so frequent and well grounded that the appointment of a Post Surgeon, whose duty it would be to organize the medical staff of each regiment, inspect and vaccinate the recruits, attend the sick, and instruct the regimental surgeons, assistant-surgeons, and hospital stewards in their duties, on their being appointed by the Surgeon-general, was decided on, and the writer was selected for that position, by the heads of the departments. In making this selection they were influenced by the facts of his having been in the British army as staff-surgeon and his having served at the Cape of Good Hope during the Kaffir War, where duties of a similar character were performed by him, and where his efficiency and capability earned and received the public commendation of the "Horse Guards," the name given to the heads of the British army, analogous to the war department of the United States. For those services, and for wounds received on the battle-field, he was permitted to retire from the service with an honorable discharge and an annual pension.

During the performance of these duties of Post Surgeon at New York, and of Medical Director in Virginia, entailing on him the care and treatment of the wounded, with the innumerable duties and responsibilities contingent thereon, the incidents related in the following pages came under his notice, and it was his good fortune to be able to soothe the last agonies of many hundred officers and soldiers of the army, and to bear the parting message of affection and dying blessing to many a bereaved parent or sister who would never again, in this world, meet the manly and beloved form sent out in the full enjoyment of health and spirits to fight the battles of his country, and, alas, to become a victim of that civil war, now desolating this once happy and prosperous land.

In the recital of these facts the author has carefully avoided the introduction of all political or sectional discussion, deeming it beyond his province and unsuited to this faithful record of facts, which will be found often ludicrous, sometimes pathetic, but always interesting. And that the reader may so consider them is the wish, and will be (for the labor of relating them) full compensation for the

AUTHOR.

NEW YORK, March, 1863.

INTRODUCTION.

A nation that for many years has enjoyed the blessings of peace, and whose standing army, if it deserved that name, was scarcely sufficient to protect its frontier from intrusion, and keep in check the uncivilized tribes of Indians forming a part, though a troublesome element, of its population, could not be expected to possess the martial spirit, or knowledge of the profession of arms, rendered necessary to grapple with and subdue a rebellion or civil war of that magnitude which sprang into existence in 1861, by the secession of the slave-owning States of the South, the first overt act of which was the bombardment and reduction of Fort Sumter, in April of that year. Nor could it, with justice, be supposed that the machinery found sufficient for the management and direction of a few thousand troops, or the officials having its direction and government in their charge, and who for years had trodden in the beaten path of routine and old fogyism, would prove capable of organizing and equipping the vast army, recruited from an agricultural and commercial population, which was created on the call of the nation's chief magistrate; many of whom were actuated by patriotism, but not a few responded from that necessity or want of employment which the interruptions of trade and total stagnation of commercial enterprise, through the war, had produced; others, influenced by less worthy motives, adopted the life of a soldier more from the facilities it was supposed to afford them to lead a life of idleness or dishonesty, than from the desire to aid their country in its hour of trying darkness, and the government in its often well-meant but imbecile efforts to crush the gigantic struggle that threatened the disruption of this vast and hitherto prosperous republic. Nor was the latter class confined to the rank and file, for many of the commissioned officers were men whose lives had been passed in gambling-houses, or bar-rooms, and who, from the supposed possession of political influence, had obtained from the Governors of their respective States commissions in the volunteer army, on which their ignorance, incompetency, and total want of honesty, has brought disgrace, and to which, in many instances, the defeats sustained by our troops, and their demoralized condition, can be traced. Among the many ingenious comparisons to which life has been subjected, and which, if we do not clearly understand, it is not for want of "reasoning by illustration," none among the resemblances which at moments to a quiet contemplator suggests so clearly the image of a whirligig or roundabout, in which each participator of the pastime, seated on his hobby, is always pursuing some one before him, while he in turn is pursued by some one behind, as the efforts of these pseudo-politico officers, who by every contrivance endeavored to supplant or overreach each other, that the successful one might obtain, as he hoped, a more extensive field for his thieving operations. In contradistinction to this too numerous class, there were many noble and striking exceptions—men who abandoned lucrative positions, and a well-paying occupation or comfortable homes, to rally round the flag of their country, and defend the government from its threatened annihilation and the Union undivided. Nor were these disinterested gentlemen alone found in any one particular State or political party of the Union; for I can recall to mind many from the agricultural West, the manufacturing East, and the commercial Middle States of the Union, who, possessed of wealth, promptly and cheerfully responded to the call, and willingly braved the rigorous and irksome duties of camp life, with the chances of that possible fatal future which has been the lot of so many brave and unselfish heroes, who have become martyrs to a war that has entailed misery on thousands, and that appears as likely to continue to sap the life's blood of the nation as it did before the hundreds of thousands of lives, and the thousands of millions of money which it has cost, had been expended.

The writer's position having brought him in contact with most of the volunteer regiments raised, not alone in the State of New York, but in the Western and New England States, he is led to the conclusions here expressed, by an unlimited intercourse and exchange of sentiment with the officers and men composing those regiments: and he does not hesitate to express the opinion, that the material of the army, both physically and in intelligence, has never been excelled, if it has been equalled, by any nation of the world; and, if the government (at whose desire it was called into existence, as if by magic) had but evinced an ordinary amount of prudence or ability in the command or disposal of this mighty force, it would have, by concert of action, struck the death-blow to the rebellion, and peace, now despaired of, would ere this have been restored to us. For the leaders of this rebellion—which has grown into gigantic dimensions, not so much from its own innate strength, as from the stupid blundering and guilty mismanagement of the Federal forces—would have been forced to lay down their arms and seek an early opportunity to renew their allegiance to this then united, but now disrupted nation.

The preponderating amount of testimony from which these opinions are formed, has been collected from the most intelligent officers of the army, very many of whom fell victims to that criminal ignorance and blind obstinacy which has characterized the conduct of the war, and which has made the military acquirements of the American people a by-word and reproach.

The Southern people, who, by education and their peculiar state of social life, are eminently qualified to command, were not slow to take advantage of these Federal blunders; and the unconstitutional inroads made on their institutions gave color, if not indorsement, to their appeals, describing the war as one of invasion and extermination. Nor have those appeals been made in vain to the able-bodied population of the Southern States, who have responded with alacrity to the supposed defence of their rights, liberties, and firesides.

Every patriotic lover of his country must deplore the course pursued by the President's constitutional advisers in sending forth the firebrands of emancipation proclamations, which have proved barren of all good results, and has but served to inflame and intensify the hatred of the Southern people, and divide irrevocably the population of the loyal States; nor can it be claimed for these injurious pronunciamentos that they have, in the smallest degree, benefited the slaves, for whose amelioration they were ostensibly issued, as from their very tenor and spirit they are alone intended for that portion of the Southern States over which the Federal Government has no control, nor ability to enforce them. The Southern slave, too, if we may judge from the experience of this rebellion, has but little desire to avail himself of this unexpected liberty; and the fact is incontrovertible that no attempt at a servile insurrection has been made, though the facilities for producing it must in many places have been ample. Whether we are to attribute this to the generally mild form of slavery, the fitness of the African for a life of bondage, and his unfitness for an independent state, or to the distrust of the negro in the philanthropic exertions of the advocates of abolition in his behalf, the writer does not pretend to decide; but the fact remains patent, that the negro, for whose emancipation this war is now avowedly carried on, has proved himself but a poor auxiliary in its prosecution, and often an unwilling participator in its boasted benefits.

The writer deems it fitting here to state that on an impartial comparison, drawn from extended personal observation of the condition of the African in his native land, in the Northern free States, and Canada, or in the Southern States now in rebellion, he has become convinced that in none of these conditions are the negroes as happy or well cared for, taken as a body, as in the cotton and sugar growing States of the South. Nor are these convictions hurriedly made or recently arrived at—they are the growth of years of reflection; for the writer, when he left his English home in 1842, was as warm an advocate of the doctrine of anti-slavery as ever left the shores of happy and free Albion.

These introductory remarks are made to show the reader that the facts and thrilling incidents related in the following pages are not dictated by any political or party spirit, but are, as they profess to be, leaves from the diary of

AN ARMY SURGEON.

LEAVES FROM THE DIARY

OF AN

ARMY SURGEON.

CHAPTER I.

In the month of October, 1861, pursuant to the orders of the commandant of New York, I commenced the discharge of my duties as surgeon of the post, which included the medical supervision of the several camps in the city and on Staten Island. Camp Washington, at the latter place, first claimed my attention. It is situated on an inclined plane of the northern end of the island, well suited for the purpose, and on which the State authorities had erected a wooden barracks, capable of accommodating 1000 men, with the necessary buildings for officers' and surgeons' quarters. This station had been occupied by the Sixth New York, known as "Billy Wilson's Zouaves," and at this time contained a portion of the Volunteer Engineers and the nucleus of two or three other military organizations, as yet in a state of infancy, but which had not reached the number entitling them to the exclusive services of a surgeon; and as the medical officers of the two first mentioned regiments had no interest in the condition of the camp beyond its sanitary condition while occupied by their regiments, I was not surprised to find it in a disordered state; but neither was I prepared to meet with the absence of all regard for the health, cleanliness, and comfort of the troops, that presented itself on my first visit, which the natural position of the ground, from its proximity to the water, had made a matter of easy accomplishment. My first care was to inspect and reform the cook-house and mess-room, hitherto totally disregarded, and to make daily examination of the cooked rations, supplied by the contractors, the quality of which was of the poorest kind, and had given just cause for repeated complaint and dissatisfaction among the men; and here, at the outset of my duties, I was met with the most determined hostility by the contractors, who dreaded that the threatened inspection of the food would oblige them to supply a better and more wholesome article, and put a stop to the shameless frauds practised on the soldier in their department. The sum paid by the government—40 cents a day—was liberal, and enabled the contractors to realize a handsome profit while supplying a good and wholesome quality of food. But the temptation was too strong, and the representations I made to the head of the subsistence department of the unfitness of the food, and the unclean and ill-arranged mode of cooking and issuing it, was met with the most determined and systematic opposition, backed by false statements of the interested parties; but perseverance and the judicious use of the power I possessed, succeeded, and I soon had the gratification to see that my daily visit during dinner to the mess-room, secured for the soldiers a clean and wholesome meal. The alternate offers of threats and bribes were alike unavailing to turn me aside from the plain path of my duty, in this first essential step to promote the health of the troops. The contractors themselves, after some time, finding it of no avail to continue their opposition, became reconciled to the change, as they learned that the improved discipline of the men put a stop to the frequent outrages committed on their cooking house and utensils by disorderly or drunken soldiers, who, in this way, revenged themselves on the contractors for the inferior quality of the provisions.

CHAPTER II.

Camp Washington, the situation of which is described in the foregoing chapter, was, about this time, on my suggestion, made a depot for military organizations, while in a formative state. Its isolated but healthful condition, the facility with which it could be guarded, and its easiness of access to the city, recommended it strongly for this purpose,—the only connection with the city being by ferry-boat, a small guard could at all times prevent stragglers or deserters from reaching the city, and the temptations held out by the villages on Staten Island were not more numerous or attractive than could be expected from the large number of troops stationed in its several camps; even these the commanding officers could always keep in check by the assistance of the civil authorities, which was promptly rendered. When those means have failed, the soldiers themselves, when suffering from imposition by the keepers of these groggeries, or when released from the confinement to which they had been sentenced as a punishment for drunkenness, not unfrequently "abated" these rum-shop nuisances by the demolition of one or more of them. But this illegal and unjustifiable course often led to a conflict with the owners, and the personal injuries received in the encounters have often swelled the morning sick report. I succeeded in procuring, by requisition on the medical purveyor, a liberal supply of drugs for this station, and in having appointed a post-hospital steward, who not belonging to any regiment, remained permanently with me. I also had a building fitted up for a hospital, and by these and other much needed reforms, was enabled to take care of the sick, and in time issued to the other camps on the island whatever drugs or hospital supplies I needed for the treatment and care of the sick at those stations.

Under orders from the State surgeon-general, I assumed, at this time, the medical charge of Camp Scott, situated about four miles from the Vanderbilt Landing on Staten Island; and found, on my arrival, that over one hundred men of the 6th New York Volunteer Cavalry, better known as the 2d Ira Harris Guard, were sick with measles, together with the assistant-surgeon and hospital-steward of the regiment, which was in tents and destitute of any hospital accommodation. Colonel Devin had taken command but the day before, and the total want of discipline, aggravated by the unclean condition of the camp, which recent rain had made almost impassable, increased the labor of getting this station into a healthful condition. My efforts to procure a building suitable for a hospital were unavailing. The building in use for the purpose was partially occupied by a portion of the Sickles Brigade, for whose use it was erected; the roof being leaky and the building in a dilapidated condition, it was totally unfit for a hospital, nor was it until I personally assumed the cost of the necessary repairs, that I had any place to accommodate the very large number of sick, most of whom were distributed among the company tents, thus spreading this contagious disease, which assumed a malignant type. However, by continued personal supervision and daily close attention to the improvement of the sanitary condition of the camp, and enforcing habits of cleanliness among the men, I had the gratification of checking its spread, which the hitherto indiscreet intercourse of sick and well had greatly increased. For the month which this regiment remained at Camp Scott, my daily labors were exceedingly onerous; as the entire duty of inspecting the recruits, vaccinating the whole regiment, and the treatment of the sick, together with arduous sanitary inspections daily made of the tents, the appointing and instructing hospital-stewards, obtaining hospital supplies, all devolved on the writer. The officers of this regiment, before leaving the station, presented him with a flattering testimonial of their appreciation of his services, and made liberal acknowledgments of the reforms made, and the perfect organization made in the medical department. The surgeon-general also acknowledged those services, and in refusing the unanimous application of the officers for his appointment to the regiment, stated as his reason that the position occupied by him could not be filled by any other surgeon as well versed in its duties. During this period not a single death occurred in any of the camps under the writer's care, notwithstanding the average number of troops was over 3000. Camp Ledlie, at Palace Garden, New York city, was another of these stations, and to it his first morning visit was paid. It contained about 400 of the 12th New York Volunteers, and about 700 of the 87th New York Volunteers, commanded by Col. Dodge.

CHAPTER III.

THE command of Camp Ledlie, Palace Garden, at this time, devolved on Lt.-col. Henry Weeks, of the 12th New York Volunteers, which had been removed from Camp Washington to increase its recruiting facilities; this regiment was in part made up from the Twelfth New York Militia, that had served in the three months' campaign, under the command of Col. Daniel Butterfield, its gallant conduct procuring for him a brigadier-generalship. This camp was stationed at Palace Garden, on Fourteenth-street, near 6th Avenue, in New York city, and had been previously used as a place of public amusement. It was poorly adapted for the accommodation of the troops. The quarters were two low and badly-lighted halls, without proper ventilation, and entirely destitute of bunks, which obliged the soldiers to spread their mattresses all over the floors, that were often wet and but seldom cleaned. This, and the many temptations to drunkenness held out to the men by the adjoining bar-rooms, greatly increased my labors, and materially swelled the daily list of those reported sick and asking exemption from duty. There not being any accommodation for the officers in the camp aggravated those evils, as their absence at night, when the men returned to quarters drunk and disorderly, frequently permitted rows, often attended with serious personal injury. The many devices resorted to by the men to procure short furloughs were such as could not fail to provoke a smile for their novelty and ingenuity. If an appeal to me for a pass failed, I would often hear of the same applicant having obtained one from the commandant, on the plea of the sudden illness or death of a near relative which had no existence in fact; or it might be that the pass was obtained on the presumed knowledge of the whereabouts of one or more deserters; or an assertion of the applicant's ability to bring one or more recruits, and as the positions of these line officers were dependent on the number mustered into their companies, these applications were usually successful. The mode of recruiting and granting commissions adopted in this State was as follows: The governor granted authority to any person, on application, who was supposed to possess the influence to raise a regiment, with the understanding that if successful he should be commissioned as *colonel of the regiment.* This colonel would then issue similar authority to persons to raise companies, with the promise of the captaincy when the minimum number required by the United States Army Regulations were mustered into the United States service, and as the captain, in time, would make like arrangements with applicants for the 1st and 2d lieutenancies, it was the interest of all to procure as many recruits as possible. As the duty of examining these recruits, on their joining the regiment, devolved on me, and as I was inexorably strict in my examination, I frequently have given offence to those line officers, and they resorted to many subterfuges to evade my examination; nor were the officers alone interested in passing any and every recruit, as it became of vital importance to the colonel of the regiment, as an order was issued at this time to consolidate the several organizations, those having less than a given number to be merged into the larger. This order, had it been carried out with impartiality, would not alone have given general satisfaction, but have been productive of much good. But with the same system of favoritism that has cursed the army, many were given positions totally unfit for the service, to the unjust exclusion of more competent and experienced men. Under this order the 12th Regiment New York State Militia, reorganizing for the war, under command of Colonel Henry Weeks, and which occupied this camp for three months, were consolidated with the 12th New York Volunteers, a Syracuse regiment, whose ranks had been thinned and reduced to 400. The Syracuse regiment, commanded by Lt.-col. Richardson, was stationed at Upton's Hill, Virginia, and the New York portion left to join them; the surgeon, Dr. Reese B. Berky, who by this consolidation was rendered supernumerary, was transferred to the 4th New York Volunteer Artillery, commanded by Col. Doubleday, encamped at Staten Island. Dr. Berky, for some time, acted as my assistant at Palace Garden, and I embrace this opportunity of testifying to his professional ability and solicitude for the comfort and health of the men, and sanitary condition of the camp. With the officers of the 12th I had formed a most agreeable acquaintance, and felt indebted to them for their cordial co-operation in my exertions to keep the camp free from an epidemic made imminent by its insufficient ventilation and drainage. They left for the seat of war with the best wishes of many citizens of New York, and with none warmer than the writer's. It has been my lot to meet many of them since in Virginia, and I know of no single regiment, that had been stationed at this post while I was post surgeon, in whose officers and men I felt a greater interest, or whose military reputation I felt more concern and pride for; many of the poor fellows who left the Palace Garden in high spirits have since met an honorable grave on the truly-called sacred soil of Virginia. Soon after the departure of the 12th from Palace Garden it was taken possession of by the 2d battalion of 3d New York Volunteer Artillery, commanded by Colonel James Ledlie, numbering about 400 men, recruited from the agricultural districts of Western New York; their stay at this station was but for three weeks, and since their departure its use as quarters for troops has been discontinued; nor is this a matter of regret, as its position in a populous part of the city, and its unsuitableness for barracks, made its selection for the purpose alone justifiable on the pressing plea of necessity.

CHAPTER IV.

CAMP SCOTT.

SITUATED in a valley and approached by a drive of three miles from the Vanderbilt Landing, along a beautiful road, which passes through the village of Clifton, the encampment named in honor of General Scott, is located. The brigade raised by General Sickles, was the first quartered here, and on its proceeding to the seat of war, the Ira Harris Guard, or 5th and 6th New York Volunteer Cavalry Regiments (then in a state of formation), were ordered to Camp Scott. Stables had been erected, and a wooden building adjoining the old homestead, called the "Stone-house," was used as cook-house and mess-room. The condition of these buildings, and the food issued to the men, I found, on my first visit of inspection, to be very bad, and I learned that the same contractors who supplied Camp Washington had a monopoly of this station. Feeling satisfied that the extraordinary large number of sick in camp was, to a great extent, owing to unwholesome and badly cooked food, I issued an order that the officer of the day should at each meal be present and inspect the food. This had a twofold advantage: it obliged the contractor to furnish better rations, fearing a report being made to me on my daily inspection, and also preserved order among the men; the want of which had been urged by the mess-man as an excuse for the filthy condition of the mess-room.

The wooden building used as a guard-house, I found one of the most wretched and filthy holes imaginable; the roof leaky, the boarded floors had been torn up and used for kindling-wood, by the prisoners confined in it, and all those who for weeks had been locked up there, had accumulated a heap of filth, composed of the rejected food and offal of every kind, which sent forth an intolerable and unhealthy stench. I at once determined on the removal of the prisoners to better quarters, and on examining the dozen or more unfortunates, ordered four to the hospital, and recommended to the commandant of the post, who accompanied me, the discharge of four others. The remainder being deserters, confined under written charges preferred against them, who, at great trouble and expense had been brought back from Boston, he had no authority or desire to liberate. To obtain a suitable building to use for a guard-house, was a matter of no small difficulty, there being but three others near the camp: one, the hospital, I had nearly full of patients; another, the post sutler's establishment, was too large, and was indispensable to the camp, as most of the officers' and all the hospital food was cooked in it. I found, however, a smaller wooden building, which belonged to the former sutler of the Sickles Brigade, and recommended the commandant of the post to take possession of it and make the necessary changes to adapt it for use as a guard-house.

Having made these arrangements, and having had the hospital building repaired and heated with large stoves, and the bedding properly cared for, I was able to control the epidemic then raging; and, before two weeks had expired, the sick report decreased from one hundred and six to sixty-four. There was still another fruitful source of disorder and disease, which, though not in the camp, exercised a wonderful and pernicious influence on the men. On the roadside which led to the steamboat landing, and within an eighth of a mile, there stood a frame cottage, in which the vilest liquor was sold, and from whence it was daily smuggled into camp, causing drunkenness with all its attendant ill consequences, and sickness from exposure, as the men, on getting intoxicated, would ramble off into the adjoining woods, and there lie down on the damp ground, certain to awake in the morning with a violent cold or the prevalent sore throat; besides these ill effects, the officers found this place a source of great annoyance, and I was not at all grieved on passing the place one day, where this rum-mill had stood, to find it torn down. On inquiry, I learned that the evening previous a fight occurred between the keeper of the place and some of the soldiers, who, maddened with the vile stuff drank on the premises, proceeded to blows, and in the *mēlée* which followed, the cottage was entirely gutted, and then levelled to the ground. Several of the men who participated in this affair, were, I found, on my daily visit to the guard-house, doing penance for it: but, as a few days showed that the removal of the groggery was a blessing to the camp, they were let off with a lighter punishment than would otherwise have been their lot.

The isolated position of the camp was one of its strongest recommendations, and went far in influencing the selection, in spite of the soft, muddy nature of the ground, and the difficulty in guarding it against desertion by the men, and thieving by the Staten Islanders—a nest of whom from Rocky Hollow made nightly visits, and generally succeeded in carrying off some booty. One night it would be a government saddle; another, a sack of oats, or even a horse; the aggregate loss to the government, by these depredations, was considerable, nor could the utmost vigilance of the officers prevent it.

Camp Scott continued to be occupied by the 6th New York Volunteer Cavalry until the 23d of December, 1861, when they left for York, Pennsylvania, where they remained some months. They have since been in active service, and proved themselves, as they promised to be, one of the best disciplined and bravest regiments in the army of the Potomac. A terrible snow-storm raged on the day of their leaving Staten Island, the inhabitants of which parted from them with regret, and many ladies of the island braved the storm to witness their embarkation, which, owing to some mismanagement in the quartermaster's department, was attended with unnecessary delay and exposure that cost the lives of many of the men of this splendid regiment, perfect in its officers, men, outfit, and discipline, and possessing, at the time of its departure, as thoroughly organized and as efficient a medical staff as any regiment that left the State. In consequence of their being unable to be moved, I kept back fifteen sick members, and also retained the hospital steward, Mr. T. E. King, to take care of them, the whole being under the command of Lieut. Wright, detailed for this and recruiting duty. In a couple of weeks they were able to travel, and their leaving broke up Camp Scott, which was not again used as a military station until by the Corcoran Legion, in the summer of 1862.

CHAPTER V.

Camp Arthur, another of the stations under my care, is situated on Staten Island, at the Quarantine Landing. It was named after the quartermaster-general of the State, Brigadier-general Chester Arthur, whose services in fitting out the New York troops and courteous treatment of all having official intercourse with him, has made him very popular. The Commissioners of Emigration consented to the use, by the volunteers, of the buildings and grounds of the old quarantine establishment, which had not been consumed by fire when the people of Staten Island "abated the quarantine nuisance," in 1858, while the citizens of New York were wild with the joyous excitement of the Atlantic cable procession. The buildings that escaped the fire were four in number; these, with the store-house, a three-story brick building, and two smaller ones, were converted into barracks for the volunteers. The 52d New York Volunteers, commanded by Colonel Paul Frank, and other troops, had occupied this camp before my taking charge; it was, at this time, in the possession of the 78th Cameron Rifle Highlanders, afterwards consolidated with the Van Buren Light Infantry—104th New York Volunteers, and by the Scott's 900, United States Volunteer Cavalry, commanded by Colonel James B. Swain, by whose name they were at this time better known; besides these the Marine Artillery, commanded by Colonel Manchester, occupied one of the buildings before mentioned. These three organizations, in one camp, totally independent of each other, was a daily and fruitful source of annoyance, as the orders I found it necessary to issue for the sanitary regulation of the camp were but partially obeyed, each of the commandants claiming that the duty required belonged to one of the other regiments.

Strange as it may appear, there had not been any hospital established at this post until I took charge of it; the sick were previously either allowed to remain in the quarters, to the danger and discomfort of the men, or crammed into a small room of the building used by the boatmen employed by the health officer. Owing to the kindness of Dr. Gunn, the port physician, I got the use of this building, and, at a trifling cost to the State, converted it into a very good hospital, in which I accommodated the sick of the three different regiments in the camp. I continued in the discharge of the onerous duties of this and the other camps, until recruiting was stopped by order of the Secretary of War, when I turned it over to Dr. Walter Kidder, for whom I had procured the appointment of surgeon to Scott's 900, which at this time was nearly recruited to its full number, and which soon left for Washington, where it has since done mounted provost-guard duty.

I now devoted my time to compiling a statistical report of my services as post surgeon, and on their being completed proceeded to Washington and personally presented them to the surgeon-general, who was so well satisfied with the manner I had discharged the duties of the office that he requested me to proceed to the Peninsula in a professional capacity. This was a change of location I had not expected, but as obedience, in my opinion, is the paramount duty of all military men, I hesitated not to comply. Making a hurried visit to my home, in New York, I returned to Baltimore and took the steamer

Georgiana, for Fortress Monroe, where I presented my instructions to Dr. Cuyler, the medical director at that place. I then visited Norfolk, commanded by General Viele, which but a short time before had been retaken from the rebels; and while here went through the navy yard at Gosport, on the opposite bank of the Elizabeth river, adjoining Portsmouth, which is reached by a ferry. This splendid yard had been burned by the Confederates before its surrender; the loss sustained by this uncalled-for and barbarous destruction of property was immense. On driving through the yard I was struck with the magnitude of the buildings, machinery, and docks, which were now lying in a heap of confused ruin, and the desolation saddened and disgusted me. I was accompanied by two officers of the Brazilian navy, whose ship lay at Fortress Monroe. We returned slowly to Norfolk, where the incidents related below occurred. I copy from my diary of the 27th of May.

A really pleasant incident occurred at General Viele's head-quarters, last evening. About nine o'clock, in a pitiless northeast storm, a deputation of citizens, composed of some of the most respectable persons in the community, called upon the general, and desired to take the oath of allegiance to the government. A more impressive scene can scarcely be imagined than that presented in the general's room, on the occasion alluded to. About forty persons were there assembled, embracing a fair representation of the solid men of the place; and the heartfelt earnestness with which they pledged themselves to sustain the Constitution of the United States, gave evidence that loyalty was the sole incentive to the renewal of their plighted faith. Some were aged citizens, who had passed long years of their life under the blessings of the Union, and who were anxious to close their days in the enjoyment of the benefits so long vouchsafed to them, but of which they have been so ruthlessly deprived by this existing infamous rebellion. Others were in the meridian of life; while others were just entering upon the stage of active duty,—and all were deeply impressed by the importance of the act in which they were engaged. General Viele addressed to them a few words of encouragement, and assured them, that the protecting arm of the government would be effectively extended over them in the future. After a pleasant interview of half an hour, the party departed, highly gratified with their visit, and confident that other deputations of a like character would soon follow their example.

Intending to return to the fort next day, I spent the evening and next forenoon in looking over the old city of Norfolk, and grieved to see the deserted state of its streets and emptiness of its stores and warehouses. Nor did my uniform escape the notice or jeers of the Secession ladies who still remained in the city. Passing the corner of one of the streets, in the western part of the town, I saw a lady sitting at an open window, with a bright and beautiful child playing on the sidewalk under the casement; feeling irresistibly attracted by the little fellow's pleasing face and merry gambols, I stopped to speak with him, and one of my Brazilian companions handed him an orange. We were, at this time, ignorant of any relation between the sickly looking lady in the window and the child; but before we had resumed our walk, she had stepped from the house, and raising the child in her arms, she took from its little hands the orange, and returned it to the donor, with the cutting remark, that "she and her child could do without any favors from the enemies of her country and plunderers of her home!" The scene was so sudden and unexpected, that I was hardly able to reply for my gentlemanly companion, who did not speak English; but I informed the lady that he was not an American, and visited Norfolk not as a belligerent but from curiosity, and his kindness to her child, dictated by courtesy alone, was so badly received, that it must make a most unfavorable impression on an officer of another nation's navy.

We were informed that the boat for Fortress Monroe started at 3 P. M., but on arriving at the wharf, learned that General Wool had taken possession of it, and had left at one o'clock. The day being Saturday, and I having arranged to return, and my companions being anxious to get to their ship, we were much disconcerted. Thanks to Quarter-master Morton, of General Viele's staff, a tug-boat was placed at our disposal, in which we safely reached the Roads and were received on board the Brazilian corvette Parasia with demonstrations of welcome. I was here made acquainted with the officers of this splendid ship, built in Rio Janeiro, and manned, from captain to cabin-boy, with Brazilians, with but one exception—a Mr. Williams, an Englishman, engineer of the vessel, and who was highly spoken of by the officers. On our arrival at the fort, rumors were in circulation that a fight was in progress or expected, on the Chickahominy, and with impatience I retired to rest, the steamer for the White House not leaving until morning. Before I had been an hour in bed, a terrible thunder-storm commenced, which frightened the inmates of the Hygeia Hotel, where I stopped,—in fact, the only hotel at Fortress Monroe, the greater part of it being occupied as a hospital, under the charge of Dr. Bountico,—so that the portion used for an hotel was limited, and miserably furnished. It was kept by one of the Willards, of Washington, who added nothing to his reputation by the management of this hotel. It rivalled in filth and exorbitant charges any California ranch that the reader has ever heard of. In consequence of the crowded condition of the house, I was the joint occupant with two others, of a dark, small-sized room. Fortunately they were acquaintances, and one of them, a Mr. Cook, of New York, on hearing the very loud thunder, arose from his bed; scarcely had he done so, when a much louder clap and the most vivid flash of lightning lit up the room, this was soon followed by a crackling of broken timber and hurried voices in confusion, which we learned proceeded from a government stable near the hotel, that had been struck and set on fire by the lightning. The uproar caused by the fire, lasted through the greater part of the night, and morning broke long before we expected it. Swallowing a hurried breakfast, I proceeded to the steamer John A. Warner, bound for the White House, which, after a pleasant, though tedious passage, on the most tortuous river I had ever seen, we reached at six o'clock. Anxious to press forward to the sphere of my duty, I landed without delay, and found spread over the railway track, on the wet and muddy ground, over three hundred wounded from the first day's fight after the battle of Chickahominy, or by some called Seven Pines or Fair Oaks. In order to give the reader a clear idea of the engagement I copy from my diary of this date, and would here state that I am indebted to officers who were on the field, and to Mr. Farrell, of the New York press, for the subjoined graphic description of this bloody and fiercely contested fight, in which so many brave fellows fell, and which will be long remembered by every man of the left wing of the army of the Potomac.

CHAPTER VI.

THE BATTLE OF FAIR OAKS.

The army of the Potomac which, since the battle of Williamsburg, had encamped on the Chickahominy creek, with its left wing resting on that stream, were suddenly and unexpectedly attacked by the rebels, under General Joe Johnston; the attack began by driving in the pickets of Casey's division, and so sudden and fierce was the onslaught that before the line of battle could be formed the enemy had fired several volleys into, and killed many in their tents. So great was the consternation and confusion caused by the charge, that the brigade which formed the centre of the division was thrown into disorder, one or two regiments of which broke and run, but the 88th New York, 83d Pennsylvania, 5th New Hampshire, and 3d Maine Volunteers, succeeded in rallying to the fight and checked the panic and dismay caused by those two regiments turning their backs on the enemy. The engagement now became general along the line, and the corps to which these regiments belonged, under the command of General Sumner, were soon under a heavy and murderous fire. The commanding general soon learned of the assaults on his left wing and the unfortunate disorder into which Casey's division was thrown, and ordered a reinforcement to support the columns, which had now borne for two hours the hottest part of the fight. The soft and muddy state of the ground along the creek, and at Seven Pines, rendered the movements of the artillery a most difficult task, and the day was far spent before sufficient numbers arrived to prevent Johnston, the rebel general, carrying out his design of cutting off the left wing from the centre and thus whipping them in detail. The sultry heat of the atmosphere told terribly on the men and horses, and increased the fatigues caused by the condition of the ground. But notwithstanding these impediments the charges of the rebels, though made in a style of daring, and with a gallant bearing seldom excelled, were met by our men with the most unflinching heroism, and on two occasions the order given to dislodge the rebels from the copse-wood adjoining the Seven Pines, from which the battle takes its name, was conducted with unhesitating alacrity and spirit, and the hotly contested possession of the ground, cost the lives of many hundred brave fellows. In one of these affairs, a corporal of the 88th New York Volunteers, Irish Brigade, got separated from his company, by pressing onward too eagerly when the rest of his column were ordered to halt, and before he could recover his position found himself surrounded by over a dozen Confederates, who loudly ordered him to surrender; without replying to their demand he stepped aside and, aiming his musket, shot a sergeant of the 11th Mississippi, and then retreating behind a tree, where, for a few moments, he was concealed, he reloaded his piece, again advanced, and taking aim picked out another, who fell from the mass of yelling rebels; by this time his regiment had regained the ground it temporarily lost, and he, again falling into its ranks, advanced to the edge of the wood, from which the enemy had been driven, but to which they soon returned strongly reinforced, and, in turn, drove our men from their vantage ground. A minié-ball having struck one of the officers of his regiment, this corporal, and a companion, lifted him from the ground to carry him to the rear, and while so engaged he was shot through the ribs; in this condition, and side by side with his captain, he was, after a tedious delay of many hours, carried to the railway station, and placed on board the freight car, with 300 others. I met him when the train arrived at the White House, and during my professional attendance on his mortal wound received from him the foregoing facts. The train that brought this humble but brave corporal, brought down 65 of the wounded of this regiment and over two hundred of other regiments of the division. All of these were wounded in the repeated contests for the possession of the copse-wood, but as it afforded good cover for the enemy's riflemen it was deemed important to dislodge them from it.

Saturday night closed in on the contending forces, and the result of the day's fighting was clearly in favor of the rebels. The Union loss could not be less, in killed and wounded, than 3500. The rebel loss was not so large, though their loss in having their daring leader, General Johnston, wounded, was a heavy blow. During the night the men slept on their arms, and a heavy thunder-shower deprived them of the rest so much needed after their day's hard fighting, and, if possible, made worse the condition of their muddy camping-ground. Sunday morning broke bright and clear, and a glaring summer's sun shone down on the mud-stained and begrimed ranks of the contending armies. Orders having been issued by the commanding general, McClellan, to attack the enemy, a hurried breakfast was swallowed, and the long-roll being sounded, the line was formed of fresh troops, the ranks of those regiments engaged the day before being sadly thinned by the casualties of the fight.

The attack on General Casey's division, which it appears numbered only about six thousand men, was made suddenly by a force of about thirty-five thousand rebels. General Casey's camp was located in a corn-field, surrounded by woods; and the enemy, after driving in his pickets, which were a mile in advance, made a sudden dash on the camp, with the above-named immensely superior force. The troops of General Casey fought splendidly, the general himself and his field-officers braving danger without flinching; but in the face of overwhelming numbers, they were forced to fall back until reinforcements arrived, as mentioned in General McClellan's official report, when the fortunes of the field were speedily turned by the action of Heintzelman's, Richardson's, Sedgwick's, Kearney's, and Keyes' corps, and a complete victory of the Union army was the result. All acknowledge the importance of that victory, though our loss was undoubtedly heavy. The bayonet charges made by Richardson's and Sedgwick's divisions on the flower of the rebel army, commanded by Generals Huger, Longstreet, and Rains, were magnificently executed, and although the enemy stood the fire of our troops bravely, they broke before the vehement charge of the bayonet, at every point. The loss on both sides during this portion of the action, was very serious, the rebels suffering terribly.

Saturday, May 31st, 1862, is distinguished to the future as the first day of the hard-fought battle of the Seven Pines. This battle was an attempt of the rebel generals to force our lines and to drive back upon the Chickahominy river, now swollen greatly, the left wing of the Union army. Many suppose the present high state of the Chickahominy river not to be natural, that the rebels by some contrivance of dams near its head, have flooded it, and that their strategy went so far as to involve our original passage of the stream, which they are thus thought to have permitted that they might swell the stream behind us, and then, by an overwhelming attack, cut off and destroy the whole of General Keyes' command, and whatever other troops might be in its rear. Perfectly informed of our position and force, they chose a point for their attack that could least bear it. They intended the blow to be desperate, and made it with their best troops. Eighteen thousand men of the rebel army in one division. Men from North Carolina, Georgia, Alabama, Mississippi, Florida, and Virginia,—men of high courage and admirable discipline, led by General Longstreet, left Richmond at daylight, on that Saturday, and went out to battle. They went also to ruin, failure, and defeat. Never did simple courage more deserve success than they did; never did soldiers falter less under fire or show a better front than they did through five long hours of that day. But they returned to Richmond, save that large proportion of them that, side by side with so many of our own brave men, "look proudly to heaven from the death-bed of fame."

Returned to Richmond, and far to the rear of the left wing, the Chickahominy tumbles turbulently on: the Union lines are drawn closer than ever; the Gaul is still at their gates. Though the battle of the Seven Pines may not be the bloodiest of the war, it is the most important battle yet fought, and it is the one in which the armies of either side have had their hardest fight. Nor will it fall far behind any other fight in respect to loss, as our own will amount to eighteen hundred killed and four thousand wounded, while the loss of the enemy was even greater than this. Nearly all of our men are accounted for, and the number of our missing is consequently small, while of the enemy's men we have taken from a thousand to fifteen hundred prisoners. For a short distance beyond the Chickahominy river the highway to Richmond, known as the Williamsburg road, runs directly west to the rebel capital. Seven miles east of Richmond, on this road, is the place known as the Seven Pines; a common country road, known to us as the Nine Mile road, crosses the main road, and on the left (our left) runs through the woods towards White Oak Swamp. On the right the road runs in a northwesterly direction by Fair Oaks station, on the railroad to Richmond. By this road it is nine miles from the Seven Pines to the city. In the northwestern angle of this road and the main road is a house, and farther up the same road, beyond a swampy wood, is another house. A third house stands to the right of the Richmond road, half a mile nearer to Richmond, and a fourth on the left-hand side of that road. Beyond the latter house was a large open cultivated field. Towards Richmond both these fields are bounded by a thick wood, the edge of which had been felled to form an abatis and obstruct the approach of the enemy. Dense woods run all along our left, but nearly all the battle-field has once been cultivated, though in parts of it there was a high growth of wood when we came up; this was felled and formed abatis. General Casey's pickets were in the edge of the wood, beyond the house before mentioned, and his camp was formed with his first brigade on the right, his second in the centre, and the third on the left of a line across the plain in the rear ot some inconsiderable earthworks hastily thrown up soon after his occupation of the point.

These works,—a redoubt on the left, and a line of rifle-pits,—were planned by Lieutenant McAllister, of the United States engineers, and executed by Lieutenant E. Walter

West, acting engineer on General Casey's staff. It is necessary to speak of the condition of General Casey's command; and it will not, perhaps, be amiss to say of it, what is not true of any other division of the army, and what will not be true of that division, after a few weeks of rest. It was made up, when first organized, of very raw troops—the latest enlistments of our immense army. There was no cohesive strength, even in the regiments; discipline was lax; and the men, as soon almost as the division was formed, were pushed into active service, made to march and starve with our year-old regiments; to bivouac and fight, side by side, with those who had been out so long as to consider themselves veterans. Numbers, consequently, became sick, and this weakened his division considerably. Moreover, it had, on the day of the battle, an unusually extensive picket line, and nearly every regiment had out three companies on picket or fatigue duty,—from these various causes this division had not in the field, on Saturday, more than six thousand effective men. General Longstreet, of the rebel army, left Richmond with the whole effective force of his command (six brigades), purposely to drive the Union forces across the Chickahominy. Other troops also came, and a number of prisoners state the force in the field at five divisions. They advanced down the Williamsburg road, and thus the whole brunt of the first attack fell upon General Casey. It was about noon when we first heard the scattered fire of our pickets in front. For two or three days before, there had been skirmishes between the pickets near the road in front, and this was mistaken for another affair of the same kind, and thus some time was lost, for, instead of the dispositions that should have been made, a regiment was simply ordered out—the 103d Pennsylvania, to support the pickets. This regiment went out quickly, was formed near the road, and almost stumbled upon the enemy advancing in line of battle. Before the men had even loaded their pieces the One Hundred and Third re ceived a full and steady volley, from the effects of which it did not recover. That one fire, delivered almost as a complete surprise, and which our men could not return, cut down perhaps one-fifth of the regiment and demoralized the remainder. No more service was had from the One Hundred and Third that day, and what was worse, the men began to stream to the rear, with the old story of "cut to pieces;" it is a shibboleth with many, in which they boast their own disgrace, though in this case it was somewhat different. Of course this stream of men had no good effect upon the spirits of their fellows, and thus the day began in misfortunes.

But that one volley, while it annihilated the regiment, told, quicker than courier could carry the news, the mistake that had been made, and that the enemy were upon us. Casey's force was turned out in a hurry and formed, and Colonel Bailey, of New York, Casey's chief of artillery, had the enemy's line under his fire before it had gotten through the first wood, and before the line was completely formed.

Spratt's battery, which was posted in a field to the right of the road and near the edge of the wood, and Regan's battery, which was also in the same field between Spratt's and the house, got into action immediately, and were supported by the 100th New York, in the road to the left, by the 11th Maine and 104th Pennsylvania on their right, and by the 92d New York in the rear. Both batteries did splendid execution, but the enemy's line advanced silently and steadily, receiving the fire with apparently perfect coolness, and firing in return with great effect. As the enemy's line came into fire of our infantry, regiment after regiment gave it to them in fine style, but still if there was many a gap in their lines, there was no break; fire after fire tore through their ranks but could not break them, and our regiments engaged at that point, fell back, a little shaky perhaps, but in good order. Spratt's battery was composed of Napoleon guns. Four hundred yards in front of where it was posted, there was rather a difficult rail-fence, which the rebel line had to cross. As they came up to it, the four Napoleons played upon them fearfully with grape and canister. They could not pass the fence. Every time they came up to it, the new discharge tore their lines asunder, mowed wide gaps through their formation, and held them there beyond the fence. They did not pass the fence till Spratt's grape and canister were gone. He could not be supplied again, for the wagons were beyond the Chickahominy. So the rebels passed the fence, and Spratt with his four Napoleons fell back to the redoubt. Regan's battery still maintained its fierce fire. But now the enemy dressed his line in the most perfect manner, and made for that. Should he have a few more pieces? Not if fire could prevent it, and the fire of the battery became warmer, while that of the four infantry regiments that supported it was redoubled. But fire could not prevent it. General Casey saw that, in spite of what he could do, the battery was gone. The old hero, conspicuous on his large gray horse, and by his white hair, rode in the thickest of the fire, formed the four regiments, the 92d and 100th New York, the 11th Maine, and the 104th Pennsylvania, into line, gave the word, and led the charge in person. *Fire could not save the battery, but the bayonet did!* Back went the rebel line, driven fairly out of existence. Plenty were behind however to take its place, and still the enemy came on. And now a new line appeared on the right flank of Casey's front, and Regan's battery and its supports fell back. Another attack came simultaneously on the left flank, held by the 98th and 96th New York, and they too retired, still in good order. Casey's division was thus fairly driven into his first line of defence, and the enemy advanced against that in the redoubt. On the left was Bates' battery of six pieces, which immediately began to put in reasons why it should not be taken. In support, were the 81st and 85th New York, and 85th and 101st Pennsylvania; Fitch's battery was posted to the right, and in rear of the redoubt, behind this line, Casey's other regiments now retired. There was a silence of a few moments, and the rebel line again began its terrible advance. Bates' and Fitch's batteries had already opened, and now also the four rebel batteries did the same; the rebel infantry, and our own infantry. Never since this war began has there been heard a more terrible fusilade. At this time the left of the rebel line was formed of Jenkins' Palmetto sharpshooters (South Carolinians), the 6th South Carolina regiment, and the 6th North Carolina. A fair view of this line was obstructed by the abatis of fallen timber between us and it; but we knew how steadily it came on, for over the obstruction of branches and green leaves, we could see the light faint fringe of smoke curl up from the continued file fire, and far above the smoke their white battle-flag fluttered proudly out and showed how fast they came. This battle-flag is, doubtless, what has given rise to the many stories of the enemy's exhibition of flags of truce in battle; it is a small square white flag, with sometimes a regimental insignia upon the centre, but at others a green cross charged with stars. The enemy reached the redoubt and the rifle-pits, and stormed both. In the redoubt was left Bates' whole battery and two of Spratts' guns, because they could not be taken away, but every gun was spiked. Out of one lot of one hundred and thirty-eight horses, only twenty-eight were left alive. Casey's resistance was now pretty well done with; his batteries were all *en route* rearward, and the majority of his regiments were completely broken, but we must not overlook what the gallant old soldier had already really done. General Keyes had apparently not been from the first very sanguine of his ability to hold Casey's position, and had given his whole attention to see that Couch's line of battle behind Casey should be such as to hold the enemy and check him there at least. Thus Casey was so far left alone, save some assistance rendered by the New York 62d, 55th, and a regiment from Kearney's division. But this assistance was completely ineffective.

The attack began shortly after twelve o'clock, and the battle was in full fury at two; for three hours and a half, General Casey, with six thousand raw troops, had sustained the whole weight of the rebel onset, an onset made by a force at least triple his own, and with the very oldest regiments of the Southern army. From Casey's front to the point of his last resistance it is not half a mile, and it had taken the enemy three hours and a half of hard fighting; he had lost by casualties nearly every fourth man he had in the field. He had lost many of his best officers, including his gallant and capable chief of artillery, Colonel Bailey, and now, at last, he was compelled, with a heavy heart, to relinquish the unequal struggle. During the quiet that ensued, after the loss of Casey's last position, General Heintzelman arrived upon the field and assumed the command that had been previously held by General Keyes.

General Couch, upon whose command the enemy was

next to fall, had upon the field parts of twelve regiments. The brigade that contained his oldest troops, General Devin's, had only the 7th and 10th Massachusetts, and the 36th New York, on the field, and each of these regiments had three companies out on picket. Peck's brigade also, and Abercrombie (lately Graham's), were both weakened in the same way; but General Couch, ready for any emergency, prepared to do his best upon the first intimation of the enemy's advance, his division was quickly turned out and posted. Two lines of rifle pits, rather inadequate for the purpose, had been constructed in advance of Couch's camp, and in open fields to either side of the main road and in front of the cross-road; in the pits to the left of the road the 55th New York and the 62d New York had first been placed, but when they went ahead the Massachusetts Tenth were placed behind the pits with the 93d and 102d Pennsylvania on its left and rear; in the wood on the right and a little in rear of the 10th, was posted battery C, 1st Pennsylvania Artillery, Captain McCarty. In the pits to the right of the road, and nearest the road, was the 36th New York, to the right of the 36th the 7th Massachusetts, in rear and to the right of the 7th was Captain Miller's battery of light twelve pounders. Farther to the right, in advance and resting on the Nine Mile road, was the 23d Pennsylvania, and behind it the 1st Long Island. The 31st and 61st Pennsylvania and the First Chasseurs, were also on the right towards Fair Oak station. Brady's battery was in the same neighborhood, and Flood's battery was placed behind the Nine Mile road, near to its junction with the main road. Such were the positions taken by the respective parts of Couch's command.

At two o'clock the Williamsburg road was lined with a stream on their way to the rear. Many were wounded, and they seemed to show their wounds as the explanation of why they went in that direction. Others were sick, and others again were the fragments of the broken regiments, the 103d, 104th, and other Pennsylvania regiments, for it is only simple justice to say that the Pennsylvanians were in the majority in this stream. Casey's division, however, was composed, in a very large degree, of Pennsylvania troops. General Keyes and Couch both endeavored to arrest this rearward stream, at first by moral suasion, and subsequently by guard. Lieutenant Eccleston, the efficient provost marshal of Couch's division, was posted in the road with his men, and did what could be done in the matter. General Keyes, accompanied by his staff, rode to every part of the field, and did much, by the example of entire indifference to the enemy's fire, to inspirit the men.

It was little more than half-past four when the renewed advance of the enemy brought them to Couch's line. His line was not drawn exactly parallel to the enemy's advance but was obliqued in such a manner that its right became first engaged. Once more the woods were alive with fire. Colonel Neile, with the 23d Pennsylvania, was first into it, and by his presence kept up the spirit of his men. His fire had been reserved until the enemy were very near him, and only six rounds had been discharged when his own men and the enemy's were fairly face to face. Then the colonel gave his men the word to charge and went in ahead to show them how to do it. Again the cold steel was offered, and again the men of the South refused it. They gave way and scattered before the Twenty-third, and the way was clear, but now Neile had the fire of the enemy upon his right and left and began to suffer severely as he fell back to his place. Many of his men also had gone down in the charge besides those that were hit, for it was over difficult ground and as they came up again did not find their regiment. Thus the Twenty-third was weakened but fell back fighting, and Colonel Neile, *with his colors and less than a hundred* men, formed on the 1st Long Island, the next regiment to his line, and in a few minutes later our whole right was in hot battle. There the fight seemed to have formed a nucleus, and supports were poured in from the left; the 93d and 102d Pennsylvania, and the 62d New York, were hurried across; and a brigade of Kearney's division, Birney's brigade, then on the railroad, was ordered to push ahead and get into action at that point.

While these occurrences were going on, on our right, another misfortune happened on our left. From its place near the rifle pits the Massachusetts Tenth was ordered into a piece of ground nearly surrounded with abatis, and with the thick wood on its left, the 93d and 102d Pennsylvania were ordered to the right. Thus the Tenth were left in a bad place and entirely without support. As the enemy advanced firing and torn by the firing of Flood's, McCarty's, and Miller's batteries,—for Miller, from his side of the field, when he could not get a clear shot at the enemy in his front, threw his missiles clear across the field, and with awful effect, too,—as the enemy advanced under his fire and the Tenth became engaged in front, a body of the enemy made their way through the woods on its left. Lieutenant Eccleston first discovered this body and rode desperately over the field to find General Couch, that he might get an order for the Tenth to move and so save it. But his exertions were vain, General Couch was in the thick of the struggle on the right, too far away to be reached in time.

Colonel Briggs was not aware of the approach of this

body, but as he knew the position that Peck's regiment had held, he deemed the report incredible, and went in the woods to see. He had not far to go. There they were, not only in the woods but through it, and ere an order could be given they delivered their fire in the full rear of the Tenth. Utter confusion was the result. The regiment broke, but it proved itself to possess that power which has been denied to Volunteers, and claimed as the especial attribute of old and so called "regular" soldiers, namely, the power of regeneration. It was rallied and became once more a complete regiment, with only those out whose bodies lay upon the field. Nay they did it repeatedly. Four different times they were broken on that day, and four different times the gallant Tenth were rallied and went back into the fight. Thus re-formed the Tenth went back into the rifle pits to the left of the road. But the left now rested upon others. Kearney was in and at it. Berry's brigade, and a portion of Jameson's, now held the left, and the Tenth was soon called across to take part in the bitter struggle at that point which was then our right, but which, by the extension of our line, by the arrival of fresh troops, on both sides, eventually became the centre. After the brilliant fight of the 23d Pennsylvania, which is described above, the enemy brought up a large reinforcement of fresh troops, and advanced again in the same good order that had been observed in his line throughout the battle. Miller's battery, a splendid battery of Napoleons, formed in a field in advance of the Nine Mile road, and tore the rebel ranks terribly until the rebel artillery got the exact range of it and hit the pieces every time. Then it changed its place, and Brady's battery to the right kept up a rapid fire. Soon the 36th New York, the 7th Massachusetts, the 1st Long Island, the 1st Chasseurs, 61st, 31st,

33d, and 102d Pennsylvania, 62d New York, and 10th Massachusetts, were all hotly engaged at that point. Three batteries also played on the advancing line, *and still* it came on, it seems as if nothing can stop it. The scene at this time, was awfully magnificent, the faint smoke of the musketry fire arose lightly all along the line, just so the heads of the men could be seen through it, sudden gusts of white smoke burst up from the mouth of cannon, all around bullets shredded the air and whistled swiftly by, or struck into trees, fences, boxes, wagons, or with their peculiar chuck into men, and far up in the air shells burst into sudden flame, like shattered stars, and passed away into little clouds of white vapor, while others filled the air with a shrill scream and hurried on to burst in the rear. Every second of time had its especial tone, and every inch of space was packed with death. It seemed that the enemy's advance was checked, for he was fairly stopped in the swampy ground, near the Nine Mile road; but he had gained too much to give it up easily, and he tried again, and again our line gave way. The 1st Long Island broke, but two of Jameson's regiments, the 57th and 63d Pennsylvania, would have more than retrieved it; but Colonel Campbell, of the Fifty-seventh, was soon down, but Colonel Hays, of the Sixty-third, kept the men in their places, and inspired all around him; yet the fire was fearful, the regiments seemed to melt.

At this point it was that Colonel Devins received his wound. Hardly a man remained mounted, for every horse was shot, and the regiments were thinned and thinned terribly; but a few brave men stood there for their country, and kept their places. Birney's brigade, of Kearney's division, when he advanced, had been ordered to advance by the railroad in full time to have reached this point of our hardest fight. Had he reached it, his fresh troops poured in after the hard fight already made, must have turned the tide, and the enemy would have been routed then; but he did not, he halted. Patterson's brigade, formed into Birney's left, went into the swampy woods and almost impassable thicket and pushed on still, while Birney with a fair dry road, and the fight not a mile away, halted and sat down.

It is not certain that our men would not still have held the point, but now they were ordered to fall back, rallying and forming as they went, so that they gave ground and kept their order. The fight in that part of the field on the Williamsburg road for that day ended a few hundred yards farther on. For hour after hour, the enemy with continued accession of fresh troops had pushed on, and now after he had pushed us a mile, we still went fighting him, step by step, and in good order. His impulse was spent and he stopped. He occupied our camps that night with troops who had not been in action. When the enemy finally forced our position on the Nine Mile road, the greater part of Couch's division fell back in the direction of the Williamsburg road. But the general himself, with a smaller body, being nearer to Fair Oaks station, fell back across the railroad, and was thus cut off from the army. As soon as this was ascertained, he prepared to make the best of it. He examined his position carefully, sent men to beat up all the roads, and especially along the New Bridge road, to see if Sumner might be near. The force with Couch was found to consist of four regiments: the 1st New York Chasseurs, Colonel Cochrane; the 62d New York (Anderson Zouaves), Colonel Riker; the 7th Massachusetts, Colonel Russell; and the 31st Pennsylvania, Colonel Williams; and Brady's battery of four pieces. His position was in a large open field, in an angle between the railroad and a road that runs northward towards New Bridge. On the west was a dense wood from which the enemy might emerge any moment; and on the south was the railroad and a fringe of wood, through which they could cross for a flank attack. Whether he had any road for retreat, the general did not know. So he formed two lines of battle,—one towards the railroad, with a section of Brady's battery, supported by the Massachusetts 7th; another towards the wood to the west, with the other section of the battery, supported by the Anderson Zouaves, with the 31st Pennsylvania and the 1st Chasseurs formed close in the edge of the wood, under cover of a rail-fence. Lieutenant Edwards, who had ridden down the New Bridge road, came back with word that Sedgwick's division was only two miles away. Couch knew he could hold his ground till they came, so he was saved the misfortune of defeat. They hurried on, and came up at half-past five o'clock, General Sumner with them. No change was made in Couch's dispositions, save in the comparative strength with which either line was held. The 1st Minnesota, Colonel Sully, was formed on the right of the Chasseurs, and Ricketts' battery of Napoleons to the left of the 31st. All the rest of the division was formed on the line towards the railroad. Shortly after six o'clock the enemy advanced through the woods, on the west—in what force, it cannot be said with certainty. Prisoners report it at eight thousand. As we caught two brigadiers, the number is, perhaps, not overstated.

As soon as the line of the enemy's advance was known, Ricketts' battery opened, and threw grape and canister into the wood with great effect. Brady was not idle either. One wounded man, of a North Carolina regiment, taken from the field the next day, says, "that he fell at the first fire; and, that his regiment only went a dozen yards beyond the spot where he fell, until it broke." It could not be rallied. But the line kept on until it was in the edge of the wood, and within ten paces of where the 31st Pennsylvania, the 1st Chasseurs, and the 1st Minnesota, lay on their faces, between the rebels and the battery. The rebels could not see them, and as they came to the edge of the wood, they delivered one volley at the Anderson Zouaves, in the field further out. That volley killed Colonel Riker, and the Zouaves broke and ran. Yet they ran only twenty yards, when they were rallied, and went right up to the edge of the wood and opened their fire. No sooner had the rebels by that volley emptied their guns, than the three regiments that had been lying down arose to their feet, and poured a volley in at almost no distance at all. "That volley settled that fight." Through the woods in front, the rebels lay dead and wounded in heaps. Brigadier-general A. C. Davis was found dead there; and Brigadier-general Pettigrew, wounded and his horse killed, was there taken prisoner. When the rebel line advanced in the wood, Gorman's brigade, from the line of battle on the railroad, was thrown forward on the right flank of the rebel line, to turn it; but when the musketry broke that line, and the rebels fell into confusion, the brigade pressed forward, and so cut off and drove in a large number of prisoners. So closed the battle for that day, and General Couch (than whom his country has no better or braver soldier) slept that night further forward on the road to Richmond, nearer to the rebel capital than he had done any night before. Both armies lay upon the field. Many wounds were dressed at Savage's, which had been made immediately a hospital, and between that point and the battle-field many remarkable experiences were compared. Perhaps the most notable was the great number of officers hit. Brigadier-general Devins received a bullet in the right leg, but kept the field for two hours afterwards. Brigadier-general Wessels was struck by a ball in the shoulder, but not disabled. A musket-ball passed across General Couch's breast, and only cut his coat. Colonel Briggs, of the Massachusetts 10th, was struck in three places, and disabled finally by a rifle-ball that passed through both thighs. Colonels Riker of the 62d New York, Dodge of the 87th New York, Bailey of the 1st New York Artillery, and Ripley of the 61st Pennsylvania, were all killed. Colonels McCartey of the 93d Pennsylvania, Rowley of the 102d Pennsylvania, Van Wyck of the 56th New York, and Hunt of the 92d New York, were wounded. Majors Ely of the 23d Pennsylvania, and King of the 85th New York, were also severely wounded. The loss of horses tells where the officers who rode them were. General Keyes had a horse hit, and Captain Suydam, of his staff, had his horse killed. All the gentlemen of Couch's staff, Captain Walker, and Lieutenants Edwards and Burt, had horses shot. General Peck's was hit three times. General Casey's horse was hit, also General Devins'. In the fight of Saturday, the bulk of the losses on either side took place, and show the terrific severity of the fighting. Our loss for that day will scarcely fall short of 3000 killed and wounded. Upon the field of battle the enemy's loss was estimated at probably two to one for our own, and the appearance of the field made the estimate seem reasonable.

On the second day, which was Sunday, our men stood to their arms before daylight. As the enemy chooses Sunday for his battle-days, we expected him; but we knew that if he did not advance, there would be no battle, as

Sunday is never chosen for a movement on our part, and would not be, apparently, to win back our camp. So, from very early on Sunday it began to look, what it proved to be, an affair of three days. Our men, at dawn on Sunday, were disposed as follows:

On the left, stretched across the Richmond road, the Sickle's brigade was in face of the enemy, at scarcely two hundred yards' distance, posted on a slope, so that the rise of the ground towards the enemy served as a complete cover. To the right of Sickles, in a thick swamp, was Patterson's New Jersey brigade. Both of these brigades faced towards Richmond, and this was the point at which our men had been pushed the hardest and furthest. To the right of Patterson was Richardson's brigade, the line of which was drawn at right-angles with the line of Sickles and Patterson. Richardson faced towards the flank of the force in front of these two brigades. Sedgwick joined on to Richardson, and a part of his division assisted to strengthen Couch's line, in the wood from which the rebels had been driven on Saturday afternoon.

Our first anticipations had scarcely settled into the conviction that the enemy intended to give Sunday to care for the dying and dead, than we heard the pickets at it. It was in front of Richardson's division. Richardson's line ran, as we have intimated, parallel with the railroad, and was on the northern side of it. The enemy was in our camps on the southern side of it, and in a strong position, covered by a swamp. Force was immediately sent forward to support the pickets, and became engaged in its turn. The enemy formed his men in line, and was disposed to feel us again. Our men had risen from sleep in anticipation of battle, and their minds were ready for it. They were not green troops, and the day gave promise of hard work. Soon the fire became general, and spread along the lines of the Irish Brigade, French's brigade, and the brigade of General Howard. This day, also, the enemy's fire was well directed and severe, but was returned with certainly equal effect, and our men pushed forward across the railroad, and down into the swamp; and now the enemy in his turn gave way. It was very difficult ground, and the men could not, at all times, keep the line, and were often up to their waists in water, in the advance through the swamp. Yet still they kept on. Sometimes, too, there may have been a weakness under the fire, but the gallantry of the officers kept the men up to it. This was once or twice the case in Howard's brigade, but by his gallantry he gave an example which restored all: two horses were shot from under him in this advance, and he received two rifle-balls in his right arm, but he bound up the shattered limb in a handkerchief, and kept the field. With the continual din of the musketry, as it pealed up and down the lines on either side, no order could be heard, and only example served. Thus the mounted officers were compelled to keep ahead, in the advance, to show the men what was wanted. There was the Irish Brigade, in all the glory of a fair, free fight. Other men go into fights finely, sternly, or indifferently, but the only man that really loves it, after all, is the green, immortal Irishman. So there the brave lads from the old sod, with the chosen Meagher at their head, laughed and fought, and joked, as if it were the finest fun in the world. We saw one sitting on the edge of a ditch with his feet in the water, and the sun and the water, too, very hot, and he apparently wounded. As we rode by he called out to know if we had ever seen a boiled Irishman. From Richardson's division the fire spread around to the New Jersey brigade, on the front which the enemy had pushed so far the day before. Nobly did the Jerseymen stand up to it, and push on closer and closer, and the enemy fell back through the thick swamp slowly and steadily. On this front the fire was not so severe as on Richardson's, but still it told heavily on our brave fellows, though it did not prevent the advance. Still further to the left was the Excelsior Brigade, and General Sickles with it. Though on, we believe, his first battle-field, the general had not the air or manner of a novice. He was all activity, and thought only of the way to win. Sickles' men apparently lost their patience, and we suppose the officers did, and General Sickles especially. When men advance across a battle-field, loading and firing as they go, they naturally do not go fast, and the Sickles brigade voted the gait to be decidedly slow. So the order was given to fix bayonets and charge, and they did it, not mincingly at all, but in terrible earnest, and with a glorious cheer. Some of the rebels stood it and held their places, some stood long enough to fire their pieces and then run; but the mass ran at once, scampering away through the woods like so many squirrels.

That ended the fight for Sunday in that direction, for it would not do to let the men go rashly too far into the woods. We did not know what little arrangements of artillery, &c., the enemy might have made there in our absence, so with a wise caution the Sickles brigade was drawn back to the edge of the wood, and laid there snugly, and there it spent its Sunday, ready for visitors, though none came, if we except several innocuous shell that the enemy threw into the wood, over their heads. On Richardson's front, also, the fight dropped off very much as it had begun. It was apparently not the design that we should make any general advance on Sunday; so we merely drove the enemy away as he came up, and then fell into our places again with a true Sunday calm. It was only nine A. M., when the calm came, but in this short fight much had been done. Howard's brigade alone, lost, in this fight, in killed and wounded, over five hundred and thirty-six men.

General McClellan had ridden over very early on Sunday morning, and when the fight first began, he immediately rode down the Williamsburg road, and over the whole scene of action which he directed. His presence excited the most intense enthusiasm in the troops, both on the field, and later in the day, when he rode along the lines, and looked kindly on the shattered regiments that had been in Saturday's fight. To these brave fellows, "few and faint, but fearless still," the young commander addressed a few words of pleasant encouragement that thrilled every ear, and then rode away. The scene in the woods on Sunday told a sad tale, which will, no doubt, be heard with sad ears throughout the South. There lay in heaps the dead, and those in mortal agony, terribly mingled, men young and old, mostly young, from every Southern State.

All day Sunday, after our own men had been seen to, we had out parties in the woods, with stretchers (which had been sent to us from the White House), bringing in the wounded rebels, and other parties engaged in burying them. Our enemies, tired of the fight, employed the greater part of the day in the same way. And so went out the second day of the battle of the Seven Pines. On Monday morning our position could be summed up about thus: Two divisions, much reduced in strength from various causes, had been attacked by a greatly superior force of good troops, and driven fully a mile from the first point of attack; but by the arrival of fresh troops the enemy's course had been arrested, and his purpose to drive us into the Chickahominy decidedly defeated. Yet he occupied our camps and the position he had taken. On Sunday he had again attacked us, and been compelled to retire with loss. But though Richardson's division had driven him on the railroad, and Sickles' brigade through the woods on the Williamsburg road, he still held nearly all, and certainly much the greater part of the ground taken on Saturday. Some men of the 10th Massachusetts regiment went into their camp on Sunday, and brought away a ham; on their return they were greeted by some of the boys of one of the New York regiments with the well-known popular chorus—

Johnny stole the ham,
Sickles killed the man.

This exploit was quoted as a piece of dexterity, so near were the enemy to the place; and the camp of the Tenth was in the rear of all Couch's division. So now, on Monday morning, we were apparently to begin the week well, to go forward and reoccupy, alive or dead, the position from which the enemy had driven us. Resolution was on every face, and all buckled themselves up with a full determination to do a full share of the work, and not only to retrieve what had been lost, but to win more. It was still dim and misty when the lines were under arms, and but little later when the advance of skirmishers was thrown forward. Cautiously the men went on, every step being made completely sure before the next was taken, until a position was gained on the Williamsburg road, where a battery could be posted. There a battery was accordingly placed so as to command the whole road, and again the men went on further and further, and the enemy fell back, his pickets in sight. It began to look very much as if the third day—the day of reoccupation, was to be a bloodless one. And so it proved, our men pushed on, step by step, pushing the rebels on before, with a light exchange of fire, but no serious resistance, until we were once more entirely at home. Then they pushed on again, through camp and beyond it, and once more they were on the road to Richmond; and they kept on it, and that night our pickets were posted within four miles of the rebel capital, and near to a line of works that we fancy is, or represents, the celebrated last ditch where the rebels were to make a final stand. Thus the affair became complete, we had lost our camp, the enemy held it, and now it was retaken, ours once more, and we felt a satisfaction in the result that would not have been greater if we had retaken the camp as bloodily as we had lost it. His departure was a full acknowledgment that he had failed, and was defeated in the purpose for which he came. Here lay yet a large number of the rebel dead, even some of their wounded were still alive and uncared for on the third day.

CHAPTER VII.

INCIDENTS AT THE WHITE HOUSE.

THE Richmond and York railroad crosses the Pamunkey river at the White House. This place, made memorable by being the residence of Mrs. Custis, who became the wife of Washington, on his visit of three days to the family mansion, which, up to the time of writing, stood on the bank of the river, was surrounded by a handsome and well-kept garden. The house itself was a two and a half story frame building, containing six rooms, with out-offices, and, by order of General McClellan, was guarded against intrusion, in compliance with a promise made by him to Colonel Lee, of the rebel army, who is a descendant of Mrs. Custis. The river at this point is quite a large stream, very deep and muddy. The opposite bank is but little above the level of the stream, which now bore on its winding waters a numerous fleet of steamboats, barges, schooners, and every imaginable kind of vessel used in transporting troops; and the horses, mules, guns, gun-carriages, locomotives, railroad cars, and the immense amount of hay, grain, and commissary stores necessary for the army. Over one thousand vessels, of all sizes, were afloat on the river,—some freighted with ordnance stores, and many others packed with live cattle and mules, which from their unceasing uneasiness seemed to suffer from the heat and confined quarters. The landing of the cattle was an occasion of much sport among the hundreds of idlers on the bank; and as each one, tied by its horns, would be hoisted over the vessel's side into the river, a shout of merriment would rend the air.

With the exception of the dwelling and out-houses described, and from which the place derives its name, there is not a dwelling for a mile round. And the shanties, erected by sutlers and refreshment dealers, were the only shelters from the burning sun, if I except the pine-trees along the river's bank, beneath which, and extending to the railroad, the quarter-master, his assistants, post-office, telegraph, and a host of other officials, had erected large and comfortable tents, in which the business of their departments was carried on.

About a mile beyond the White House there was erected a large number of hospital tents, in which were treated the sick sent down from the advance. The wretched water and miasmatic condition of the Chickahominy kept these tents well filled. The rebels having destroyed the railroad bridge across the river, the cars were run down to the river-side, filled with the wounded, after the battle of Fair Oaks. It was here, lying around on the track, as they had been taken out of the freight-cars in which they were transported from Savage's station, I found over 300, many of them in a dying condition; and all of them more or less mutilated, and still enveloped in their filthy and blood-stained clothing, as they were found on the battle-field. Some of these had been attended to by the surgeons, but by far the greatest number were sent down to the station before receiving any surgical care. On learning that there was not any medical officer detailed for this duty, I consulted with Colonel Ingalls, the chief quarter-master, and Dr. Alexander, the medical purveyor, and with their advice proceeded to have them taken care of, first telegraphing to the surgeon-general and Dr. Cuyler, the medical director at Fortress Monroe, the exact state of affairs. I found that there was lying in the river a large number ot steamboats, chartered for the purpose of transporting them, but having no orders remained totally inactive. Colonel Ingalls at once placed the harbor-master under my orders; and by his aid I got the steamers State of Maine, Elm City, and Whildin alongside of the railroad wharf. On board of these boats I had the wounded men carried on litters by all the civilians I could press into the service, and a detail of the 93d New York Volunteers, promptly given me by Lieut.-colonel Butler of that regiment, which was stationed as a guard over the stores accumulated here.

The agents of the Sanitary Commission, on board of their boat, the Wilson Small, were also in the river, under the guidance of Frederick Law Olmstead, Esq., the efficient secretary of the Commission. He responded to my call in the most prompt and effective manner, and labored with me, night and day, to relieve the sufferings of the unfortunate. The general agent of the society, Mr. Knapp, Mr. Mitchell, and Dr. Ware, were also untiring in their exertions. Nor can I ever forget the devoted and self-sacrificing services of the ladies of the Commission, Mrs. Griffin, Mrs. Howland, and Miss Woolsey, and the invaluable aid they rendered in making nutritious beverages and cooling drinks for the parched lips of the fainting and exhausted wounded for forty-eight hours, without intermission or rest. They quickly and cheerfully responded to my innumerable calls on them for clothing, bandages, lint, &c., and their intelligent and fatiguing self-imposed duties were discharged with a courtesy and endeavor I have never seen equalled. By their aid I was enabled to have the men well provided with clean under-clothing, and freely supplied, on arrival in the cars, with tea, coffee, lemonade, &c. Many a poor fellow's life was thus saved, and the hundreds of blessings asked for these ladies, by the parched lips of the exhausted but patient heroes, will doubtless be granted. Without food or rest, at all hours, and often under the most trying and disagreeable circumstances, they labored cheerfully, carrying hope and comfort to the wounded and weary. Before three o'clock, Monday morning, June 2d, I had loaded and dispatched the Whildin, under Dr. Smith of Pennsylvania, the Elm City, under the care of several physicians and surgeons of the Sanitary Commission, and the steamer State of Maine, under the care of Dr. McDonald. These vessels carried away about twelve hundred, but they continued to arrive from the field by hundreds. I felt terribly the want of assistants, and called on the surgeons of the gunboats Sebago, Marblehead, and Currituck, anchored in the river, who quickly lent their aid. I am under obligations, of no ordinary kind, to Dr. Quin, of the Sebago, for able and unremitting assistance. He worked with me steadily and with great skill, for three days and nights, and not until exhausted nature compelled him, did he relinquish his humane efforts; and again, as soon as he had snatched a few hours of rest, he returned to his post. In this manner, for the seven successive days and nights, did I work, not stopping a moment to eat or sleep, performing the necessary amputations, providing steamers, after inspecting them, procuring surgeons, stewards, and nurses for each vessel, and supplying it with commissary and medical stores, and the equally important articles bountifully contributed by the Sanitary Commission. This engagement was the first that really tried the resources and efficiency of this truly good and useful association, and nobly did it respond, through its officers and supplies. The amount of ice, luxuries, and necessaries, freely given and judiciously selected for the wounded, was immense, and I joyfully bear my unqualified testimony to its usefulness. There was at this time, in some of the cities, an unjust prejudice against the association, which was even entertained by army officers, but it has fully proved itself to be the most needful and well-conducted charity that has ever been organized on so large a scale. This is, in a great manner, owing to the character and usefulness of the gentlemen connected with it, and the truly noble ladies, who, at the risk of life and health, and total self-denial and surrender of every personal comfort and necessary accommodation, have contributed their invaluable personal services. The incidents crowded into this eventful week were so very numerous, and the writer's time was so completely occupied, and his mind continually on the stretch to meet the multitudinous wants of the occasion, that he had but a scanty opportunity to make note of them, and the following are but some of the most striking, which from being imprinted on his memory, he has been enabled to reproduce, without claiming them to be free from the errors inseparable from the confusion attendant on a scene of carnage of such magnitude.

Among the many wounded brought down from the battle-field I had abundant opportunity, while attending to their wounds, of learning the true state of things on the Chickahominy, since it was quite necessary I should know whether our army was falling back, as in such case the White House would be abandoned. Reports to this effect having been freely circulated, I lost no opportunity to inform myself of the facts, by interrogating such officers as, from their position on the field, were likely to be best informed. From Col. Champlain, of the 3d Michigan Volunteers, who had received a flesh wound of the thigh, I received the following sketch of his regiment's engagement. Captain Nolan and Lieut. Mason, of this regiment, who were also brought down wounded, corroborated this statement. In the latter, I met a schoolfellow whom I had not seen for twenty years, and our meeting under such circumstances was very affecting.

Col. Champlain's Statement.

After Couch's Division had fallen back, on Saturday, Berry's Brigade was brought forward, consisting of the 1st, 2d, 3d, and 5th Michigan, and 37th New York Volunteers. The 3d Michigan (Col. C.'s regiment) was thrown into the battle in advance, and about half an hour before the others arrived. General Kearney directed them to attack the enemy on the left side of Bottom's Bridge road. The rebels opened fire from among the fallen timber, where they laid concealed. On the right wing of this regiment, not distant over ten rods, an advance was ordered in double quick on the enemy's position. The centre and left wing extended to a thick growth of young pines, and by the time it was formed in line was within thirty feet of the slashes. The rebels now opened a murderous fire on the centre and left, causing a heavy loss, and thinning the ranks of the 3d; but the boys received the fire in a most unflinching manner, and before the enemy had time to reload, the right charged on them with the bayonet, reserving their fire until the concealed foe were drawn from their cover, and as soon as they were in sight delivered a deadly volley. This made them break and run like sheep, leaving the slashes filled with their dead and wounded. The right continued to load and fire at the rebels, who made several ineffectual attempts to reform their shattered ranks, but at each volley they again broke and ran. Thus driven out of the slashes, they fell back still further, and held in this position until reinforced by the balance of their brigade, when they still continued to retreat, until we had recovered the ground lost by General Couch on that side of the road. While this was transpiring the enemy was gaining ground on the other side of the road, and our brigade was in great danger of being flanked; on perceiving which, General Berry withdrew his brigade within the slashes, which he held till relieved, as night came on.

As the colonel finished relating the foregoing, a wounded rebel of the 11th Mississippi, who lay on an adjoining mattress, called out, "That is true. I got this wound running out of those pines. I was not with my regiment, having got separated. As I was told if I shot the one-armed General Kearney I would be promoted, and seeing him in the field the other side of the road, I left the ranks, entered the wood on the opposite side just as our men were leaving it, and, turning to run back, I was shot in the thigh. Do you think the bone is broken, doctor?" To which I replied that I feared it was; and on close examination found it fractured for four inches of the shaft, and was obliged to amputate it. He bore the operation with great fortitude, and, on being dressed and returned to his bed, minus the left leg, he cheerfully said, "Phil Kearney is better off now, with his one arm, than I am."

On the adjoining bed there lay a young, delicate-looking fellow, a corporal in the 3d Georgia Volunteers, who had lost an arm on the battle-field, in Saturday's fight, and whose father, also wounded, was at the time on board of the Daniel Webster, the steamer I selected for use as a receiving ship, as it afforded facilities not possessed by any of the other steamers; and having dispatched all the steamers there were in the river adapted for floating hospitals, I was obliged to have a receiving ship for those that would arrive. Even this was insufficient. So that I was obliged to make requisition on the quarter-master's department for forty Sibley tents, which I had erected along the railroad track, to protect the wounded from sun and rain, and have their wounds dressed and their clothing changed without delay. Some of these men had been lying on the battle-field uncared for for two or three days; nor could this be avoided, as the ground was alternately in the possession of the Union and rebel troops; and their condition, on arrival at the White House, was filthy in the extreme, their wounds alive with maggots, their clothing saturated and stiff with congealed blood and dried mud.

The captain of the Georgia regiment before mentioned, on hearing my dialogue with the Mississippian, asked me what was his destination, or where I intended sending him and the other wounded Confederate prisoners. I told him I had arranged to have as many of the Confederates left at Old Point and Portsmouth, Va., as those hospitals could accommodate. He expressed great satisfaction at this announcement, and seemed terribly unwilling to go North. I was anxious to learn the cause of his hostility to the Northern people; and while engaged with a patient in an adjoining bed, made some inquiries of him as to the feeling existing in his State. He described it as intensely and unanimously hostile; of many years' growth; and stated that he personally was opposed to war, and had been, for his peace proclivities, looked on by his neighbors with suspicion of entertaining Union sentiments. "But," said he, "Doctor, when I found it had to come to blows, I raised money on my plantation, equipped and mounted a com pany of young fellows I had recruited, and have paid them from my own means ever since." He further said, "I have but that one boy you see lying there with his arm shot off," pointing to the corporal; "and if I had a dozen, or was worth a million of dollars, I would risk and lose all before I would again consent to live under the United States flag." I told him I hoped he would change his opinions before his wound was sufficiently healed to allow him to be exchanged, and I trusted yet to see him a good Union man. When I visited the Chesapeake Hospital, some weeks after, he recognized me, and renewed the conversation; and in reply to my inquiry, if he was yet converted to Unionism, he said there was little hopes of it, but if any thing would have such an effect on him, it would be the good care and kind treatment he and the Confederates had received from me and the other surgeons since they were taken prisoners. As an offset to this deep-rooted hostility to the Union, I will mention the case of a rebel surgeon, a Doctor McPhail, of Georgia; he had been taken prisoner with a couple of wounded rebel officers he was attending on the field, and all three were sent down to the White House, from whence I forwarded them to the Fort, on board the steamer Kennebec, in charge of which I had placed Dr. Middleton, Asst. Surgeon U. S. A., and Dr. Alvord, of Michigan, who had philanthropically volunteered his services. Dr. McPhail remained on board of my receiving hospital-boat with his friends, and I allowed him all the liberty and extended to him any courtesy in my power. On his going aboard of the Kennebec, when about to start, he came to bid me farewell, and thank me for my kindness. I asked him to what State he belonged, and stated I was sorry to see him in the rebel service. He replied, he was from Georgia, and was ashamed to tell it, as he believed the war, which had cost the lives of many dear relatives, could have been avoided, but for some unscrupulous politicians from his own and other Southern States.

The arrival of wounded and sick continuing unabated, I determined to send away none but the wounded. To put in the hospital the sick, for whom room had been made by my repeated drafts on it for convalescent soldiers to act as nurses. I also obtained from Assistant Quarter-master Broadwood fifty contrabands, to aid in carrying the wounded, and distributing the lemonade, as the men detailed from the 96th New York Volunteers were entirely worn out with the fatigue of the last three days and nights; but I found the colored men poor substitutes for the willing boys of the ninety-sixth, who, under the orders of their efficient officers, rendered most valuable aid. A number of acting assistant-surgeons arrived this day in response to my repeated telegraphic requests for them, but I found, on an interview, that a very large majority were young and inexperienced, and totally incompetent to take charge of a steamer. I consequently recommended them to proceed to the advance, where the demand for dressers was very great, and requested Captain Sawtelle, assistant quarter-master, having charge of the transportation, to inform me of the arrival of any surgeon under orders to join the advance. By this means I was able to secure the assistance of some few surgeons, and thus give a respite to those gentlemen who had worked so long and faithfully with me. The news of the great battle, spread over the nation through the newspapers, brought hundreds to the White House, each one fearing his or her relative or friend had fallen a victim; the repeated inquiries by these persons, to many of whom I could offer no consolation, nor impart any intelligence, seriously hindered me, while it was of but little use to them. I adopted a plan: by having my clerk learn from any officer that came down in charge of the wounded, or of prisoners, the names of the regiments engaged, and by taking a list of those that had arrived, I was frequently enabled to give the desired information. Judging from the number of dispatches I hourly received from Dr. Cuyler, at the fort, he must have been similarly importuned. As far as I could I used the cooking apparatus of the receiving steamer, the Daniel Webster, to cook food for the nurses, where the beef-tea and other necessaries for the wounded were prepared; and as there was not any hotel or place to procure a meal at the White House, it soon became known that if any thing could be had to eat it was on board the hospital boats. This brought many field and line officers, who for days had not tasted cooked food, and from them I learned the latest news, and probable number of wounded I would be obliged to make provision for.

The Congressional committee on the conduct of the war had paid a visit to the White House, accompanied by Hon. John C. Tucker, assistant secretary of war, and other gentlemen. Two members of it, the Hon. Moses F. Odell, M. C., of Brooklyn, and Hon. John Patten, M. C., of Pennsylvania, worked unceasingly to aid in getting the wounded from the cars to the boats, and preserving order. In this they were ably seconded by Col. Wm. Borden, of New York, agent of the Fall River line of steamers, two of which, the Canonicus and State of Maine, were being used as hospital boats, and both of them were models of cleanliness and order, and well worthy the imitation of others.

The number of wounded was so great that I was obliged to have mattresses spread on the saloon floors of the steamers, on each of which a patient was laid. And finding it much cooler and easier, I selected the worst cases for these beds. Frequently I have heard the poor fellows, who now lay helpless beside each other, recount the bloody deeds of those two days; and on one occasion I was called to separate two who had quarrelled. Both were Irishmen, and had been friends, working for a stevedore. One went to Mobile, where he entered the Confederate service; the other, remaining in New York, joined the Irish Brigade. They had not met for seven years, and their recognition, under these peculiar and trying circumstances, was the opposite to friendly, and I have no doubt, if able, they would have had a set-to. Each reviled the other for having taken up arms on his side, and freely used the names of traitors and turncoats. This turbulent scene had scarcely been ended by the removal to another part of the vessel, of one of the belligerents, before another, of a very different nature, occurred. It appears that a private of the 15th Massachusetts Volunteers had, on the death of his wife, some years ago, gone West, taking his two children with him. One, a daughter, had married in Detroit; the other went to Grand Rapids, the father returning to Boston. The son, on the breaking out of the rebellion, joined the 3d Michigan Volunteers, and the father the 15th Massachusetts; and here, after a separation of several years, they met on board the hospital steamer, both wounded. The meeting was very affecting, the old man, with a severe wound of the shoulder, and a flesh wound of the leg, crawled from his bed to embrace his son, who lay terribly mangled by the explosion of a shell, from which he died the following morning. There arrived this day, with the wounded, a private of one of the Pennsylvania Volunteers, who had become a raving and violent maniac from fright.

The shock to his nervous system was more than he could bear. His exclamations of terror were piteous and heart-rending, and caused such discomfort to the other sufferers that I sent him on shore to the hospital, to do which six of the strongest men were barely sufficient.

Mr. Clement Barclay, of Philadelphia, has been most active and untiring in his exertions in aiding the transportation of the wounded and carrying out my suggestions, which he asked and cheerfully acted on, he enabled me to devote to the operations the necessary time; he also sent for me to the Secretary of War several dispatches to have steamers and surgeons sent on, and rendered such services as only could be contributed by a gentleman of ability and whole-souled philanthropy.

The staff of volunteer nurses was increased this day by several ladies: one, the wife of Lieut.-col. Chas. Sampson of the 3d Maine Volunteers, was most active and useful, and did much to alleviate the sufferings of the brave fellows, all of whom bore their wounds, and subsequent exposure and want of care on the field, with wonderful and uncomplaining heroism. Where their parched lips received the cup of tea, gruel, or lemonade, or, as in many cases, a stimulating drink, they were truly grateful, and expressed their thanks to the lady nurses in a very flattering manner.

On Thursday night, at 11 P. M., I received a dispatch from the advance that a cargo of 250 wounded had left for the White House at 6 P. M., and asking if they had arrived, as the officer in charge had failed to telegraph his arrival, as ordered. I proceeded, with about fifty nurses carrying lanterns, along the road for a mile, the rain pouring in torrents, not meeting the train. Several of them sat down, myself among the number, and soon fell asleep, the first I had since the Saturday night previous. I had lain on the wet ground for about an hour, when I was awakened by the shrill whistle of the locomotive, making up in speed for the loss of time it had sustained by running off the track near Dispatch station. When these had been received and cared for, I determined to return with the train to the advance, to learn, by personal observation, the number of wounded still remaining. We started at three in the morning, and after a tedious ride of three hours reached Fair Oaks station. I then procured a horse and orderly to visit the hospitals and learn the number each contained. To do this it was necessary to pass near the battle-field, the odor from which was insufferable. For over a mile, the ground was thickly strewn with unburied men, mules, and horses, whose decomposing bodies infected the atmosphere for miles. Having collected all the wounded together fit to be removed, I proceeded with two hundred of them to the White House, the rest to follow the return of the train. I had them conveyed on board of the Louisiana, one of the largest and best boats chartered by the government, and determined on the arrival of the others from the advance, to proceed in person with them to a Northern hospital. My reasons for so doing were, that I had received all the wounded who for some time would be fit for removal, and as among those last sent down, were very many of the most dangerous cases,—many of them having lain on the battle-field uncared for for several days,—and as all the surgeons in whom I could place confidence had been dispatched with the other steamers that took away over four thousand of the wounded; I decided on going with these myself, taking Dr. Bates, surgeon of the 15th Massachusetts, and Doctors Case and Robinson, of Buffalo, as assistants.

Wednesday night the train from Fair Oaks station, with over two hundred wounded, was delayed nearly three hours by the following causes. It appears that a rebel cavalry company of Stuart's brigade conceived the idea of cutting off the communication between White House and head-quarters, and made a sudden dash at the train, which, in consequence of the track having been washed away with the late heavy rain, was proceeding at a very slow pace. A shot from one of their carbines disabling the engineer, the fireman stopped the locomotive, and the rebels proceeded to rifle the cars. Ascertaining that it contained wounded, they were not very close in their scrutiny, and failed to discover a paymaster's safe, containing thirty thousand dollars of government funds, which Paymaster Taylor was returning to the White House with, having been obliged, by the confusion consequent on the battle, to suspend paying the men of the brigade to which he was attached. The attack on the train was so sudden and unexpected, and the means of resistance at hand so feeble, that the paymaster, leaving the safe with the money behind him on the car, sought refuge in an adjoining wood. The train, after some delay, was allowed to proceed to its destination, and the valuable, but much-coveted prize, was found in one of the freight cars, and handed over to Captain Sawtelle, of the quarter-master's department. The frightened paymaster made his appearance at the White House in a state of great trepidation for the supposed loss of the money; but, after some bantering and ridicule for his cowardly desertion of the treasure, was informed of its safety, to his great and unconcealed joy.

Among the wounded which arrived from the field on Wednesday, was a young private of the 1st Long Island regiment, son of Captain Stillwell, of that corps, who had been shot through the body. He was carried on board while I was busily engaged in extracting a musket-ball from beneath the frontal bone of a young fellow of the 103d Pennsylvania Volunteers. His father, who was sick at the White House, having been sent off the field in a feeble state, was a friend of Hon. Moses F. Odell, who was working with unflagging and laborious zeal. This gentleman requested my care for young Stillwell. The family resided in Brooklyn, New York. I was unable to give any reason to hope for his recovery, as he was then sinking, and died in a few hours. The body, through the exertions of Mr. Odell, was embalmed, and was taken by me on the Louisiana to Fortress Monroe, on the following Saturday, where I was obliged to leave it, in consequence of the previous orders issued forbidding the transportation North of dead bodies. I was, however, enabled to recover it on my return from Philadelphia, from which place I brought his brother on the steamer, and with the aid of Mr. Martin, of New York, a most careful and considerate undertaker, had his remains removed to Brooklyn for burial. Mr. Martin had accompanied Mr. James Cooke, of New York, who was now returning to the White House, to renew his valuable labors, of no ordinary kind, for the soldiers. Mr. Cooke's kind and cheerful compliance with the many requests of the suffering, and his untiring attendance on them, was a most valuable assistance, and a blessing to many, who gratefully remember his kind and encouraging nursing, promptly rendered, without hope of reward but that arising from the pleasing knowledge of soothing the agonies of a suffering fellow-being

Another member of the 1st Long Island regiment, which had suffered so terribly, was eagerly sought for by his father on Wednesday, but I had not as yet received him. It was Corporal Samuel F. Bouton, of Brooklyn. He arrived on Thursday, and as I had taken the receiving ship, the Daniel Webster, down the river to load the Spaulding from her, and then turned her over to be cleaned and fumigated, —rendered necessary by the intolerable stench arising from the hundreds of wounded that had been treated, and the large number of operations performed on board of her—her main-deck and saloon being used for this purpose,—I had Corporal Bouton, who was dangerously wounded, carried on board the Louisiana, and appropriated enough space in the upper saloon to his use. His deeply distressed father claimed the privilege of nursing him, to which I assented, and detailed a nurse for his special assistance. The ball having passed through the substance of the right lung, his breathing was distressingly difficult, and his being able to reach his home alive depended on his being kept perfectly quiet. No surgical aid could be rendered him, the ball having passed out below the shoulder-blade, and medical skill was alone useful in relieving the distressing symptoms. His father watched and waited on him with the most solicitous affection during the week he was on board the Louisiana, until our arrival in Philadelphia, when he had him carried to the Camden and Amboy railroad, *en route* for his home, in a very feeble condition. The fatigue of the journey was too much for his fast-failing strength, and as the Amboy steamboat came within sight of his native city, opposite to Staten Island, he breathed his last. His mother, to whom, at Mr. Bouton's request, I had telegraphed from Philadelphia of his having started for home, was denied the privilege of seeing him alive. Her grief must have been heart-rending when she beheld the lifeless body of her handsome son. Too many mothers, alas! have thus sadly been bereaved since the breaking out of this unholy war, which has spread desolation over the land, and swept away the brightest flowers of its youth and manhood.

Among the wounded Confederate prisoners I brought down to Fortress Monroe was a major of a North Carolina regiment, as noble and as fine-looking a fellow as I had ever seen. He had been shot in the thigh, fracturing the thigh bone very badly, and rendering amputation necessary, which I performed before leaving the White House. After the operation was over, and he had been removed to his bed and made comfortable, he thanked us for our attention, stating that he had not expected such kind treatment at our hands, but said, "Your men will never take Richmond, unless they do it over the dead and wounded bodies of fifty thousand Southern soldiers. They have resolved upon it and will perform it at any cost of life." He was very communicative, and was evidently a gentleman of fine education and good social position. He deplored the war and its necessity, but said it had been brewing for many years, and that sooner or later it should come, and that the Northern and Southern people were so dissimilar in their habits, sentiments, and social organization, that they never could, nor should they be commingled as one people and one nation. He argued that the Union had been held together, for the last twenty years, by a dislike on the part of the Southern people to go to war with the North, and that the concessions, which they had from time to time made to the North, had only put off the evil, but not remedied it—that Webster, Clay, Calhoun, and the statesmen of the last generation, had foreseen this rebellion, and had succeeded in postponing it by advising compromises of the just claims of the South to the peaceful possession of their slave property, guaranteed to them by the Constitution, which he claimed had been violated by Northern abolitionists.

CHAPTER VIII.

VOYAGE TO FORTRESS MONROE AND PHILADELPHIA.

We started at 6 P. M., on Saturday evening, for Fortress Monroe, and during the night performed several operations.

Just before leaving, a young private of the 3d Maine Volunteers, named Gordon, who had been struck in both legs by minié-balls, and whose legs were amputated above the knees, died. On the voyage down the river: five more breathed their last, having sunk under their wounds and exhaustion, and were buried at the fort, which we reached on Sunday forenoon. I at once called on Dr. Cuyler, the medical director, and was most kindly received by him: he knew from the number of wounded I had consigned to him, and the daily reports of gentlemen arriving from the White House, the extent of my labors, and made full acknowledgment of them. I also visited General Dix, who had relieved General Wool at this station, since my departure from it. He came on board the Louisiana, talked kindly and sympathized with the wounded sufferers, and expressed his full commendation of my services and the orderly condition of the vessel. On consultation with Dr. Cuyler, we decided on removing to the hospitals, at the fort, 85 wounded Confederates I had on board, and to take an equal number from these hospitals, who would thus benefit by a change to a more northern hospital. A sudden and violent storm sprung up, which made the steamer part her moorings from the dock, and run into the steamer Flushing, previously sunk opposite the fort. The storm continued with unabated fury for three days, and obliged us to run the steamer to Newport News, as she had lost both her anchors at the fort. On Wednesday, the weather giving promise of a change for the better, I took on board the wounded Union troops and started for Philadelphia with my precious cargo, all of whom had, notwithstanding the storm, greatly improved from the sea-breezes and care bestowed on them, and the attention paid to their wounds. On the way down from the White House, the Confederate wounded had also picked up in spirits, and became more communicative with our men; the dialogues between them were of the spiciest kind, each claiming for his side all the bravery, and each having some instance of cowardice of the troops of their opponents to relate. I was busy the whole night in getting through with the operations, and, on their completion, in taking a correct list of all on board for my own use, a copy of which I supplied to the press. During the hours spent in this weary task, many of the men being too sick or too sleepy to disturb, I heard a Confederate soldier, on the lower deck, singing for his own, and the amusement of some dozen others in adjoining beds, the following Secesh song, of which I obtained a copy, and now give it for the reader's edification.

Secesh Song.

CHIVALROUS C. S. A.

Air.—Vive la Compagnie.

I'll sing you a song of the South's sunny clime,
Chivalrous C. S. A.
Which went to housekeeping once on a time,
Bully for C. S. A.

Like heroes and princes they lived for awhile,
Chivalrous C. S. A.
And routed the Hessians in most gallant style,
Bully for C. S. A.

Chorus.—Chivalrous, chivalrous people are they,
Chivalrous, chivalrous people are they,
In C. S. A. In C. S. A.
Ay, in chivalrous C. S. A.

Oh, they have the finest of musical ears,
Chivalrous C. S. A.
Yankee Doodle's too vulgar for them, it appears,
Bully for C. S. A.
The North may sing and whistle it still,
Miserable U. S. A.
Three cheers for the South now, boys, with a will,
And groans for the U. S. A.
Chorus.—Chivalrous people are they, &c.

Thursday morning broke bright and sunny, and found us steaming up the Delaware river. We reached Philadelphia at nine o'clock, and dropping anchor in the stream, I proceeded on shore to report my arrival to Dr. King, the medical director at that city.

Hardly had the Louisiana touched the Callowhill-street wharf, when the citizens of Philadelphia, among whom the news of her arrival had spread like magic, crowded the wharves and streets adjoining, all eager to catch a glimpse of the mutilated heroes of Fair Oaks. With the concurrence of Dr. King, I determined on giving furloughs to all the wounded who were able to proceed to their homes; and as many of them belonged to Pennsylvania regiments, this privilege was gladly accepted by nearly half the number on board. Experience had taught me that men suffering from wounds and the long-continued privations of camp life, would recover much sooner under the kind care of home and friends than in a military hospital, and thus return to their duty in far less time than if kept in general hospitals. The result proved the correctness of my conclusion, and a vast expense was thus spared the government, while it afforded much gratification to the soldier and his anxious friends. The Philadelphians, true to their well-earned reputation, behaved most generously on this occasion. The police force attended and preserved order, and afforded full opportunity for us to avail ourselves of the promptly tendered services of the fire department, who turned out *en masse* to convey, on their carriages, to the different hospitals those poor fellows unable to walk. The citizens, generally, vied with each other in bestowing kind attentions on them, and before leaving for the seat of war, I received, for the benefit of the wounded, bountiful contributions of every imaginable luxury and necessary indispensable for their use. The Sanitary Commission, through its philanthropic and benevolent agent at this city, also sent to their general agent liberal supplies of articles most needed, and thus replenished the stock on which I had largely drawn at the White House. Among those who had fallen or been wounded in the Fair Oaks' fight, there were many residents of Philadelphia, the friends of whom heaped the kindest and most generous courtesies on the writer. Among them was the family of Colonel Lee, who had lost a noble son, Lieutenant Lee, of the 81st regiment Pennsylvania Volunteers, and whose eldest son, Captain Robert Lee, had received a severe wound from a minié-ball, which had lodged between the bones of the leg. This exemplary family received the kind sympathy of many, and elicited my sincere condolence for their bereavements. Their delicate and kind attentions, tendered through their friend, Joseph P. Loughead, Esq., to me, during my brief stay in their hospitable city, will ever be gratefully remembered. It was, indeed, a rich reward for my services, and I sincerely grieved that the pressing necessity for my return to the Peninsula, alone prevented me from paying my respects in person to that venerable gentleman, Colonel Lee, whose sorrow-stricken face, when I first met him, at Fortress Monroe, bearing manfully up under the twofold afflicting visitation, was a true index to his warm and patriotic heart, and bespoke him the worthy father of a worthy son, whose heroic and uncomplaining fortitude had endeared him to me, as it had to his regiment. There were many noble wounded under my care at the White House, but you, Captain Robert Lee, stand out in pleasing prominence on my memory.

It being necessary to have some repairs done to the boilers of the Louisiana, she was taken to the Richmond boiler-shops, and this delayed our departure until Monday. The assistant-surgeons and nurses, as soon as we had landed our wounded, eagerly sought leaves of absence, which I could not refuse; and, with some few exceptions, they went to pay short visits to their families. This prevented my leaving, and obliged me to telegraph for my wife to meet me in Philadelphia, to allay her anxiety for my safety, as I had not been able to write to her for many days; and she knowing I was at the great battle, naturally felt solicitous for my return. On her arrival, in the night train, she was struck with the changes which fatigue, exposure, and the loss of rest, for ten consecutive nights, had effected on me. I had hoped, on leaving the White House, to have obtained some rest on the voyage, but the many severe cases on board, requiring my constant care, the illness of Dr. Bates, my first assistant, and the inexperience of the others, prevented my snatching an hour's sleep; and while in Philadelphia, the demands on my time were so numerous from the friends of the soldiers, that I had but little time to recruit my strength, so much needed on my return to the Peninsula.

Visit to the Philadelphia Hospitals.

At the invitation of the surgeons in charge, I visited the hospitals in which the wounded volunteers from the several steamers I had dispatched from the White House and from the Louisiana, were cared for. On my arrival at the U. S. hospital, corner of Fifth and Buttonwood streets, I was unexpectedly greeted with a hearty cheer from the poor fellows, as they lay on their comfortable beds. Many of their faces were quite familiar to me, but the number I had attended during the preceding eventful week was so large that I could not possibly recollect them all. They, however, generally recognized me, and expressed their thanks. I found here Col. Cross, of the 5th New Hampshire Volunteers, who had been wounded in the leg, while leading on the brigade of which his regiment formed a part, and of which he was then in command. I was gratified to find him fast recovering from the effect of his wound, but suffering mentally from some unjust statements, in relation to his regiment, that appeared in one of the New York papers of the day previous. Jealous of the well-earned reputation of his gallant corps, and of his own valorous conduct, he stated the particulars of his part in the engagement, which I give in his own words:

"My regiment, the 5th New Hampshire Volunteers, was detached from Howard's Brigade on Saturday evening, and on Sunday morning occupied the extreme right of the line formed by General French, when we skirmished with the enemy, and took quite a number of prisoners.

The battle had raged some time, when orders came for me to go to the relief of a portion of French's Brigade. I moved quickly down the railroad track, passed General French, and halted on the track, face to the enemy, in rear of the position just occupied by Howard's two regiments, the 61st and 64th New York. Being in command of the brigade, I sent an order by Adjutant Gregory, of the 61st, for the two regiments to clear my front as soon as póssible, and I would take their place. This was done at once, and while the movement was going on, the Irish Brigade came up in my rear. The 69th New York formed on the right of my line, and the 88th on my left, but in rear of my line, where they halted. The 5th New Hampshire then entered the woods, solitary and alone, the regiments on the right and left remaining in their places. About 200 yards from the railroad track we came upon the dead and wounded of the 61st and 64th New York, and a few yards farther on we met the enemy. Twice we drove back their line, and it rallied; the third time it broke. Most of the firing took place at twenty yards range. While advancing the second time on the enemy's line, the 69th fired a volley right into the backs of my men, for I had obliqued my line to prevent being flanked. That volley mortally wounded many of my best men. Fortunately, being on the railroad track, their aim was high. I expected the two regiments on my flanks would have entered the woods with us, but they did not; and why, I never could learn. When the enemy ceased firing, my regiment broke by the right of companies to the rear, and filed out to the railroad. It was here I received this ugly wound in the thigh, that made me acquainted with you, Doctor. My boys carried me to the track, in front of the regiment. On the track we found the two regiments; and here two men of the 69th relieved my own men, and carried me to the rear. The Irish Brigade, while on the track, lost four killed and twenty-seven wounded. The 5th New Hampshire lost nearly two hundred killed and wounded, among them myself, the major, and many other officers; and yet we have hardly been mentioned as having been in the fight, and there, as you see (handing me the newspaper), grossly misrepresented. No other regiment was sent into the woods. This ended the fight of Sunday. The 5th bore their part in its closing scene, and not till then did I turn over the command of the 1st Brigade to Col. Parker. It is true that the brave Howard's Brigade bore the brunt of Sunday's fight, and no doubt the official reports will do justice to the 61st and 64th regiments, which fought so well and lost so heavily. But I do want to see justice done the 5th, and no more. We did our duty, and want our country to know it; and I owe it to the mothers, wives, and sisters of the brave boys I took with me from New Hampshire that the truth should be told."

The recital of the above consumed all the time I could spare to this well-ordered establishment. It had been a coach factory, and was converted into a hospital. The wards were large, and kept well ventilated. The patients, one and all, were loud in their praises of the care they were receiving, and of the kind attentions bestowed on them by the ladies of Philadelphia, many of whom I saw tenderly nursing the wounded, to whom the change from the bloody field of Fair Oaks to the comforts they were then surrounded with, must have been as striking as agreeable.

Departure from Philadelphia.

The Louisiana having received the necessary repairs and taken in coal, was again hauled into the Callowhill-street wharf, to take on board the generous contributions of the Philadelphians for the sick and wounded, the necessary commissary stores, and the supplies for the Sanitary Commission at the White House. The quarter-master having received directions to forward, with all possible haste, a number of artillery horses, sixty were put on board, in boxes or stalls, fitted up on the main-deck. With this cargo, so unsuited to a hospital boat, we started from Philadelphia on the afternoon of Monday, June 16th. The wharves were again crowded with a dense throng of people, to bid us farewell, and send messages to their friends in the army, and to obtain promises that all the Pennsylvania wounded would, in future, be sent to Philadelphia. A number of gentlemen, Mr. Binney, Mr. Loughead, and others, came on board, some with their ladies, to see the Louisiana, of whose size they had heard much. Nor did they come empty-handed; their carriages brought down many luxuries for the use of the medical staff on board, and valuable contributions for the wounded. Steam being up, and the word "all's ready" having been given, the gang-plank pulled in, we moved out of the wharf, and amid the deafening cheers of the crowd, the Louisiana steamed majestically down the Delaware on her mission of mercy and relief.

I subjoin a list of the medical staff and nurses on board, when we started for Fortress Monroe, which we reached on Wednesday:

List of Medical Staff and Nurses.

Surgeon in Charge—Dr. Thomas T. Ellis.

Acting Assistant Surgeons—Case, Janner, Maury, Tyson, Corson.

Acting Hospital Steward—Sankey, 49th Penn. Vols.

Clerk to Surgeon in Charge—G. A. Wood, 40th N. Y. Volunteers.

Dresser—Platt Raymond, 5th Wisconsin Volunteers.

Nurses—E. Graves, E. H. Post, L. Port, G. Foot, Wm. H. Boyd, O. L. Guild, C. H. Miller, F. E. Wheeler, G. L. Welden, T. Rhae, J. Potts, J. Bliven, L. H. Clapp, E. S. King, J. Myerby, E. Emerson, W. P. Barnes, M. H. Conley, J. G. Abbott, L. Raymond, J. Legarey, Wm. Billings, Patrick Lyons, E. Almsted, E. Barclay, J. Gaylord, F. W. Carpenter, S. G. Peterson, G. W. Gillen, L. Haven.

These men were members of volunteer regiments, and the greater number of them I had obtained from the hospital at the White House.

The following Philadelphia ladies requested to be allowed to proceed to the White House as volunteer nurses, but returned, without rendering any services: Mrs. Corson, Mrs. Phillips, Miss Caldwell. In addition to these, we had on board, Mr. Jas. Cooke, Mr. Martin, Mr. Taylor; Major Brinten, U. S. paymaster; Mr. Goddard and Mr. Alexander, his clerks; and Mr. Stillwell, of Brooklyn—the death of whose brother I have mentioned—and who was now proceeding to Fortress Monroe to recover his remains, which, through the kindness of Dr. Cuyler, he was enabled to do.

Our trip was a most agreeable one. Having partially recovered from the fatigue, and not having any care but the discipline of the nurses to attend to, we enjoyed the beautiful sail down the Delaware river and bay, and arrived on Wednesday at the fort, well supplied with every requisite for our future labors.

CHAPTER IX.

FORTRESS MONROE—RETURN TO WHITE HOUSE.

On our arrival at Fortress Monroe, I anxiously inquired for the latest news from the army,—fearing a renewal of the fight had taken place, as I was satisfied that the failure of the rebels to achieve their design in cutting off our left from the main body of the army, though for the present foiled, was not totally abandoned; but I learned from General Dix, to whom I introduced the ladies and gentlemen from Philadelphia, that all had been comparatively quiet since my departure, and that, with the exception of some shelling of the pickets and slight skirmishing of the outposts, matters were as I had left them. As a couple of hours would necessarily elapse before starting for the White House, in consequence of our intention to tow the hospital-ship St. Mark, which lay in Hampton Roads waiting for a tug, it was spent by the Philadelphians in viewing the Fort. Fortress Monroe, as most of my readers are aware, is built on the sandy promonotory forming one of the southern boundaries of Chesapeake Bay, and which has been better known as Old Point Comfort,—but a few years since one of the most popular and fashionable Southern watering-places, to accommodate whom a large wooden hotel, with a circular front ornamented with Corinthian columns, was erected. This hotel, the only one at the place, was capable of containing 1,200 guests, and such was the rush to the "Point," that frequently 1,500 persons have been accommodated at one time. It contained a fine dining-room and concert-room, with all the necessary public apartments usual in an hotel on a scale of such magnitude. It was at this time, and had been for some months previous, used as a United States hospital, under the charge of Doctor Bountico, an excellent surgeon, who spared no trouble to prevent the ill effects of its want of ventilation, in a great measure owing to its peculiar shape, and in consequence of which it was soon after abandoned for hospital purposes. Two or three other general hospitals were situated near—the Chesapeake and Seminary. The reader can hardly imagine a busier scene than that going on at this time at Old Point: thousands of soldiers, sutlers, camp-followers, and contrabands hurrying to and fro in a state of confusion; the steamboat wharf—the great rendezvous—continually crowded with passengers going to or returning from the Peninsula. This was the outer gate of the army lines,—all passes to which, were here issued, on proper authority, by the Provost Marshal, Major W. P. Jones, U. S. A., who performed his arduous duties with unusual suavity. His forbearance must have been frequently overtaxed by the unreasonable requests for passes from persons having no better claim than curiosity. The general satisfaction given by Major Jones caused much sincere regret on his leaving, when General Wool (of whose staff he was a member) was relieved by General Dix. The major's office was in the hotel building adjoining the hospital; and between it and that portion of the building used as an hotel by Willard, the other staff officers, viz., the quarter-masters and commissary, were distributed around among the cottages formerly used as family residences, or were accommodated in temporary buildings, a large number of which had been erected for these and various other purposes, such as store-houses, post-offices, express-offices, harbor-master offices, &c. Their number and unfinished appearance, scattered around without any reference to order, gave the place an appearance very unlike what it presented when used as a watering-place before the commencement of the rebellion, and bearing a striking resemblance to San Francisco or Melbourne in the early days of the gold fever. The Rip Raps, on which Fort Wool is being erected, lies in the roadstead opposite the fort. It is a small, bare rock, and presents the appearance, at a distance, of having been artificially constructed. It is used as a military prison, the inmates being obliged to work on the fortifications: cut off from all communication with the mainland, they must lead a terrible life. Besides the steamboat wharf there is another, the light-house wharf, the approaches to which were equally thronged, and, taken in connection with the crowds of shipping and steamboats which lined the wharves and filled the roadstead, presented a scene of animation that could not fail to strike a visitor as peculiar, and only to be accounted for by its proximity to the army of a great nation in time of war.

As the Fort was used as the depot of supply for all ordnance and other stores, the offices of the heads of each department were continually crowded, and any one having business to transact with these gentlemen suffered an unavoidable loss of time, trying to their patience; and in some cases the outbursts of temper caused by the delays created amusement, and helped to pass the time spent in waiting. Having completed my arrangements on shore, we started for Yorktown, where we left the St. Mark, and reached the White House next day after another scorching trip up the tortuous and muddy Pamunkey.

Back again to the former scenes of our busy labors. But how changed an appearance every thing wears! No hurrying to and fro from the hospital steamers; no arrivals of trains with wounded; every thing peaceful; and the bustle and confusion at the quarter-master's, and other offices, seems to have quieted down, as if the scorching sun had produced a lethargy which the employees of the departments could not shake off. Even the contrabands, horses, and mules were visibly affected by the heat; and the oppressive calm seemed an ominous precursor of the storm that soon broke over this placid scene.

I found that but a few wounded had been received from the advance during my absence. They were now lying on board the steamer South America, at the railroad wharf, waiting until enough had been sent down to load the vessel. My letters had been sent on board the Sanitary Commission steamer Wilson Small, as was usual while I was here; but she had gone to Yorktown with Mr. Olmstead and Dr. Vollum, and would not return until next day. The short distance from the Louisiana to the post-office occupied some time in getting over, as I met many well-known faces, and was frequently saluted with, "Welcome back, Doctor." Most of these gentlemen had labored with me,—many of them day and night,—and we consequently had become better acquainted than an ordinary intercourse of years would have made us. From them I learned that Dr. Chas. Tripler, Medical Director of the Army of the Potomac, had been down to the White House, having, as I suppose, heard of the commendations I had received from the members of the Committee on the Conduct of the War, and of the censure he received for not having made provision for the discharge of the duties I assumed on my first arrival. I have stated, in a former chapter, the condition of things on my first getting here. I at once telegraphed to the surgeon-general, Dr. Cuyler, and Dr. Tripler. From the two former I received orders to act as my discretion would dictate; but Dr. Tripler took little or no notice of my letters and dispatches. The former, however, were sufficient authority for me to act on. The amount, quality, and necessity for the services I had performed had received the commendation of the authorities and the country. Of this Dr. Tripler was aware; and, in order to neutralize it, he appointed for those duties a Dr. Watson, who was in charge of the hospital at the White House, and who, as he expressed it, had more duties than he could perform. The opportune arrival of Dr. Vollum, at this time, set this matter to rights; and the relief (as medical director of the Army of the Potomac), of Dr. Tripler, by Dr. Letterman, which occurred a few days after, was the most convincing decision in my favor.

The excitement at the White House to-day, and for the last twenty-four hours, has been intense. The story is abroad that the ubiquitous Stonewall Jackson, with a large flying *corps d'armée*, is approaching the White House, with the general idea of capturing the stores here for the Army of the Potomac, or of destroying them, or of breaking up our communication with the advance, and thereby of starving out the army, and of clearing out things in general, besides killing all the troops, camp-followers, &c., &c., as a sort of by-play. What adds to the excitement, is the fact that a gravel-train, that went up the railroad from here this morning, has just returned, and brings back the story of the taking by the rebel troops of Dispatch Station and a down train. Be this as it may, it is certain that a train leaving before the one captured had three army paymasters on board, with about $6,000,000 between them;—this would have been a good haul for Jeff. Davis. On receipt of the above intelligence, orders were given civilians to leave. The fact of the taking of Dispatch station needed only to be told them to insure prompt compliance with the order. There has been, too, a sudden diminution of the fraternity of sutlers, who have skedaddled in an agony of fright. The mail-boat, which left very late, never went away so well loaded. There is a general movement of all the vessels, that have been so long lying in the Pamunkey river, towards the mouth. Every thing possible to be moved has been, or will be, sent down to Cumberland or West Point. All the tugs and steam-vessels have been busy as bees, and things look rather lively on the water. The river is now comparatively free from vessels, and if the famous "Stonewall Jackson" does come, he will find little in the river to tempt his cupidity. On the land there has been quite a general clearing out. Quarter-masters, and other officers, have placed their effects, private or official, upon steamers, ready for an instant start, so soon as the rebel bayonets gleam near us. The woods lining the shores of the river have been cut down to give the guns of the gunboats a chance to work, and every precaution has been taken to insure Jackson a warm reception. There is certainly a great fright on every one's face. But I fancy there is little reason for it. Perhaps, as a precautionary measure, all this general evacuation may be well enough; but it strikes me, a looker-on in Venice, that it would have been as well to have sent troops enough here to guarantee safety, when it could have been done. It is certainly a singular oversight to leave a base of operations, and a point so essentially important as this, with a force which may not be deemed sufficient to protect it against small raids of partisan corps. It may have been an oversight, but after the "scare" which the presence of a roving band of rebels caused, some weeks since, it seems to be a blunder that precautions against a recurrence of the movement should not have been taken. We are stronger to-day, of course, but it seems by military minds not to be deemed strong enough. Eight or ten thousand men ought to be at this point guarding it, as well as the railroad to the front. There is undoubtedly heavy fighting going on, on the right wing of the army, to-day. The enemy are endeavoring to turn our right flank; but from all accounts they are not meeting with success. It is very generally believed the grand battle is soon to come off, and may be now going on; if so, the result will soon be known. May it be a glorious one.

CHAPTER X.

TRIP TO WASHINGTON ON THE JUNIATA.

HAVING received orders to proceed to Washington and make a personal report of my duties while acting medical director at the White House. I turned over the charge of the Louisiana to Dr. Middleton, assistant-surgeon United States Army, and started in the Juniata, which Captain Sawtelle, assistant quarter-master, placed at my service. The trip, which occupied two days, was delightful, the clear bracing sea-air was a most agreeable change from the hot and sickly banks of the Pamunkey. I arrived at 5 P. M. on Monday evening, and had been at the Kirkwood Hotel but an hour when I was called on by Dr. Alvord, of the office of the Interior, already mentioned, and who had, with Judge Clark, his associate (as a committee), to look after the interests of the wounded Michigan Volunteers, efficiently aided me. They had also written from the White House a very strong letter to Senator Chandler, making favorable mention of my services, and now called to introduce me to him. Between Senator Chandler's rooms and that of Mr. Odell the evening passed away, and, according to appointment, I reported at the Surgeon-general's office the following morning at nine o'clock. My reception by Surgeon-general Hammond, was cordial in the extreme; he stated he had heard of my valuable services from quite a number, mentioning Mr. Odell, Paymaster King, Mr. Olmstead, and others, and said I had proved myself a highly competent and efficient surgeon, and that he was deeply grateful to me for assuming the duties at the White House as I had thereby saved him and the country everlasting disgrace; that he supposed there was a surgeon at the White House, detailed by Dr. Tripler for that duty. That it would afford him pleasure to forward my claims for promotion, if I desired it, and that he advised me to take some rest after my unusual labors, and tendered me transportation to my home in New York for the purpose, which I accepted, and after considerable conversation with him and the assistant surgeon-general, in relation to reforms needed among the nurses, with whom I had had great trouble to keep sober, and other matters connected with the department, I left the office to return, by appointment, at three o'clock for a second interview. Leaving the Surgeon-general's office I proceeded to the capitol to meet, by appointment, the Committee on the Conduct of the War, some members of which, as I have stated, were at the White House when the wounded from the battle of Fair Oaks were arriving, and witnessed my exertions. I was introduced to the committee by Senator Chandler, who spoke highly of my services. I replied to several questions from members of the committee, and urged on them many needed reforms. I then was brought into the Senate chamber and introduced to many senators. The confirmation of General Shields as a major-general, was under discussion, and I learned before leaving the capitol that it had fallen through. Mr. Forney, the secretary of the Senate, who had been written to by Mr. Loughead of Philadelphia, showed me much attention, and promised me any influence he possessed to insure my promotion—this he redeemed so far as writing letters for me. But I found, that for some reason then unknown to me, the surgeon-general, who, I suppose, feared being censured for not having provided suitable care for the wounded, was most anxious for me to leave Washington, under pretext of his giving me leave of absence, with the hope that the session of Congress would have adjourned before my return. He was proceeding to Philadelphia by the train of this evening, and desired me to accompany him, which I did. After a few days spent at home, and in official visits to Albany and Boston, I returned to the White House in time to witness its evacuation.

CHAPTER XI.

EVACUATION OF THE WHITE HOUSE.

Since the 15th of May, the White House has been the base of operations and the grand depot of supplies for the Army of the Potomac. It now is being abandoned. This has been determined on for some days, for the reasons that it is too remote from the main body of the army, and being easily approached by many avenues, afforded superior inducements of attack by the enemy, and required too large a force to guard it. Yesterday, forty or fifty cargoes of Quarter-master and Commissary stores were sent down the river, which were in danger of capture, and worth three or four millions of dollars, of just such supplies as the rebels most need.

The raid made by the rebels under General Stuart and Colonel Lee, two weeks ago, convinced General McClellan of their anxiety to cut him off from, and capture the large amount of supplies stored here both ashore and afloat. The enemy have commenced their flanking movement, which has been purposely met with but slight resistance; but when they do get possession of the White House, it will be to find it a mass of ruins, and thoroughly empty of the valuable prize they hope to come in possession of. General Casey assumed command here two days ago, and at once gave orders for the felling of the trees along the river's bank, to give play to the gunboats, so that if attacked before the stores are all removed, the rebels will get a warm reception. Colonel Butler, the Provost Marshal here, to whom the order was given, has a large force now engaged of the 93d New York Volunteers and 6th Pennsylvania Reserves in cutting down the lofty pine-trees under which so many men found shelter from the scorching sun. The axemen of these two regiments commenced on the lawn in front of the White House, and the sound of the chopping is plainly heard, as one by one the lofty trees of a century's growth—oaks, elms, and pines—topple over and fall with a fearful crash.

Others are engaged in the erection of a high signal-station, from which the movements of the enemy can be watched, and a lofty cupola on the roof of the White House or Lee House, from which a splendid view of the river for its full length and the surrounding country can be had. A detachment of the signal corps from the gun-boats are now stationed in both of these, to give notice to General Casey's head-quarters and the vessels on the river, so that they can act in concert, and, if necessary, drop down beyond the reach of the enemy's guns.

Other active preparations for departure are going on: the freight-laden schooners and transports are one by one starting for Fortress Monroe, and many exclamations of surprise issue from the lips of those ignorant of the order to evacuate, but as yet little or no panic exists. The rail-road over which so many hundred wounded have been carried, with its locomotives and hundred freight-cars, and which carried all the supplies, men, and horses to the advance, is now busily engaged in bringing back such supplies and wagons as can be shipped down the river, and are not required in the purported change of front by the army. These active preparations have not escaped the notice of the hundreds of sutlers and camp-followers, the bustle soon becomes general, and vessels of every kind are being rapidly loaded at the wharves. The papers and personal effects of the chief officers here are being put on board of the steamboats, and the heavier articles on the schooners, barges, &c.

The contrabands are being put on board of canal-boats. The order was sent this noon to their camp, about an eighth of a mile from here, and with their camp equipage they are busily hurrying to and fro from the boats. One old white-headed darkey was the first to go on board. He was closely followed by a motley crowd of men, women, and children, each carrying some household article or piece of dilapidated furniture. This colored stream continues, and soon all of the three or four thousand "culer'd pussons" will bid farewell to this part of Dixie. Judging from the grin each face wears, I think they don't regret their exodus from the Old Dominion. But the negro loves excitement, and nothing is now thought of but the sail down the river. The excitement has increased so much that many of the laborers, panic-stricken, refuse to work, fearing to be taken prisoners. Colonel Butler has a band playing airs around the camp, which seems to inspire them with confidence as to their safety.

Saturday Morning.—All the night was spent in getting the stores on board, and by the crowd in getting ready for the start. The fighting we know has been going on for two days, but we are in suspense as to the result. A report has just come in that a train laden with commissary supplies, which started early this morning, has been captured; and another, laden with railroad truck, went as far as Tunstall's station, but was sent back by General Stoneman, who commands a brigade of cavalry and flying artillery, detailed to watch the enemy's flanking movement made yesterday against General Porter's corps. The rebels were pressing on to the White House, and had captured Dispatch station. General Stoneman consequently ordered the return of the train, and requested that as soon as it reached the White House the locomotive should return, so that he might ride up the railroad to reconnoitre, which was complied with. He had proceeded but a few miles, when he found himself within musket-shot of the enemy.

The removal of the sick in the General Hospital began to-day. Many of them being well able to walk to the river, were permitted to do so; the remainder, several hundred in number, were carried in ambulances or on litters, as their cases required. The whole number were quietly and comfortably removed, and by the arrangements I had made were well accommodated on the hospital transports. When they had been all placed safely on board, the large tents of which the hospital was composed were struck, and conveyed on board of the barges provided by the Quarter-master's Department for this purpose. I here mention with pleasure my acknowledgments to Captains Sawtelle, Rankin, Farnsworth, and Wagner, for their prompt co-operation on this and other occasions, and cannot omit making mention of their efficiency and the perfect order preserved by the employees under them.

General Stoneman has just arrived from Tunstall's station, with an escort, and is now holding a consultation with General Casey, at his tent on the lawn in front of the White House. He ordered supplies to be sent up for his command, and says he can hold the enemy in check until we have all left here. At the same time he recommends all possible dispatch.

The gunboat Commodore Barney has been added to our

fleet. The Currituck is about a mile above the railroad bridge. The others are in position below, with every thing in readiness for an attack, should the enemy force our protecting lines. The signal gun, for all to embark, has just been fired, and hundreds, taking advantage of it, are making a fierce onslaught on the sutler's stores, stripping them of dry-goods, groceries, and whiskey. The soldiers and laborers vie with each other as to who shall make the largest haul of the miserable stuff, and if not prevented in their depredations, we will have a boisterous time. Each one on loading himself starts for the boats, and his place is quickly filled by another. The stores cannot long hold out, at the rate they are disappearing. Already many thousands of dollars' worth must have been carried away. The officers interfered to prevent this waste of property, but too late. The commissary stores, to a great extent, were got on board; but a large amount, stored in a wooden building, were destroyed, as they were said to be partially damaged. The building, outside, was heaped up with bales of hay, on which whiskey was spilled, to hasten its destruction.

Colonel Morris, this afternoon, under orders from General Casey, commenced the destruction of the government property, by the men of his regiment, the 93d New York. They began with the large water-tank, built to supply the locomotives. The post-office and quarter-master's tents, the officers' and sutlers' tents, the negro quarters and railroad shanties, then the White House itself, were given to the flames. The flame, smoke, and noise from the crackling and falling timbers, made the scene one of the grandest imaginable, throwing a lurid glare for miles around and over the river, in strange contrast with the sunlight. Added to this, was the frequent explosion of shells and other ammunition. The light from the fire continued until after dark, and lit up the heavens, making visible for miles the scene of the destruction. The White House itself, situated as it was on a high bluff must have been seen blazing at a great distance. Many mourned its destruction, which, I learn, was contrary to the orders of General Casey, but the torch was set to it by some one of the many who had for a long time complained of its being so jealously guarded by Union sentries, and it the property of a rebel leader—claiming that it could, with advantage, be used as a hospital. There was some justice in these complaints, for although the building was small, and would accommodate, comparatively, but few, yet it could be used for the worst cases, or as medical head-quarters, apothecary shop, &c.; and a large number of hospital tents could have been erected on the lawn, beneath the shady trees with which it was covered. This would have afforded an agreeable and cool shading to the sick; and the well of spring water on the premises, the use of which was denied, would have prevented many cases of dysentery that occurred on the gunboat fleet and among the employees on the boats. These complaints were urged with considerable pertinacity at Washington, and the surgeon-general issued an order for its occupation by the Sisters of Charity, who have been, for a couple of weeks, devotedly nursing the sick and wounded.

The work of destruction being nearly complete, including the explosion of three splendid locomotives and the burning of over one hundred railroad cars, General Casey, with his staff, are getting on board the Knickerbocker. Colonel Ingalls and his department have gone on board the Circassian, and we start down the river, which is filled with the transports. As we turn the winding of the crooked stream, forests of masts can be seen, bound for Fortress Monroe. Looking back at the White House, we can still see the bright flames flying upward, lighting up the banks of the muddy stream, now loaded with a fleet, resembling more closely the approach to a large commercial city than a quiet inland river of Virginia. We soon dropped anchor for the night, it being unsafe to proceed further.

As soon as daylight returned we started for Fortress Monroe, which we reached at 10 A. M., Sunday. Colonel Ingalls started at once up the James river to learn how matters were going, and, if possible, the result of the battle before Richmond, which has been raging for the last two days. Orders were received to send but a portion of the fleet, with supplies, up the James river—the remainder to remain at Fortress Monroe awaiting orders.

CHAPTER XII.

THE SEVEN DAYS' FIGHT

THREE or four days have again passed witnout any thing of any great importance occurring here, except a very lively skirmish between the pickets, which came near bringing on a general engagement. I was at some distance from the scene of the skirmish when it first commenced, but the rapid booming of cannon, which lasted nearly an hour, told me that something was occurring in that direction which I should know. As I approached the late battle-field I became convinced that the heavy firing was from our side altogether: it proved so upon my arrival. It seems there is a redoubt of great force, and mounted with heavy guns, which the rebels have got an eye upon: in fact, I learn they have had an eye upon it ever since it was commenced, as it is in plain sight of their pickets, who have attempted to capture it no less than four or five times, each time being repulsed with great loss. The last attempt will probably remain the last until the great battle takes place, as they should, by this time, know its little use; but if they should try it again they will find as warm a reception both here and elsewhere as heretofore.

At five o'clock yesterday afternoon the pickets of the 2d (Troy) regiment, Colonel Carr, New York State Volunteers, relieved those of another brigade. They were about four hundred strong, those on the right of the redoubt commanded by Lieutenant-colonel Olmstead, and those on the left by Major Otis. About six o'clock the enemy made a feint on the left pickets, to draw the attention of the reserves in that direction. Almost at the same instant they attacked the right, and in a few minutes the whole line was engaged. The enemy were full six hundred strong, as no less than eight companies were seen by our pickets. The pickets commanded by Major Otis were outnumbered and driven in, retreating in good order, and placing themselves on the right of the redoubt, the enemy out of range from our battery and rifle-pits. The troops under Lieutenant-colonel Olmstead maintained their position from first to last. Three or four companies of the rebels followed the retreating pickets beyond the skirt of the woods, exposing themselves to view, and commenced a galling fire of musketry on our rifle-pits. When within range our men returned their fire, and the enemy still advancing, they approached so near the redoubt that the orders of the officers could be distinctly heard. Now was the time: the musket firing had lasted about three minutes, drawing the enemy on, when the artillery, from a redoubt in the centre, opened upon them. This was instantly followed by a charge of canister from the redoubt on the right and shell on the left, making a cross-fire, the musketry, from the rifle-pits, still continuing. Nothing could withstand this; as shot, shell, and canister, with deadly aim, flew among them, mowing them down and scattering them like chaff before the wind, they retreated in great disorder. The firing was continued some time longer, when the pickets who retreated to the rifle-pits were sent to their original positions, holding the ground until relieved this morning. The enemy's loss, in killed and wounded, must be very great. They were seen from the first removing them to the rear, and even to the end, as they supposed, carried off all their dead and wounded with them; but early this morning our pickets observed a man lying upon the ground, waiving a white handkerchief. He was brought in, and found to be a rebel sergeant. He was badly wounded in the groin, by a rifle-ball, and his recovery is very doubtful. He reports a great number of the enemy killed and wounded, and states that he heard the cries and groans of the wounded and dying all night, and that they were all carried off but him. According to his account, there was one Georgia regiment and four companies of the 2d North Carolina engaged in the fight, and they had volunteered their services to take the redoubt. When they saw our pickets on the left retreat, they yelled like madmen, and, no doubt, thought that the redoubt was already won. Our noble fellows fought bravely. Two were killed and seven wounded, their names are as follows: George Murray, Company B, killed, shot in the breast; Henry L. Dunham, Company B, flesh wound in arm; Jesse G. Huse, Company F, slightly, in face and hand; James McGann, Company D, wounded in hip, seriously; George Paine, Company D, wounded badly in the arm, the ball entering at the elbow and coming out at the wrist, shattering the bone; Francis Megott, Company D, wounded in the hip; Michael Barrett, Company D, shot through the hand; John McGovern, Company D, slightly in the face. The other that was killed belonged to the Third Excelsior, and was shot in the breast, while on picket, just before the skirmish commenced,—I could not learn his name. Murray was from Schaghticoke, Rensselaer county, unmarried and about thirty-five years of age. He lived about an hour after being shot. The wounded are all from Troy, N. Y., and were the advanced pickets. There is no doubt but that if the enemy had succeeded in capturing the redoubt, a general engagement would have been the result. I forgot to mention, that the first notice of any thing unusual was the appearance of several officers, apparently making a reconnoissance, and the chief officer sending aids to the right and left. Two horses, belonging to the rebel officers, were brought in by the pickets this morning, they having found them straying riderless in the woods. One was a splendid animal, and the other desirable. A few days since two companies of this regiment, Company D, under command of Captain McGuire, and Company E, by Lieutenant Wilson, drove the enemy, after they had driven in our pickets, skirmishing through the woods, back to their own rifle-pits, without losing a man. Colonel Carr, of this regiment, is acting Brigadier-general, as General Patterson was taken sick and has returned home.

I have just seen a number of rebel prisoners and contrabands, who are on their way to Fortress Monroe. The contrabands were so stupid and thick-skulled that nothing could be gleaned from them, and the rebels so bitterly secesh that equally as little could be learned from them. Of their appearance there as prisoners, however, I learn that some have been captured by our pickets; some were of the 1st Virginia cavalry, and had been hunted down, as they termed it; while others—honest, quiet farmers—had been torn from their homes, because they said they would not take the oath of allegiance, but were, probably, supposed to be connected with, or know something of that little affair down the road the other evening. They are terribly secesh, as I said before. They appear to delight in boasting of their connection with the rebel army, their intention never to take the oath of allegiance, and their hatred and contempt of the Northern army and people.

One man said, "*Richmond* is not yours yet, nor can it ever be." Upon asking one, who appeared more intelligent than the rest, if he did not think we would be in Richmond before long, he said: "Yes, I think you will, but the same way as I am here," meaning as prisoners. They did say they did not expect the kind of treatment from us that they received. Yet they act as though they despised it. It will be well to remark, that after General McClellan had paid his accustomed visit to our troops in this direction, on Wednesday afternoon last, when he was greeted with such bursts of applaüse, the rebels attempted, and succeeded, in driving back, with an immensely superior force, our pickets to their reserve. The rebels engaged in this affair consisted of a whole brigade, while our picket and reserve did not outnumber a whole regiment. What the motive for this attack was cannot be divined, unless it was to learn the cause of the immense glee in our camp. "Secesh," probably, imagined that reinforcements were arriving for General McClellan, and the reconnoissance in force was for the purpose of ascertaining the extent and nature of the reinforcements. At all events, the effort, whatever may have been intended, was a perfect and entire failure, the shells from our batteries driving them like chaff through the woods and swamps, and enabling our pickets to obtain an advanced position. On Friday, Orderly Sergeant H. D. Hanahan, Company I, 2d South Carolina Volunteers, Colonel Kennedy, of Kershaw's Brigade, was found in the woods, wounded in the legs, where he had been since Wednesday night. His legs were amputated by the surgeon of the 1st California. He was found, by Captain W. P. Tomlinson, Company F, 1st California, in an emaciated condition. The prisoner expressed a great desire to have one fact noticed, which was, to disa buse the minds of the Southern soldiery, who believe, from representations of their leaders, that their wounded do not receive merciful and charitable attention at our hands. He desires to express his thanks for the noble and generous treatment extended towards him since he has been a wounded prisoner in our hands. He believes the loss of the rebels severe, in the skirmish of Wednesday, as the shells from our battery exploded right among them in their retreat through the woods.

As an incident illustrative as well of the fearlessness as of the vigilance and activity of General McClellan, during Wednesday he rode to the outer line of our pickets and pulling off his coat mounted a tall tree, generally used for reconnoitering purposes by our officers and men, with all the agility of a well-trained "salt of the ocean," and ascended into its topmost branches, where he had a splendid view of the enemy's position and defences, and also of his army's Paridisian city of Richmond, the heart of the the rebellion. The rebels were no respecters of his valuable presence in the tree, for their volleys flew thick and fast around and among its clustering boughs, happily without injury to the chief above, who was taking notes. The object of their most recent movements is judged, by our generals, to have been to capture a quantity of commissary stores, which they presumed laid near Fair Oaks station. Our picket lines, during the whole of last night, resounded with the crack of musketry, mostly from the rebels, who, from motives of spite, seem determined to prevent our forces in camp from enjoying their nightly sleep. These constantly recurring alarms in camp are now, however, taken cheerfully by the men, and the line of battle is uniformly formed after a few shots have been exchanged between the pickets. While the position and strength of our forces are at present such as to dissipate all fear for our own safety from any attack which the rebels may make upon us, a reinforcement of fifty thousand fresh troops would insure the immediate reduction of Richmond, which is generally conceded here, and with much less loss to our side than it could be accomplished otherwise. It is idle to deny the fact that the rebels outnumber us, though in effectiveness our army is superior to theirs in the field. I am glad to see that some of our regiments have been provided, as a measure of protection from the fervent heat, with a neat and light straw hat, with the name of the regiment neatly printed on its black band. I noticed the 16th New York, in regimental line, this morning, and they presented a really neat and tidy appearance with their new chapeaus. If any thing can be said to be hopeful about the rebels, the fact that yesterday they allowed the blessed Sabbath to pass, or at least the devotional morning hours of the same, without the resort to the messenger of death, would indicate a change for the better on their part. The health of the troops has slightly improved.

Wednesday, June 25th, was signalized by another glorious struggle between the rebels and the Union troops, in which the latter were twice victorious. About six thousand of our men encountered (on that day) two divisions of the rebel army, a short distance beyond Fair Oaks, and drove them back a mile. By a very remarkable blunder, we relinquished all the ground we gained as soon as we had obtained possession of it, and then when the error was sifted and understood, our gallant lads went at it again and corrected the mistake. Upon our retirement, the enemy had once more swept in over the field like a recurrent tide-wave, and for a second time we drove him back, step by step, over all the ground originally won, and maintained our position there at night. But little artillery was employed, and the casualties are therefore not so numerous as might be supposed from the duration of the fight. As the artillery that was used was mostly ours, the enemy's loss is, doubtless, considerably heavier than our own. Ours will, perhaps, reach the neighborhood of eighty killed, and less than two hundred wounded. It should be clearly understood what this particular fight was for. It was not an interruption of our march to Richmond, in which, as might be supposed, the rebels threw themselves in our way and stopped us at a mile from our original line. It was a fight for a position; a determined struggle for a piece of ground which it was deemed necessary that we should "have and hold." This piece of ground is barely a mile beyond our former line, and we have it and hold it, for what purpose I cannot state. It will be remembered, that the field on which the battles of Fair Oaks and Seven Pines was fought, was bounded on the side towards Richmond by a line of woods. This wood extends on either side of the Williamsburg road for a mile, and beyond it is a piece of open country. Our outer pickets have hitherto been posted in that edge of the wood which is farthest from the "sacred city," and the line of rebel pickets was drawn only a little farther in the woods, and so near to our lines that the men could talk to one another. It appeared to be well understood that any further advance on our part would bring on a general engagement, and in that view our line was kept stationary. But, finally, it was deemed necessary that our pickets should be posted at the outer edge of the wood. Accordingly, General Heintzelman was ordered to advance the pickets on his front to the point named, and to advance the pickets on his left in a line with those in front. At seven A. M., therefore, the greater part of his two divisions was in line and ready for action; but the advance was not made by so large a force. Two brigades of Hooker's division, Grover's and Sickles', did nearly all the work, though some other brigades were slightly engaged before the day was over. Sickles' brigade is composed of the five "Excelsior" regiments, the Seventieth, Seventy-first, Seventy-second, Seventy-third, and Seventy-fourth New York. This gallant body of men has lost so heavily in previous battles, and by illness, that it mustered for Wednesday's fight only fourteen hundred men. Grover's brigade is composed of the First Massachusetts, Colonel Cowdin; the Second New Hampshire, Colonel Gilman Marston; the Twenty-sixth Pennsylvania, temporarily commanded by Lieutenant-colonel Wells, of the First Massachusetts; the Massachusetts Eleventh, Colonel William Blaisdell, and the Massachusetts Sixteenth, Colonel Wyman. This brigade mustered about four thousand men for duty. At a little before eight A. M., the word was given, and these two brigades moved forward. Sickles' line was formed across the Williamsburg road, and he advanced in the direction of that thoroughfare, his second regiment on his right, the Fourth next to it, and both these regiments on the right of the Williamsburg road. To the left of the road in the order in which they are named, the Fifth, First, and Third were formed. Sickles' left stretched about three hundred yards to the left of the road. Grover's line joined on to Sickles' left, and was formed of the First Massachusetts on the right, and the Eleventh Massachusetts on the left. His other regiments were at hand ready for use anywhere. Both brigades advanced in line of battle with skirmishers out in front. Never was there a day better fitted for a fight. Two or three tempest-like showers in the few days previ ous, seemed to have washed all that was disagreeable out of Virginia. Nature and the cool, fresh air, filled our Northern lungs with life. It was just cloudy enough, too, so to temper the sun's heat without making it a dull day, and there was just breeze enough to lift the smoke. As the line moved out across the field that lay between the point and where they had been drawn up and the wood, it presented a beautiful spectacle; the light-blue of the uniforms contrasted with the brilliant green of the field; the light reflected from their gun-barrels in a silvery sheen; and their glorious standards blown out in the breeze, gave the whole scene the gayety and show of a Fourth of July parade. In a few minutes the whole line disappeared in the woods, Sickles' part more slowly than the others, for the left of his line had to move through an abatis that was very difficult, and was thus detained. Through this means, also, the regularity of his line was broken, and did not get into action so soon. Only a few moments, however, had elapsed after the disappearance of Grover, when the scattered "pop," "pop," told that he had reached the enemy's rifle pickets. This little fire only continued a few minutes, rattled rapidly once, twice, thrice, and down the lines and was over, and Grover went on. The enemy's outer line was driven in.

Slowly and cautiously the advance was continued. When the pickets were driven in, they formed on the picket reserve some distance in their rear, and after some little delay, with difficult ground and necessary caution, Grover's skirmishers came upon their second line. They disputed the ground tenaciously. Nearly all their front appeared to be held by North Carolina troops, whom we have found to be by far the best and bravest troops of the Southern Confederacy. These gallant fellows stood to their posts and kept up a rapid and accurate fire that galled our lines severely, until they were fairly driven back in rout by Grover's steady advance. The stout resistance of these pickets gave ample time for the formation of Hill's division, to which they belonged, and which is made up in great part of North Carolina troops. This division, supported by that of General Huger, now advanced to meet our line, and in a little while the ball was fairly opened. So rapid was the rattle of the fire this time, that the sound seemed to be without cessation, without pause, or interval, one continuous rattle of rifles. This fire was very severe, and wounded men now began to find their way to the rear; some on stretchers, others leaning on the shoulder of a comrade, and others again, with a brave pride, determined to help themselves, and "go it alone."

The head-quarters were established in the open field near to Fair Oaks, and there General Heintzelman, very quietly, and with a very business-like air, "taught the doubtful battle where to rage." The two houses at that point were used as hospitals, and numbers of the wounded were laid on the ground in the oak grove that gives name to the locality. There, many wounds were dressed and the soldiers made comfortable; and there, also, many a gallant fellow breathed his last. More commodious hospitals were established further back, and the ambulances passed hastily between field and camp with such good effect that the wounded men were all cared for with admirable dispatch. General Sickles, for the reasons heretofore given, did not become engaged as soon as General Grover, and when the very heavy fire was heard on the latter's front, the Excelsior Brigade was still under the irregular picket fire of the enemy's outer line. By degrees, as they advanced, this fire became hotter, until it broke into the rattle of several thousand rifles; a fire fully as severe and intense as that on the left. On Sickles' front it was straightforward work. He had only to keep his men up to it and push on, and this was well and gallantly done. When Grover advanced his line, it was understood that Kearney's line, which joined Hooker's at that point, was to have been advanced also; but, as it did not keep up, Grover's position became dangerous just in proportion to his apparent success, for his flank was left exposed to the attack of the rebels, who filled the woods in front of Kearney. To guard against mishaps in that quarter, and to establish the connection with Kearney, he threw out, on his left, five companies of the Massachusetts 16th, which regiment was held in reserve. At about the same time, as the fire continued terribly severe in front, he placed a battalion of the New Hampshire 2d on his extreme right, to strengthen his connection with Sickles' left, and placed the remainder of the same regiment between the Massachusetts 1st and 11th, where there was some appearance of weakness. Thus strengthened in front, and provided against attack on his flank, he went on. · Berry's brigade soon began, however, to push forward on Grover's left, drove the enemy rapidly and easily before it, and advanced till they completed the line from Grover's left. Robinson's brigade (late Jameson's) was subsequently pushed in between Grover's and Berry's, and continued the movement. But the enemy was not at any time in great force beyond Grover's left, so that the fight in that direction was not severe. At half-past nine our line was brought to a stand still. It was evident that the enemy was in great force along the whole line. Near that hour the 5th New Jersey was sent out as a reserve to Sickles; the 2d New York, to reinforce his advance, and a regiment of Sedgwick's division, the 19th

Massachusetts, was pushed in on his right, so as to extend his line to the railroad. Still, with occasional intermissions of comparative quiet, the fire raged along the whole front of the two devoted brigades, and seemed ever to rage with intense fury as it approached the road on which the Excelsior Brigade had advanced. During this hard-fought hour our men had not flinched at all. Every one toed the mark resolutely to do what he came for. There was not a straggler to be seen; and those even who helped the wounded off the field, helped them only to where they could get better help, and then went back. Gloriously does the conduct of these two brigades speak the praise of the gallant officers who have made them soldiers, and filled them with the soldier's spirit; and especially does their good conduct on this day redound to the honor of that noble old veteran, General Hooker.

When the rebels found that our boys were not going to give way, under any circumstances, they concluded to give way themselves. Their disposition to do so first appeared in front of Grover. It was hailed with a hearty cheer by our boys, who pushed ahead, and, now that the machine was fairly started, went on with a rush. In a few minutes they broke out into the open field, and the object was so far gained at that point. A battery was sent down to Kearney to play on the enemy's flank, and shell the masses in retreat. Grover was not, however, permitted to hold the ground he gained in quiet. An attempt was made to dislodge him, by a body sent to reinforce those previously driven out. A hard fight ensued, and the attempt was repulsed. But while the enemy were thus driven in on the left, the right did not get along so well. There the enemy's whole available force seemed concentrated in one endeavor to bear down the gallant Excelsior Brigade. Reinforcements were ordered there immediately, and Birney's Brigade went up the Williamsburg road at the double quick. As these regiments filed on, cheered by those they passed, a chorus of responsive cheers arose from Grover's brave fellows, away off on the left, as they drove the enemy before them. Sickles' boys took it up in turn, and made a stouter push at the foe. Everybody seemed exhilarated at the sound. Orderly after orderly rushed in to tell how Grover was driving them, and others to say that Sickles could hold his ground till Birney could reach them. We had the enemy fairly started, and could have driven him any distance. Just at this exciting juncture, the order was received from head-quarters, to "withdraw gradually to the original line." They alone who know how brilliantly the first dawn of victory beams upon the battle-field, can appreciate the gloom this order cast on every spirit, but it had to be obeyed, and was disseminated. It was hard to credit the news from the tongues of aids or orderlies, but it was soon verified, and the men were withdrawn. They all believed that we were beaten on some other part of the line, and that we had gone too far ahead for safety, and all retired in good order, and took up the line in the edge of the wood nearest the camp. This was about half-past 11 A. M. General McClellan and staff rode upon the field at one P. M., escorted by Captain McIntyre's squadron of regular cavalry, and the 1st Regiment New York Volunteer cavalry, Colonel McReynolds. He made his head-quarters at Fair Oaks, where Heintzelman had previously been; and there drew around him all the sources of information that such occasions furnish.

All were then in amazement at the recent unaccountable order. But he soon saw how affairs stood, and ordered, very shortly after, that the same advance should be made again. The order was received with joy on every hand. All was again activity and spirit, and every one prepared to do the thing over again, as bravely as if they had never been compelled to relinquish the almost gotten prize. Once more they went forward, in the same order in which they had already done so well. Grover, on the right, got in first again, and rattled away; but the resistance there was not so tenacious as it had been, and he pushed through, still finding, however, enough resistance to keep up the interest. Kearney, on the extreme left, found also no great resistance. But on the Williamsburg road, in front of General Sickles, the fighting was harder than ever. There the enemy had evidently gathered a strong force, and he seemed determined to hold that point at every hazard. Steadily and accurately as the battle-trained boys of the Excelsior Brigade delivered their fire, still they made no permanent impression. The place of those who fell on the rebel side were again filled, and the enemy was still there. For nearly three-quarters of an hour the hard fire was continued at this point. Thus the battle stood at a little after two o'clock, when General J. N. Palmer's (late Devin's) Brigade, of Couch's Division, was ordered up to support Sickles. The vigilant, and ever-ready commander of the Fourth Corps, had put Couch's Division under arms when the firing first began on the left, and they had awaited their chance till now. They went up the road handsomely—the Massachusetts 10th, commanded by Lieutenant-colonel Decker, in advance, followed by the Rhode Island 2d, Colonel Frank Wheaton; the New York 36th, Colonel Innes; and the Massachusetts 7th, Colonel Russell. At the same time, Battery D, 1st New York Artillery (four rifled pieces), Captain J. W. Osborn, was ordered up the Williamsburg road to shell the woods beyond our advance.

It was expected that they would throw shell directly over our advancing line into the enemy's line, and into his camp beyond. This is always a perilous attempt. Shells either fall false, or the distance is miscalculated, and misfortune ensues. So it did in this case. Several of Captain Osborn's fell false, and exploded in the rear, and even right in the ranks of our men. By this means the Massachusetts 7th, which was deployed in the woods as skirmishers, lost several men; and, by one of these shells, Lieutenant Bullock, of that regiment, received a wound which soon proved fatal. This fire was immediately stopped. Two guns of Battery K, 4th United States Artillery, Captain De Russey, were then sent up the road and into the wood, and took position right in the midst of Palmer's Brigade, and thence opened fire, which they kept up briskly for some minutes. Meanwhile there was an almost complete cessation of the musketry fire. At the same time General Sumner began to shell the woods on his front, and the artillerymen had it all to themselves. Soon the enemy also got artillery at it, and began to throw shell and shot, with considerable accuracy, all around De Russey's guns. So perfectly did he get the range of their pieces that they were withdrawn. But this did not stop the enemy's fire, Many projectiles—shell and round-shot—fell in the woods in that neighborhood, and a number of men were mutilated by them. Lieutenant Whiting, of General Palmer's staff, lost his arm by a round-shot at this time. Colonel A. J. Morrison, volunteer aid to General Palmer, had been wounded in the thigh and hand earlier in the day. The continual push of the Excelsior Brigade, and the fire of the artillery, finally forced the enemy entirely through the woods, and our line now lay just in the farther edge of it. Thus we had gained our object, and there the battle rested for a time. The fire now fell off into an occasional shot from skirmishers, and in that position matters continued until six P. M. At about that hour General Kearney led Birney's Brigade against the enemy. Pushing in on Grover's left, and between Grover and Robinson, he went at it in gallant style, and entirely cleared the woods. The fire there was very fierce for several minutes, when it subsided, and shortly all was quiet again. Thus had passed altogether a glorious day, in which we had twice beaten the enemy, twice driven him before us over the same ground. Dispositions to hold the ground, in case of a night attack, were made all along the line; and on the right, the weakened and wearied Excelsior Brigade was withdrawn, and relieved by that of General Palmer, which thus held the advance on that part of the line.

Soon after dark large bodies of the enemy were brought up in front of the position held by General Palmer, and the rebels also pushed forward, at the same point, a battery of field-pieces. Arrangements were in progress to strengthen our position there, when at ten P. M. a large force was pushed in suddenly, and delivered a volley in the line of the 2d Rhode Island and 10th Massachusetts. Some confusion was caused, but the men were soon rallied, and repulsed this threatened advance, driving the enemy back with considerable loss.

CHAPTER XIII.

CONTINUATION OF THE SEVEN DAYS' FIGHT.

THE foregoing particulars of the battles of Friday and Saturday, necessitated the vacation of the north bank of the Chickahominy, and made certain the evacuation of the White House and the York River railroad. This obliged the falling back on the James river as a new source of supplies and another base of operations. The tents of General McClellan's head-quarters, which had been pitched in Dr. Trent's field, on the Chickahominy, were moved to Savage's station at dusk on Friday. At night, as the several brigades came over the bridge and clustered on the borders of the swamp, one single tent stood on the hillside, and that was General McClellan's. At eleven o'clock a council of war was held in front of this tent, in which the general commanding, corps commanders, with their aids, among them the French Princes and the General of Engineers and Artillery, took part. A large fire had been lighted just beyond the arbor in front, and its blaze lighted up the faces of the generals as they sat in the arbor which formed a pavilion for the tent. The conference was long and seemingly earnest. This was the first council called by General McClellan since he took the field, and here he disclosed his plans of reaching the James river. The rumor soon got wind that the army was to move, and all Friday night the baggage wagons went in long trains towards Savage's station, whence they took their way over the hills to the Williamsburg road, and thence to White Oak Swamp. This procession continued all the following morning, and the large siege pieces which had come up from the White House the previous week, went passing along with ambulances, batteries, and pontoon trains—"retiring in good order"—in pursuance of the prearranged plans. The celerity of their movements, however, caused an anxious look on the faces of the initiated; and the quarter-masters, though they said nothing, appeared disconcerted. All know it requires much patience to await the tardy march of an army, even when the troops are free to go in advance and leave the teams to follow leisurely; but when the baggage-wagons lead the way, blocking up the roads, sticking in the ruts, and upsetting down the hills, the march is trying in the extreme. Such was the case on the several marches of Saturday, Sunday, and Monday, when the tedium became almost unbearable, from the anxiety to press forward. At daylight on Saturday it was known that the army was to evacuate its line of intrenchments. To do this with sufficient celerity, it was necessary to move only the most essential baggage, and leave behind every thing ponderous or bulky. An order was issued to officers to discriminate between necessaries and luxuries. Even the sick had to be told that but to few of them could ambulances be allowed. The wounded were told nothing, but the ominous silence must have convinced them that they were to be left on contested ground at the mercy of the enemy, while the army would, column after column, recede to the distant James river by a doubtful and dangerous route. None who witnessed it will ever forget the scene on Saturday morning. All knew the White House had been abandoned, thus cutting off the depot of supplies—a part of the line of earth-works were deserted, and the tentless army lay on the open field, many sleeping after the labors of the battle, but by far a greater number were grouped in anxious conversation. Hundreds, also, were limping along, or with an arm in a sling, inquiring eagerly for their own regiments. Many, very many, started on the painful and hopeless pilgrimage to the now coveted Jâmes river, where they hoped to find the Union gunboats, feeling that under their portholes alone could they find rest or safety. The long and straggling lines of these left many a drop of blood on the sandy track as they filed through brook and wood and over hill and dale, braced by the certainty of deliverance which each step secured to them. Some of them hobbled ten miles the first day upon crutches; and one poor fellow who had received a ball in the hip, and had the ankle of the other leg broken, kept up with an ambulance for eleven hours. The ambulances were crowded so full that the springs, often breaking, were all bent flat on the axle. Many poor wounded fellows sat on the tail of the ambulances, their blood-dripping feet dangling behind.

Files upon files of wagons were passing all day, and the troops sauntered along, each one bent on reaching the wished-for destination. With them the siege-guns and pontoons were commingled; the horsemen, teamsters, and negroes vied with each other in profane efforts to urge on the horses or mules. Few, if any, slept this Saturday night, for the heavy forebodings of the coming day, and each felt a terrible anxiety for the army and his own personal safety. It was reported that the enemy, advised of our plans, had pushed a large column between us and the James river, and that if we succeeded in reaching the river, Beauregard was there with a hundred thousand men to prevent our reaching the gunboats. A little rain that fell during the night moistened the dusty ground and improved the walking. At 3 A. M., the rebel prisoners in charge of Major Willard were marched off, the teams were on their way, and before two hours after, the commanding general and his staff were dashing across the country. Coming to an elevated position, General McClellan reined his horse and took a survey of Richmond and his late position. Over a thousand wounded were left in the hospital at Savage's station. This was unavoidable, under the circumstances, and every arrangement that could be made was attended to, to insure their comfort and secure them good treatment from the enemy whose bloody greeting they were a second time destined to hear. Surgeons and nurses in abundance volunteered for the duty, and but little complaint was heard even among the wounded thus unwillingly abandoned.

The Battle of Peach Orchard.

Daylight Sunday morning saw the trenches deserted and the artillery moved a mile in the rear, where it was judiciously distributed. The batteries masked and the infantry concealed by the woods which formed a part of the battle-ground of Fair Oaks, but to distinguish it is now called Peach Orchard.

At daylight the enemy were discovered coming eastward along the Williamsburg road—one column advancing down the railroad. They opened from two batteries on the left, but their artillery and musket fire was irregular and ineffective, though the latter was within ordinary range. When they reached a line of marsh about three hundred yards from our front, a terrible fire from our large guns burst upon them. They staggered, but before the full effect of one of the discharges was discernible the guns rang again, and their columns were fearfully thinned. For an hour and a half the fire was so continuous that it seemed the unbroken echo of one prolonged deafening report. A perpetual blaze of flame and flying of balls, to which the Confederates replied feebly but with determination. General Sumner passed through the thickest of the fight, and Meagher's gallant Irish Brigade stood like an unyielding row of Round Towers. The troops of Richardson's, Keyes', and Heintzelman's divisions vied with each other in the rapidity of their firing and the steadiness of their behavior. The whole fight, although it lasted from eight in the morning until noon, was like one unbroken incident when it terminated. Many a participator breathed a long breath of relief, and the nervous tension of many brave men was followed by a corresponding reaction that prostrated them. Our loss was under 200, that of the rebels must have been five to our one. His efforts to overreach us were rendered futile, as we took pains to protect our left. Our line of general retreat lay along the Williamsburg road to a creek that crosses it more than a mile from Savage's station. The enemy tried to charge through the brigades of Burns, Dana, and Gorman, but the steady fire of the regiments, conspicuous among whom was the Massachusetts Twentieth, baffled them completely. Having held the position until the teams, ambulances, heavy artillery, sick, and wounded, had crossed White Oak Swamp, the order was given to fall back leisurely to Savage's station, and again form in line of battle. So the fight of Peach Orchard ended with a clear victory to the Union troops, it was fought with but a small force of our army, and against largely superior numbers, with a comparatively trifling loss, when the fact is considered that we were the rear of a retreating army, and opposed to a foe, who, flushed with victory, supposed us flying before him. To plan and execute such a battle, in the manner it had been conducted, required more than ordinary generalship and bravery. General Sumner's large figure, mounted on a noble charger, and attended by his dashing staff, with his long and flowing white beard, was conspicuous during the fight; his appearance, as he rode down the lines, was greeted by the soldiers with the exclamation, "Boys, here comes Old Bull, give him three cheers," which they did; and his acknowledgment of the compliment made them fight with redoubled energy, and renewed enthusiasm. General Dana's cool, steady, and valorous conduct all through the engagement, won for him the loud praises of the men, the best proof of its being merited. There were many others conspicuous for their bravery on the occasion, and many who, though they were not privileged to wear a shoulder-strap, by their coolness and bravery materially aided in securing to the Union army the victory gained on this occasion. A private of the 74th New York Volunteers, seeing the last gunner of a battery shot down, sprung to the gun and rendered efficient service, dealing death to the rebel ranks.

The Battle of Savage's Station.

The battle of Savage's was much more sanguinary than that of Peach Orchard; it commenced at five in the afternoon, and lasted until eleven at night. The rebels, when we had fallen back from Peach Orchard, filed with large reinforcements and additional batteries, as well as with several squadrons of cavalry, towards several roads leading to the Chickahominy; and, covered by the thick timber, they were enabled to remain concealed until they had reached a wheat-field that stretches from Savage's to a dense belt of woods in the direction of Dr. Trent's farm, and the farms of a Mr. Dudley and a Mr. Couch. Suddenly appearing out of the edge of the timber they opened with their rifled guns on our men, drawn up in full view to the south of the railroad. Directly they ran out their batteries to commanding points in the wheat-field, and opened a rapid and well-directed enfilading fire of shell and grape, which was at first so staggering that our men could not form, nor the artillerymen bring their guns into service. The 106th Pennsylvania were panic-stricken, but soon recovered and did good service. They lost, in the beginning of the battle, a hundred killed and wounded, and a regiment of rebel cavalry galloped through their ranks, driving the regiment off and obliging them to abandon their wounded.

In the mean time, a rebel brigade was observed stealing down to the right, as if with the design of flanking our troops by reaching a position on the Williamsburg road. Captain Pettit at once planted two guns on the railroad and swept the column with grape and canister until it went back to the woods upon a run. Some of the sharpest infantry fighting of the war ensued, in which parts of Sedgwick's, Richardson's, Hooker's, Kearney's, and Smith's divisions engaged with various success. The rebels came determinedly across the field, firing as they advanced, until General Sumner ordered our troops up, at double quick, to a charge. About four thousand of them went off at once, with a roar that might have drowned the musketry. The rebels kept their position for a moment, and then fell back to the rear of their batteries. Meagher's brigade, however, succeeded in charging right up to the guns of a Virginia battery, two of which they hauled off, spiked, and chopped the carriages to pieces. The 88th, 63d, and 69th, participated in this gallant act. It was here that brave Colonel Pierce of the 29th Massachusetts regiment, formerly General Pierce, of Big Bethel fame, lost an arm; it was taken off by a solid shot. Night came on, but put no end to the carnage. The steady roar of cannon, and the sharp ring of musketry—now bursting into volleys—now degenerating to that rasping noise, made by file-firing, filled the whole air. The darkness was lit up by fitful flashes, and to complete the awful picture, the woods were set on fire by bursting shells, and conflagration painted fiery terrors on the sky. In the battle of Savage's the rebels fired into our hospitals repeatedly, although admonished by the customary red flag, and afterwards the white flag. Deaf to all appeals for forbearance, they continued to hurl messengers of death among those already past their vengeance, and the wounded were compelled to lie immovable and receive the quietus to their sufferings from the hands that had already maimed them. A few had limped away from the hospitals, but were shot down, whenever they were discovered by the blood-thirsty foe. The battle at Savage's was much heavier than that of Peach Orchard. We lost, in addition to our wounded,—all of whom fell into the possession of the enemy,—from seven hundred to a thousand men, the greater part of whom were killed or wounded. Most of the wounded and all the killed were left behind, as we had no means of transportation for them, and the exigencies of the army would not allow of delay in waiting the tardy movements of the wounded. The enemy lost severely, and several of his caissons were blown up by the effectiveness of our firing.

During the several parts of the action, we took not less than five hundred prisoners, but were compelled to let them go, for the same reasons that operated in the case of our wounded. The weary but still resolute soldiers received orders at midnight to fall back rapidly from Savage's across White Oak Swamp. The enemy was making furtive attempts to overreach them in this respect, and it was likely to become a tight race between the rebels and Unionists as to which should first cross the creek and gain the high ground on the other side. If they should be more speedy, and succeed in placing the swamp between ourselves and them, our retreat would be inevitably cut off and almost the whole army butchered or surrendered; although every soldier and officer felt this dreadful alternative so close, no one acted otherwise than as a Northerner and a man. There was no murmuring, no flinching, no undue hastening,—only the subdued talk of soldiers comparing opinions, the steady tramp of battalions, and now and then the gritting of teeth, or the hard drawing of a breath to indicate the bitterness in the hearts of all. Had some spirit supplied the torch, there was the requisite fire in the whole army to rush headlong upon immolation at Richmond and end the campaign with honor if not with consummation. At dawn, all had reached the swamp, and the enemy were coming on behind.

White Oak Swamp.

The enemy followed us hard towards White Oak Swamp —the faithful fellows of Heintzelman, Sumner, and Franklin protecting our laggard baggage and artillery. These, indeed, were compelled to keep in line of battle across the country, along the whole extent of the retreat, for the enemy was forever trying to turn us upon the right and left. Notwithstanding this, our march exhibited no symptoms of haste or fear; the trains went on duly, but not riotously, and when finally the last wagon and cannon went splashing through the creek, our teams whitened all the hills on the southern side, and the weary soldiers, having torn up the bridge, laid themselves down to rest.

It was now eight o'clock on Monday, a day arid, dusty, and closer than the panting, but indomitable, Northerners could well endure. Many of them were hungry—the water in the swamp was such, the stomach turned at it with loathing—and the wounded hobbled here and there, with dry eyes, that seemed to plead for drink. White Oak Creek runs through a belt of swampy timber, precisely as the Chickahominy flows through its encompassing morass. The creek is not more than four or six feet deep, and had been made passable by the engineer's brigade, who built a good corduroy bridge across it. A strip of bottom-land lies on both sides of the swamp, and on the north side a steep hill, crowned with a farm-house, formerly the head-quarters of General Casey, had been encircled, by our own troops, with a line of rifle-pits. An abatis also stretched across the bottom-land. Beyond the stream the country was rising, and two farm-houses lay opposite each other, at a little distance, where some of our officers stopped to rest and refresh. Beyond the most eastern house ran a small creek, supported by a thick wood. This was the right of our new line of battle, where General Hancock was posted with his brigade, consisting of the 5th Wisconsin, 6th Maine, 43d New York, and 49th Pennsylvania. Generals Brooks and Davidson lay close into Hancock, and the batteries of the division were commanded by Captain Ayres, formerly of Sherman's battery. Generals Sumner, Heintzelman, Porter, and, in fact, the whole of the army,—excepting the corps of Keyes, and an immense number of stragglers that had pushed on towards the James river and could not be rallied in time to be of service,—extended the line of battle upwards of four miles to the left, bordering the whole distance upon the swamp, with batteries ranged upon every commanding hill, and a strong picket situated at Charles City cross-roads, where it was shrewdly expected that the enemy would come out in force from Richmond.

Hancock's position was a strong one, and it would have taken a strong enemy to dislodge him. The fire commenced at this point, on Monday, when the bridge that the engineers had constructed for the passage of our army, having subserved its purposes, was removed from White Oak Creek. Previously, the railroad bridge had been burned, the culverts blown up, and a lot of superfluous ammunition and cumbrous baggage run, by train, into the Chickahominy. The enemy appeared on White Oak Swamp, strong in force, and directly opened from some twenty masked batteries, that blew up several of Captain Mott's caissons, dismounted his pieces, and raised hubbub generally, among teamsters, wagoners, cannoneers, and infantry. The 20th New York at this time made their celebrated stampede, for which next day the provost guard, by order of General McClellan, picked them up and took them to head-quarters, like so many culprits. Very soon our light batteries recovered themselves and vigorously responded to the enemy, who was soon at a perceptible disadvantage, so far as accuracy and effect was concerned. Our infantry, too, fell in line, ready to support the batteries, or meet half-way any attempt of the rebel infantry to push across the creek. Thus the battle progressed till late in the afternoon, with serious loss to both sides, more wounds from cannon-shot, perhaps, resulting than at any other battle. The rebels made some desperate efforts to cross the creek, but General Smith brought his men up to close quarters with them whenever they dared the contest, and although in each case some of our best soldiers bit the dust, there were no signs of holding off. The cannon firing was inces sant here—some of the deepest and closest of the war—and the infantry fire extended along the whole column.

The cannonading had continued several hours with fearful effect among our baggage and artillery teams. We had, however, prevented the enemy from crossing the swamp in our front, and fervently hoped he would be unable to pierce its fastness at any other point of our right or left. That this hope was ill founded was soon testified by the appearance of the enemy in strong force at Charles City cross-roads, which lies about four miles from White Oak Swamp, due south, and about a mile and a half or two miles from the James river at Turkey Island Bend. He had advanced direct from Richmond eight brigades, the first under command of the redoubtable Gen. Henry A. Wise, and, when discovered at the cross-roads, was endeavoring to work quietly down the river road between our trains and wounded and the army. Two hours previous such attempt might have been successful, when utter ruin and confusion would have ensued. Porter and Keyes were ordered up to repel these new-comers, the troops of the former still suffering from the battle of Friday in so great a degree that many regiments had no organization at all, and many brigades scarcely a regimental organization. At five o'clock they engaged the enemy, hidden by woods and the swelling of hills, and the firing from musketry and field-batteries was soon intense. The rebels did fatal execution among us, and some of our most valuable officers fell here wounded and dying. The reports of ordnance had now been heard so many days, that such chaos seemed the normal condition of nature, and painfully the battle went on. It was scarcely an enthusiastic fight, for all the romance of battle had worn off by reason of its monotony. The men fought well, however, though half dead with heat, thirst, and weariness. Some broke for the river and plunged in the cool water for an instant, then emerging, rushed back to the fray and fought like lions. Fresh troops and superior numbers seemed bearing the tide of battle against us at five o'clock, and the fate of the army hung trembling in the sunset, when a new advocate came to our relief. About five o'clock in the afternoon the gunboats, Galena, Aroostook, and Jacob Bell, opened from Turkey Island Bend, in the James river, with shot and shell, from their immense rifled guns. The previous roar of field artillery seemed as faint as the rattle of musketry, in comparison with these monsters of ordnance, that literally shook the water and strained the air. The shells seemed to be supplied with eight-second fuses, and a considerable interval elapsed between the shock of the report and the subsequent explosion of the shells. They fired about three times a minute, frequently a broadside at a time, and the immense hull of the Galena careened as she delivered her complement of iron and flame. The first few shots went wide, but the man in the Galena topmast lookout signalled the proper elevation to the guns, and soon they threw among the serried ranks of the rebels on the hills their ponderous obligations, that cut down whole lines, spreading confusion, desolation, and dismay. The fire went on with the same fatal effect, making music to the ears of our tired men, and consternation among the rebels. They, already confident of concluding their work and driving us into the James river, began to reel and grow uneasy. Their fire perceptibly slackened, their ranks seemed slow to close up when the naval thunder had torn them apart, disaffection and disappointment had already seized upon them, and every deep tocsin from the Galena added its impetus to the prevailing dread. General Heintzelman, with his whole corps, confident that a recovery of the fortunes of the time could be made, prepared to give another great effort to retrieve the losses of the day and the cause of the country. Such a charge of horse and foot was seldom seen, while our batteries upon the hill-tops far and near played incessantly upon the foe. Signals were given to the Galena to cease firing when this advance was determined upon, the Galena having already hauled off. This was done by consecutively placed signal officers all the way from the point of battle to the banks of the James river, when the thunder lulled and the great ship rested after her labors. Heintzelman made a little appeal to his generals, telling them that in the dash about to be made their confidence and courage might not only save the army, but do something towards avenging the great number of loyal men who had fallen in the several fatal encounters.

The soldiers, poor, heroic, jaded fellows, responded with a spirit that must have come from hungry hearts, and soon the grand corps of Heintzelman was in line, with the gaunt, gray figure of its commander galloping down its columns. The enemy anticipated some such dash, for they directed their fire upon this part of the line, if possible, more concentratedly than ever. Then Heintzelman passed down the order, and like the surging of a sea long embosomed in a plain, the column moved slowly, certainly, vigorously, belching fire and ball at every step, but never halting, until they came so close to the rebels that they might have hallooed the names of each man to man across the little interval. The latter came up bravely to the offered combat, but there was a destructiveness in our fire, and a vehemence in our tread, that they could not withstand. The fiery brigade of Meagher edged up gallantly on the right, using the musket quite soldierly; and General Sickles' Excelsior Brigade, already fearfully cut up, went into the action like a battalion of fresh veterans. The brigade of Hooker was ably led by that distinguished officer, and General Kearney seemed ubiquitous, as he screamed his orders here and there, always urging his men on to the foe. The brigade of General Grover, including some Massachusetts regiments, behaved finely here; but the whole corps was a unit, and Heintzelman was its genius. Pushing steadily ahead, defying all efforts of the enemy to break or turn its line, the corps had at last the satisfaction of seeing the enemy break and fly in confusion to the swamp, totally dispirited and repulsed. We took, in this engagement, over two thousand prisoners; but as our object had been gained, in covering our advance to the James river, it was not deemed of sufficient importance, in view of the risk to be encountered, to hold possession of them through the night. A large number of these prisoners, however, remain on our hands, and will serve in some way to console us for the loss of very many of our own. The battle of White Oak Swamp was scarcely inferior to that of Gaines' Mill in point of losses of life, wounded, and prisoners. We undoubtedly suffered less than the enemy, who was literally butchered, but our own loss is enormous. We lost all of Mott's battery but a single gun; the whole of Randall's battery; one gun, we believe, of Captain Ayres, and several others in various parts of the field. We could not have lost, in killed and wounded, less than 2500 men, and our loss may reach twice that amount. But we gained our point, and made the James river, despite all the enemy's attempts to cut us off therefrom. In failing to do this, he suffered a defeat. Whereas, in the pitch of battle, we beat him back with immense loss, and he was so crippled as to be unwilling or unable to fire a gun next day. The gunboats Galena and Aroostook are entitled to the most unbounded credit. They came into action just at the right time, and did most excellent service.

The region of the James is high, hilly, and bountifully marked by nature with all that vegetable opulence can supply. The ripe wheat-fields, and the long wavy stretches of clover, burst like a vision in fever upon the weary eyes of our wounded and footsore. Some fell down by the banks of the river, and lapped the bright water like dogs. Others fell upon the margin, and wept. General McClellan's tent was pitched by a beautiful farm-house at Cummings Wharf, near Great Turkey Bend, just on the bank of the river. He wrote his dispatches here, and sent them off by the "Stepping Stones," in charge of the French Prince De Joinville, the Duke de Chartres, and the Count de Paris. The general spent a part of the afternoon on board of the Galena, and as he passed along the crowded banks in the commodore's barge, all the troops, even to the haggard wounded, cheered him lustily. He doubtlessly slept peacefully that night, having saved his army and placed it more secure, and in a more convenient position. In addition to the loss of our field-batteries reported, we also lost several of the large siege-guns, that had only reached the army a few days before the action on Friday. A number of them were spiked, and rendered useless for all time to come.

There are here, at Harrison's Landing, fine wharves and roads, which will probably be the future depot of the grand army of the James. It is a fine old property, commanding a long view down the river, and there are several excellent wells on the premises. The house itself has been turned into a hospital. At the landing there are several thousand teams of all descriptions, and five hospital transports were lying off the pier. Ammunition was being landed in great quantities, and hauled to the field of battle. On Tuesday, at two o'clock, every thing on the James had assumed a condition of comparative cheerfulness. There was no strong desire to leave the place expressed either by civilians or soldiers, reviving confidence was expressed in every look and assurance. The people had comprehended General McClellan's bold plan; when it was fought out, and the reins, by unanimous consent, were restored to him, as still the only successful arbiter of our destiny. Had we had half as many men as the enemy, in the fights of Gaines' Mill and White Oaks, we would have possibly retrieved the whole fortunes of those disastrous engagements. The James river was full of transports on Tuesday afternoon, and the wounded will soon arrive in New York and other large cities.

The Battle of Golding's Farm.

About seven o'clock on Friday evening, Toombs' Georgia Brigade, one of the best in the Confederate service, drove in our pickets, and advanced, with close volleys of musketry, in two lines of battle. Hancock's Brigade, consisting of the 5th Wisconsin, 6th Maine, 43d New York, and 49th Pennsylvania regiments, was immediately under arms, as they had indeed been all day, expecting to join in the contest on the other side. They advanced over a piece of corduroy road, passed the redoubt to the right, and after traversing a bottom or declivity, formed in line of battle about a third of a mile from the redoubt, and on the ascending slope of a hill. Here they threw themselves upon their bellies, so that they could just peep over a crest by rising to their knees, and awaited the onslaught of the enemy. The pickets skirmished right into the main body, the rebels coming pell-mell after them, hoping to capture the whole force, when, just as they turned the crest of the hill, Hancock's Brigade and Brooks' 5th Vermont regiment gave them a staggering fire. At the same time the artillery from the redoubt and below opened upon them, and they fell right and left, in heaps and files, until the desperation of the Georgians changed to doubt and then to panic. As they attempted to fall back our men rose to their feet, rushed some distance, and lay down again, pouring in, as before, murderous volleys. The whole fight lasted half an hour or an hour, and ended in one hundred dead Georgians being left upon the field. Our loss was exceedingly slight, as our men were not only properly generalled, but the regimental officers of this brigade are some of the most efficient in the service, as Colonel Cobb of the 5th Wisconsin, Colonel Burnham of the 6th Maine, Colonel Vinton of the 49th New York, &c., &c.

Second Day of the Fight at Golding's Farm.

The next morning the infuriated Georgians, who had meantime heard of their success of Friday across the Chickahominy, determined to attack our lines before General Smith's division a second time, and make another effort to occupy the redoubt near Golding's house. Their dead still lay in the bottom or meadow where they had fallen the night before, and our troops had stolen around in the night to a strip of wood near a picket station, where they dug and masked a rifle-pit. About eight o'clock the Georgians formed in line of battle, commanded by Colonel Lamar of the 7th Georgia Volunteers,—whose connection with the celebrated slave case of the yacht Wanderer will be remembered,—the Seventh was the first regiment, by repute, which joined the rebel service. They did not seem dispirited by their ill success of the day before, but marched boldly up to the same inevitable fate. Terrible volleys that cut them to pieces, literally butchering them, and their enemy, though so obvious to feeling, was nowhere plain to the sight. Lying in the tangled grass, buried in the timber, prone under the sill of turf, or drawing a bead through a fence, the keen-eyed Wisconsin, Maine, or Pennsylvanian, was holding the terrible rifle, every thrill of which sent the leaden messenger through flesh and bone. In the beginning of the fight Lamar was mortally wounded, and in attempting to rescue him his lieutenant-colonel was taken prisoner. Our rifle-pit galled their retreat, a movement they were compelled to make, but all its heroic denizens were bayoneted. Lamar was a beautiful man, singularly like a woman, but he had all the fierce elements of a warrior, and died suppressing every moan or cry. His wound was a bad one, and he must have suffered terribly. General Brooks is generally rumored to be seriously wounded. His brigade of Vermonters behaved like veterans in the several engagements between Gaines' Mill and White Oak Swamp. The same indomitable pluck that instigated the charge across the dam at Warwick River, marked their course in the fight of Golding's Farm, Savage's, and White Oaks. The loss of this brigade is, perhaps, less than that of any of the brigades of Smith's division. The provost marshal's troops, commanded by Major John M. Willard, were of incalculable service in maintaining discipline on the day of the battle. They collected the tired stragglers and skulkers and sent them to their several regiments. Others who could not be turned over to their commands, were organized by some of the officers of the provost guard, and made to do guard service in the fight at Charles City cross-roads. Captain

Walcott commanding a battery, did fine execution in the fight at White Oak Swamp. They were posted on the brow of a hill, and signalized themselves among a number of batteries posted around them, for skill in the handling of their guns and general soldierly demeanor. There is no doubt as to the loss of General McCall. This gallant officer had his horse, a spirited black stallion, shot in four places during the fight on Friday. His coat was also repeatedly torn by bullets, and his aids trembled for his safety as he persisted in riding hither and thither encouraging his men. The gallant fight of these men may be traced entirely to the coolness and collectedness of their commander. He had been the victim of neuralgia for a long time, but has fulfilled his duties unflinchingly through evil and good report. General Meade, also of this division, distinguished himself for courage and activity. He has been taken prisoner. The rebel officers were so disguised by questionable and obscure costumes, that perhaps on the several engagements they lost fewer officers than we. Our officers, on the contrary, were so conspicuously clothed that they were prominent marks,—hence the great mortality in this respect.

Our troops say that, during the fight, they saw no rebel officers. Rush's regiment of lancers did good service, not only in the fight of Friday, but in the subsequent occurrences of Savage's station and White Oak Swamp. In the battle of Gaines' Mill they charged a little to the south of the old mill upon an Alabama brigade, and threw their long-handled lances with terrible effect, in many cases smiting the rebels to the ground by piercing them through and through. The scene witnessed when this fine regiment charged, may well be historical: their long lances upright, their red pennants streaming, and the riders like so many avengers, bending forward to make the plunge.

The most frightful slaughter occurred in the New Jersey Brigade, commanded by General Taylor. Colonel Tucker, of the 3d regiment; Colonel Simpson, of the 4th; and Lieut.-colonel Hatch, of the 4th, are dead; Major Birney, brother of General Birney, shot through the bowels; Major Ryerson, of the 2d, killed; Major Hatfield, of the 1st, shot in the head; Adjutant Fairly, formerly connected with General Garibaldi, wounded seriously in the head. The 1st regiment went into action with 685 men, lost 195; the 2d lost upwards of 200 men; the 7th went into action with 700 men, and came out with 70; the 3d had only four companies engaged: the brigade went into action with 2500 bayonets, and cannot now muster 1200. All this loss occurred on Friday, between the hours of five and seven P. M., and does not include any subsequent losses that may have happened in other battles. Colonel Torbert, of the 1st regiment, is safe, having been sick with a fever. He rode upon the field, tottering. The Pennsylvania Reserve corps fought on Thursday, Friday, Saturday, Sunday, and Monday, on each and all of the leading fights, and their losses are terrible. In all cases they behaved like good and gallant soldiers, and the commonwealth they represent had nothing in common with them of which she may not be proud. The Reserves did not lose more than 150 men in the engagement of Thursday, at Mechanicsville; but after the fight on Friday, they reported the almost incredible loss of 2200 men. The subsequent encounter must have increased their loss to 4000, and in this is contained three generals, including General Meade, several colonels, majors, captains, &c., &c., representing every part of Pennsylvania. Among the rumors afloat on the field of battle was one, on Tuesday, that General McCall had been killed; and it was also reported that General Meade and General Reynolds were missing. Ayres and Mott's batteries, of General Smith's Division, have been engaged in a dozen fights, and have acquitted themselves gloriously on each occasion. Captain Mott lost his battery at White Oak Swamp. In the embarrassing position in which he was placed, he fitted up temporary wheels from the baggage-wagons, and fired to the last. The charge of the 1st and 5th Regular cavalry, at Gaines' Hill, though brave and dashing, was not prudent. The 1st had but two companies; the 5th, 600 men. They charged up the hill and galloped around two divisions of the rebels, firing their revolvers at them. The rebels waited with fixed bayonets for them, and drove them over one of our batteries. The next morning the 5th reported but one officer for duty. The 20th New York, it is said, did not behave well at the battle of White Oak Swamp. Some mules were drinking at the time in White Oak Creek, and these, alarmed at the opening of the fire, galloped furiously up the hill, close to the 20th, which broke and run, scarcely less undignified. General McClellan ordered a squadron of cavalry to pick up stragglers of this organization, on Tuesday, and guard them to head-quarters. The order was carried out in its extreme conditions, and the regiment may be considered as virtually under arrest, officers and men. Colonel Gallagher, of the 11th Pennsylvania Reserves, was killed in Friday's fight; Lieutenant-colonel Porter and Major Snodgrass, of the same regiment, were made prisoners. The Bucktails report about 120 men left. Four of their companies were with Kane in the Shenandoah Valley, and six with McClellan. A whole company was taken in the fight on Thursday. Major Stone commanded during the late battle. The 6th regiment of Reserves were doing picket duty at Tunstall's station, and it is believed they all escaped harm up to Saturday, but subsequently they might have suffered seriously. General Seymour, who commanded the brigade, formerly commanded by a general of Dranesville fame, had two horses killed under him. The Reserves made several desperate dashes with the bayonet. Their ammunition gave out at six o'clock on Friday, up to which time they had discharged 100 rounds—50 in cartridge-box and 50 in haversack.

At four o'clock, on Friday, the fight beyond the Chickahominy grew desperate. The enemy redoubled his efforts, and pressed hard upon our centre and right. He evidently labored to turn us in the latter direction, and to that end pushed his left to Coal Harbor, designing to flank us and prevent, if possible, access to our bridges of communication with the south bank. Our brigade was ready to prevent any such catastrophe, and battery after battery was brought into position, until the screaming of balls baffled description: such sublime artillery practice was never witnessed. The infantry that had been skirmishing on their bellies, or firing irregularly from some concealed covert, now rose in line and poured in deadly volleys. All seemed to realize that an emergency had come, and resolved to contest each inch of ground. The scene has never been excelled on this continent. Each volley took hundreds off their feet, until the air seemed to grow clammy with the dead, and hoarse with the dying. Slowly our troops—outnumbered, but great-hearted—fell back after resigning their dead; and all the while the enemy's shell and ball played havoc in their ranks. Most of the dead, and a portion of the wounded, we were obliged to leave on the field at Gaines' Mill to the mercy of the enemy. It was a cruel necessity, but unavoidable. All the hospitals were crowded with sick and wounded, and the surgeons were busily engaged in relieving, as fast as possible, the suffering and misery of the great numbers committed to their care. The usual heart-rending scenes were witnessed at the hospitals; and, as the groans and sighs of the wounded and lacerated heroes ascended to heaven, it seemed as if the hatred of this cruel, causeless rebellion in which their lives had been sacrificed, must be deepened and intensified throughout the land. The loss of the rebels in the battle at Mechanicsville was much larger than ours; and as they by far outnumbered us at the battle of Gaines' Mill, and were for hours under a very heavy artillery fire, as well as small-arms, and exposed to repeated and determined bayonet charges, it is thought that their loss on Friday must have largely exceeded our own. It is but justice to the rebels to say that they fought well, and with a bravery which, if displayed in a better cause, and in defence of, instead of for the destruction of our national existence, would have forever secured the admiration and gratitude of their countrymen. They fought with an energy and desperation which has not hitherto been displayed by them anywhere. They were animated by the presence of "Stonewall Jackson;" and Jeff. Davis himself was on the field cheering them to the battle. The 4th Pennsylvania Cavalry, commanded by Colonel Childs, assisted in covering the retreat. At the battle of Gaines' Mill it lost ten men and twenty horses. The bridges that had cost so much labor were blown up on Friday night and Saturday—Woodbury's being the last to go up, at ten o'clock, on Saturday morning. They had facilitated our retirement; but their removal could not greatly embarrass that of the enemy, who recrossed at New Bridge and above, and prepared for their subsequent descent upon our forces at Peach Orchard and Savage's. Sykes' Regular Brigade, the gallant brigade of regular infantry men, is said to have lost forty officers and two thousand soldiers. The 2d regiment is cut down to a mere vestige, and some can scarcely turn out a corporal's guard. Lieutenant-colonel Barney of the 2d Maine is missing, probably a prisoner; Adjutant L. P. Mudgett, do., Assist.-surg. A. D. Palmer, do.; Captain Emmerson, Company E, severely wounded, and a prisoner; Lieutenant Brown, Company B, wounded and a prisoner; Lieutenant Currier, slightly wounded. All these were lost in the fight of Friday. This regiment took the flag of the 5th Alabama.

Among the killed in Franklin's division, now Slocum's, Colonel Tucker, 2d New Jersey; Colonel Goslin of the Philadelphia Zouaves; Colonel Simpson, 7th New Jersey; Lieutenant-colonel Heath, 5th Maine; Colonel Stockton, 16th Michigan. Among the wounded and prisoners are Colonel Jackson, 5th Maine; Colonel Pratt, 32d New York; Major Hough, 55th Pennsylvania. The presence of General Slocum at Woodbury's Bridge battle is a high attestation to his gallantry. He had been sick, with fever, for a long time, but when the order was given for his division to advance, he determined to lead them. The firing was hottest when they entered the field, and death made gashes in their lines. They persevered, regiment after regiment pressing on, until depleted and wasted; and the heroic Slocum cheered them on, until Nature asserted her claims, and he fell from his horse. Having been taken from the field, he recovered, after a time, and again ordered his men to place him on his horse and accompany him to the field. Perhaps no one is more regretted, in this division, than Lieutenant-colonel Heath, of Waterville, Maine. He was, of all men, the most consistent, courageous, and chivalrous. He was seen, a little while before the battle, reading serenely in the shade of his tent, a Latin copy of Cæsar's "Commentaries." His relations with his men and fellow-officers were such as only exist among high-minded gentlemen. Heath was a soldier by instinct, and a man of rare forensic powers. He had been United States consul at Quebec, during Mr. Buchanan's administration. Colonel Jackson is seriously wounded, but was in good spirits when last heard from. He has arrived at Fortress Monroe. Each of the three brigades of Newton, Bartlett, and Taylor fought like fiends, and they covered the army, saving it from still greater loss.

The reserve artillery was engaged on Thursday and Friday, and also in the great battle of Monday. Tidball's battery blew up three of the enemy's caissons, and had seven men and six horses shot. Major Robinson's battery suffered as severely. Weed's regular artillery broke two axles, whereby two pieces had to be abandoned, after being spiked. Captain Weed was wounded in the face. We captured a rebel flag, now held by the 2d Maine regiment, marked on one side "Victory," and on the other "Equal Rights." That regiment had lost one hundred and thirty-six men, from various causes, up to Saturday morning—how many since, it will take some time to decide. It was posted on the left of Martindale's brigade, in the centre of the line of battle. The 13th New York took the battle-flag of the 7th Tennessee. The rebel artillery consisted, in the several battles, mostly of rifled six and twelve pounders, seldom, if ever, of larger calibre. They practised the concentration of fire from a dozen or twenty batteries upon a single point, and their practice was most unerring and powerful. In some cases, as for a time at White Oak Swamp, we could not get under play at all, owing to the vehemence of the enemy's artillery. When the Galena's big guns opened, however, the rebels began to think we had a whole armada in reserve. Colonel Torbert, of the 1st New Jersey, is safe. He had the fever, but persisted in riding to the field, where finding his colors still waving, he seized them, in an ardor of emotion, and pressed them to his breast. He is the idol of the brigade, and the signatures of every general in his corps have been forwarded to the War Department to make him a brigadier-general. The 83d Pennsylvania regiment was raised in Crawford and Erie counties. Its colonel, J. W. McLane, of Erie, had been sheriff, and his term was yet unexpired, when he hastened to the defence of the Union. He was shot through the head, near Woodbury's Bridge, and instantly killed. Major L. H. Nagle, of New Albany, Indiana, of the 83d Pennsylvania regiment, was shot through the breast at the same time. Captain Morris, of Company B, was shot through the hip and taken prisoner. The regiment lost, in the fight of Friday, about two hundred men. It was attached to Morrell's division, and was the left regiment in line but one, viz., the 44th New York. They also suffered badly. Several companies of the 1st regiment United States Sharp-shooters, Colonel Berdan, were, early in the day of Friday's fight, deployed as skirmishers in the woods on our right and in front of General Griffin's brigade, under the immediate command of Lieutenant-colonel Ripley. They had thirty-eight of the new target rifles; and the two companies in the woods, to the left, used Sharpe's rifles. They held their position until their support had fallen back some distance, so that the rebels attacked them on the flank, as well as in front. They then fell back and formed a line with them. Lieutenant Gibbs, with the target rifles, was ordered by Colonel Griffin to pass around the reserve. This brought them into a field surrounded on three sides by rebel riflemen. Here they were employed with the artillery with great success. They were attacked by a rebel brigade, which deployed out of the woods in good order, bearing a black flag, with death's head and cross-bones. This brigade was repulsed by the united efforts of the artillery and sharp-shooters. The different companies were splendidly posted by Colonel Berdan, and were on duty the whole day, rendering good service, as usual.

The 14th New York, 9th Massachusetts, and 62d Pennsylvania were formed in the woods, on the right. About two o'clock they were attacked by a large force of rebels, who had succeeded in entering the woods. They were at first driven back, but soon rallied and charged upon the enemy, and drove them out of the woods. They held the position until sundown, when they were ordered to fall back. Early in the day Colonel Black, of the Pennsylvania 62d, was killed. He was an able and popular officer. On the opposite side of the ravine, Colonel McQuade, of the 14th New York Volunteers, assisted by detachments from different regiments of the Pennsylvania Reserves, held the position until the left was broken; and it becoming untenable, they retreated up the hill. For about an hour and a half, in the afternoon, the rebel infantry and riflemen fired by volleys, without cessation. It was one continuous sheet of fire, and the noise terrific. Dnring this time they did great execution, but the men stood it well and returned the fire vigorously. It rained shot and musket-balls. Towards night a number of the regiments, who had lost a large number of their officers, began to retreat rapidly towards the bridge on the Chickahominy, and for a time there was danger of a regular stampede. Had not this been checked the battle would have ended in a complete rout. Seeing this, Colonel Berdan, of the sharp-shooters, rallied some officers and men, and determinedly stayed the retreating mass, discharging several shots from his revolver over their heads, calling loudly upon them not to disgrace themselves and their cause by such an ignominious flight in the face of the enemy. In this he was vigorously assisted by Captain Hoyt, of General Butterfield's staff, and other officers. The disorderly retreat was checked and the men formed in line of battle, under Colonel Berdan's command. While this was going on, the enemy had collected a large force, and were preparing to charge down upon them. The men then commenced to advance rapidly, cheering loudly, and the enemy, seeing this, withdrew. Much credit is due to Colonel Berdan for his prompt and decisive action, and it is undoubtedly due to his exertions that this portion of the army was saved from the disgrace and disaster of a disorderly retreat. He was enthusiastically cheered by the men whom he had saved. They remained in position, near the hospital, until about dark, when they retreated, in good order, across the Chickahominy.

Jeff. Davis was at the house of Mrs. Price, just opposite Dr. Gaines', for three consecutive days before the battle of Thursday, in every case engaged in close consultation with General Lee. Colonel Towers, of the 7th Georgia, stated that Jeff. planned the whole attack.

CHAPTER XIV.

RETREAT TO JAMES RIVER.

In the foregoing pages I have given a full and faithful account of the movements, actions, and conflicts of the two contending armies during the ever-memorable seven days' fight before Richmond; but some detail of the individual commands will not be uninteresting to the friends of those brave troops engaged, and will serve as an impartial record of those interesting incidents of this volume of the rebellion.

While the great battles of the 26th and 27th of June were progressing on the extreme right wing of the army, there was more or less fighting along the whole line of the extreme left. The enemy was now everywhere on the offensive. In these affairs Sumner's corps, which formed our centre and front, played an important part. The sound of cannon on our right grew louder towards the evening, and it became evident that we were drawing the enemy into a trap, or that our troops were obliged to retire before them. The latter soon became apparent, when the right wing, under General Porter, were retreating after an obstinate and bloody resistance. At six o'clock, in the evening, General McClellan ordered two brigades from Sumner's corps to the right, to cover the retreat of our forces across the Chickahominy. In obedience, General Sumner sent forward the Irish Brigade and General French's. They proceeded at a double quick, with cheers, and crossed the Chickahominy bridge in less than three-quarters of an hour afterwards. Here they joined the brave fellows who had been fighting the rebels all day against superior numbers, but who were now hastily falling back, Sykes' division covering their retreat. General French's brigade was thrown out to the right. The regulars, under General Sykes, were ordered to fall back, the Irish Brigade taking their place. As the stream of dead and wounded was hurried to the rear, these fresh troops, undaunted by the panic, rushed forward with enthusiastic cheers, which the rebels hearing, and seeing the new regiments deploying before them, hesitated. This gave time for all the other battalions to reform, which they did in good order, and stoutly held their ground. The Irish Brigade at once threw one or two volleys into the rebels, and French's Brigade manœuvred in a menacing manner on their flank; thus checking their pursuit and obliging them to fall back a mile or so beyond the late battle-field. As the night closed on the scene, some of the troops were so near each other that the 30th Georgia lay down within forty paces of the 88th New York Volunteers, of the Irish Brigade; and its adjutant, and several of its men, unwittingly entered the camp of the 88th, and were astonished to find themselves prisoners of war. The orders were not to pursue the enemy, and both sides were too much exhausted to continue the combat.

The morning broke clear and cool. Our troops still held the ground beyond the Chickahominy. The rebels had returned towards the position they held on the preceding day. The losses of yesterday were heavy on both sides. We lost over six thousand, in killed, wounded, and missing. The enemy's loss, if not greater, was full as many. Early this morning the Irish and French's brigades fell back to protect the bridge, until the division of General Sykes had crossed over. This it did at daylight, in good order, but with terribly reduced ranks, and without any opposition from the enemy, who showed but little disposition to renew the fight, as they imagined our right wing had been reinforced, and supposed we wanted to draw them into an ambuscade across the creek. As soon as all the troops had safely crossed over, the engineers blew up the bridge, and then these two brigades, French's and the Irish brigades, returned to their encampments with their own division (Richardson's), and, with the rest of the army, remained constantly under arms.

It now becoming evident to General McClellan that no time was to be lost in carrying out his plan of changing his base of operations from the Pamunkey to the James river, he at once changed his front, as the ground gained by the enemy enabled him to threaten our right flank, as as well as our communications in the rear. The order, when given, was promptly obeyed. The baggage and supply trains commenced moving, while a strong force of cavalry and artillery were placed at every ford and bridge across the Chickahominy by which the enemy might effect a crossing before we were fully prepared to receive him. Skirmishing had been briskly carried on by the rebels during the night, but discontinued earlier than usual. At daylight on the 29th, most of the troops had left the breastworks and taken up their march for the James river. General Sumner's corps was intrusted with the dangerous post of covering the retreat. By four o'clock the pickets were called in, which was done so quietly that the enemy was still unconscious of our design, and imagined that we were still in full force before them. Yet they soon discovered the movement, and before long they entered the works our men had left. The march was steadily continued, under the precautions taken to cover our rear; nor did we again see the enemy until they appeared before us at Peach Orchard, on the line of the Richmond and West Point railroad. No sooner were they discovered than General Sedgwick ordered General Burns to prepare to receive them. They were distant but a mile, and beginning to show their strength; and before we were aware, a terrible shower of shells and round-shot snapped the branches of the trees above and around us. It became evident that to save ourselves the enemy must receive a check. The 1st Minnesota was thrown out as skirmishers, and the rattle of musketry soon mingled with the booming of artillery. On our side, Kirby's battery had obtained a good range, and played away, with a certainty of aim and constancy that tore the ranks of the rebels asunder; but their force was so large that the Minnesota boys were soon obliged to fall back, which they did in good order, under Colonel Sully, their commander. The 71st Pennsylvania, 2d New York, and other regiments now rushed to their assistance, which checked the advance of the enemy, and obliged him to fall back to the cover of the woods. This occurred between nine and ten o'clock, and cost us over one hundred and fifty, killed and wounded. Thus ended the first of a series of encounters, which, with the several battles described, might be said to have commenced at Orchard station, and continued, without intermission, until our arrival at Turkey Grove, on the James river. The time spent in destroying the stores which we were unable to carry with us, gave the enemy time to rest, and at about five o'clock in the afternoon he came in sight, near Savage's station, about three miles from Orchard station. We first discovered his cavalry masking a battery, and with both flanks and infantry, in the rear, marching in column of brigades, presenting a triple front of over half a mile in length. The

Minnesota boys, with Baxter's Zouaves, were again thrown out to skirmish. Smith's Division formed on our right, and Richardson's protected our left from the flanking columns of the enemy. Segdwick's Division formed the front, and well maintained its ground, though often the skirmishers were driven back upon it, by the terrific front and flanking fires of the enemy. A heavy portion of the action fell on Burns' Brigade, and General Burns was wounded by a minié-ball, which shaved off his moustache and passed through his cheek, coming out below the ear, fracturing the jawbone and knocking out several of his teeth; but though he received this painful wound, he continued to keep his seat, and, by gestures (for he could not speak), to direct his men in the face of the enemy, with great gallantry. That he was able to do so, can only be accounted for by his possessing a brave and indomitable spirit, which the occasion had nerved to its utmost pitch. His heroic conduct called forth the unqualified admiration of his men and of General Sedgwick.

The terrific onslaught of the enemy was momentarily stayed by the steady and well-directed fire of the 1st California, 2d New York, and 106th Pennsylvania, who were hotly engaged during this time, and the reinforcement now received by the rebels told upon our centre, under their terrible storm of grape and musketry. Just at this momentous time, General McClellan was seen riding in the midst of the field with the greater portion of his staff. His order to let the enemy have some grape and canister was heard and passed along the lines; and as he rode fearlessly through the enemy's fire, he was loudly cheered by the gallant 88th, under Colonel Baker, who now came suddenly on the flank of the rebels and routed them completely, taking 140 prisoners. In the mean time, other rebel regiments closed around them; and to add to their discomfiture, they were shelled from the woods out of which they emerged to the engagement. This fight occurred in an open field nearly a mile square, and the struggle was one of the fiercest ever known. It lasted over three hours, in the most determined manner, and the yells of the men on both sides, mingled at intervals with the thundering of the guns and the incessant cracking of musketry, lent an exciting interest to the scene, that held in breathless agony of suspense the lookers-on of this bloody conflict, which night put an end to; but not until the rebels were fairly driven from the field of battle. When these all-important results were procured by the bravery of the gallant Irish 88th N. Y., General McClellan, seeing that all danger was at an end, rode off the field towards the front. Our loss in this engagement was very heavy,—over one thousand men killed, wounded, and missing. The enemy's loss was also heavy, equal, if not exceeding, ours. Of this we had no means of ascertaining but by the gaps made in their ranks by our artillery and muskets. Our troops remained in the unmolested possession of the battle-field until eleven o'clock, when our advance guard of the covering column resumed its line of march to the James river. At one o'clock that night it reached the White Oak bridge; and at 3 A. M. on Monday the rear-guard, consisting of a squadron of the 6th New York V. C., crossed the bridge, bringing up with them all the stragglers capable of walking; but many were so worn out that they fell by the wayside and became the enemy's prisoners. At 5 A. M. the bridge over the swamp was blown up. This was done as the head of the enemy's column was seen advancing. Soon the troops reached a position which will ever be remembered by them, and will form a striking feature in the annals of warfare. Encamped here in the stillness of a summer's morning, the clear whistle of a steam-valve is heard at a mile's distance. One remarks, "The rebels are running the train;" to which another replies, "That cannot be the cars." "Yes, but it is," chimes in a third. But hark! another, louder whistle is heard, unlike a locomotive. It is not from the direction of the railroad. No; it is a much more welcome sound. It is from the gunboats on the James river; and now that this is decided, a loud, spontaneous, and long-continued cheer is given for the gunboats which proclaim their readiness to assist us. But our toils are not yet over. No; we have to fight the bloodiest of the seven days' battles, and that within hearing of our gunboats.

The enemy, prevented by our artillery from reconstructing the White Oak bridge, would, we thought, not molest us for a day at least. Many of our men were much exhausted from want of sleep and extra labor, and all were so weary that the prospect of even a temporary rest was a great boon to us; next to which came the beautiful weather, which kept the roads in fine condition. Quietness reigned until four o'clock in the afternoon, when we were again aroused by the booming of distant guns. We knew that the rebels could not have crossed the broken bridge, as our artillery held it. From whence, then, did this new cannonading come? Could he have got in our rear? Such were the questions quickly put to one another by the men and officers of our corps, as the shells began to fall around us. Mortified, but not discouraged at this fresh attack, a shout, clear and ringing, passed down the lines, "Here they are again, boys! Let us show them again how they must run before Yankees!" This was the spirit that animated Sumner's corps. Meanwhile the rebel guns were mowing down the trees and branches, and evèry thing that offered resistance to their missiles. Our guns were not long silent, and, as usual, soon slackened the enemy's fire. The inquiry became general, "How did they get there?" It was plain. They made use of two roads unknown to us, by which they flanked us on the right and left with their columns, while we had our wearied troops guarding the bridge on the principal road to the James river. Our troops were disposed as follows at this juncture: Richardson, with his own division and two brigades of Sedgwick's, with the bulk of Sumner's artillery, were engaged together in watching the bridge. McCall's corps was the nearest to the enemy by the by-road on our right flank as we marched towards the James river. Burns' Brigade was detailed to guard a portion of the supply train, which we now had overtaken; and Hooker's division formed our left wing, on a road almost parallel to them, by which McCall's and Burns' were advancing; and the enemy, after engaging us in the rear and on the left flank, suddenly and unexpectedly appeared in front of General McCall's forces. This was a disastrous beginning to the battle, but the sequel proved that "all's well that ends well." General Burns, seeing the danger, ordered over the 69th Pennsylvania to check the progress of the enemy, who were chasing our flying troops—artillery, infantry, and cavalry, all mixed in indiscriminate confusion—across an open field in the direction of Richardson's forces. At this critical time and place, the 69th Pennsylvania, under Colonel Owens, charged bayonets on the enemy's flank, which checked their headlong impetuosity. Astonished at the attack, they turned to fight this new foe. A fierce struggle ensued, lasting for some time, with variable results; but, finally, the 69th drove them beyond a hill across the road, which they occupied and held. While this was going on, the engagement became general along the whole line. Sedgwick's and Richardson's divisions drove the enemy back. General Hooker, at the head of his division, now came up, and seeing Colonel Owens, of the 69th, sharply asked him, "Where is your regiment, sir?" "On that hill," proudly returned Owens, pointing to where his regiment was drawn up in the form of an arc around the crest of the hill. "Well and nobly done," said Hooker, and rode away. On the left, Keyes' corps was desperately assaulted, while the fury of the rebel attack on our front was unabated. Trap after trap was set for the enemy, and our men literally mowed them down so that their wounded and ours lay in heaps together on the ground. The 2d and 34th New York regiments lost terribly, but did good service. The 42d New York also fought well, and lost their lieutenant-colonel, Mooney. The 1st California and 19th Massachusetts were placed in the space occupied by the broken regiments, and, with one of the most destructive fires ever heard, repelled the enemy after a long-contested and often doubtful struggle. Thus Sedgwick's division at all points drove them off, yet could not retake the guns we had lost. But at another point of the line some of the enemy's guns were captured, his columns driven away front and rear, and he found there was no possibility of uniting his forces, so long as we chose to prevent it, and hastened to protect one of his wings, in danger of being cut off by us. Night came to the rescue. Our object was not to pursue them; so that, after a short chase, they were allowed to retire unmolested from the field. Next morning at one o'clock our rear-guard reached Turkey Grove, on the James river. The loss to the enemy by his frequent attacks on us during our weary march and in the engagements provoked, was not less than 3,500 killed and wounded. Our own loss was nearly as heavy. When the battle of the 30th was over, we all expected an attack from the enemy along our whole line, as their best hope lay in overwhelming us before reinforcements could arrive. At this critical time McClellan rode through the ranks, inspiring confidence among the men, assuring them he had now got the enemy in the position he wanted to have them. They had played the old game of masked batteries whenever possible during the retreat of our columns. Their loss in the whole pursuit must have exceeded 20,000 up to the evening of the 30th June. Ours was not so heavy, though terribly severe, for many hundreds of stragglers fell into their hands.

The position taken up at Turkey Grove, near the James river, by our forces, was a promontory of high land formed by a bend in the river nearly opposite City Point. It was naturally strong; and in addition to this, our left wing was well guarded by the gunboats. All that was left of the brave army of the Potomac, was drawn up in line of battle on the promontory this Tuesday morning, July the 1st. Contrary to expectation, the enemy remained quiet during the previous night, thus admitting the severity of the conflict on the afternoon before. At daylight we were formed in a circular line, our left flank on the river, our right well protected by the gunboats, the reserve corps in such a position that the whole had the appearance of a half moon: the front of the line in some places was three miles distant from the river. The rebels were drawn up about a mile and a half beyond; and the sheen of their bayonets, glistening gayly in the morning sun, could be seen extending for mile upon mile: their waving banners showed where the long line rose over the wooded hill, or sunk in the slopes of the rich valleys. The picture was sublime beyond conception, and fully showed the proud pomp of war. Sumner's corps, which up to nine o'clock had been engaged in covering the retreat, now fell into its original position in the line ; and when it had done so, the enemy again assumed the offensive. Their cannonade lasted an hour, but did us little damage, as their shells either fell short or failed to explode. Our men were suffering for want of rations, and in fact every necessary. During the day there was a good deal of skirmishing along the line. At Sumner's corps the cannonade was revived at intervals until nightfall. The enemy had planted a battery on the left of his position, from which Sumner's force suffered considerably. General McClellan decided on its capture. It was planted on the margin of a wood, about half a mile from our principal line of battle. Between five and six, General Sumner ordered a battery of the 4th United States artillery, the Irish Brigade, supported by the 69th Pennsylvania Volunteers, the 29th Massachusetts, and a couple of other regiments, to take up a position near to and capture that battery. The rebel leader Jackson's eagle eye quickly discovered the movement, and he determined to prevent it, and sent forward ten thousand men, marching at support-arms, in columns of brigades. This was done to deceive us as to their object. But no sooner had they debouched from the woods which lay between their position and ours than they broke to the right and left, and opened on our men a deadly fire of shell, grape, shrapnel, and canister. The 69th Pennsylvania was the first to open fire and engage them. Such was the nature of the ground, that but one of our regiments at a time could oppose them. The rebel front was twice the extent of ours. The 69th, after a sanguinary struggle, were compelled to fall back towards the right, where they subsequently did good service on the flank of the enemy. The 69th New York replaced them, with Meagher riding at their head, brandishing his sword, and their colonel (Nugent) commanded them to charge the enemy with the bayonet. While these movements were going on, a fresh body of rebel troops suddenly appeared on the left flank of this regiment, and fired two volleys into their ranks at twenty paces, which annihilated the two left companies of the battalion; every officer of these companies fell dead or wounded, and but ten men escaped. This, however, did not prevent the bayonet charge, and the 88th, under Major Quinlan, coming up, repaid fully the death-blows dealt to the 69th regiment, making a desperate charge with the bayonet. They were with difficulty prevented by their officers from rushing on the enemy's batteries, which would have resulted in their destruction. The 63d New York of the Irish Brigade, under Col. John Burke, and the 29th Massachusetts, under Col. Pierce, now arrived; the latter here fully retrieved his reputation from the cloud thrown over it at Big Bethel, and a general charge bayonets along the line followed, producing an instantaneous and complete rout of the enemy, with a loss of 1500—one half of them were killed in the pursuit and in the incessant and ineffectual attempts to rally. Our boys cheered loudly as they followed up the enemy, and paid them severely for their temerity wherever they attempted to re-form. We captured two guns, and a number of prisoners; but our loss was terribly heavy: over 1200, in killed and wounded, fell in this bloody conflict. The officers and men behaved nobly. Meagher was conspicuous in the fight; and Captain McCoy, of his staff, had his horse shot under him by a round-shot. As night set in the rebels fell back, to attack us no more. They had failed in their efforts to turn our left, and had received a severe blow, under which they reeled back to their position. Quietness reigned in our camp that night: the dead were being buried in silence, and the wounded cared for in the temporary hospitals, as well as our limited supplies and circumstances would permit. The surgeons worked all night, and the gray morning broke on our labors. The wounds were chiefly from minié-balls, and fragments of shell. Numbers were wounded in several places, and in their prostrated condition were unable to undergo the necessary operations until recruited by rest and nourishment.

The enemy, finding our position impregnable, and our troops prepared to defend it, at once determined on a change of tactics, and commenced the erection of a fort on the opposite bank of the river, from which he could bombard our camp in the rear. General McClellan came to the determination of foiling him in this, as he had already done in all his designs. For this purpose he had the baggage ordered to a point down the river, called Harrison's Landing, where the stream is so wide that a battery on the opposite bank could receive more damage from the gunboats than it could inflict upon us at such a distance. This point is about seven miles below Turkey Grove. The baggage and heavy artillery commenced moving early on Tuesday afternoon; and at two, A. M., the rear-guard, consisting of Sumner's corps, commenced its march without molestation from the enemy. The rain had now begun to pour down. The roads were getting in a bad condition. This made the movement slow, but as we were on the best road, the enemy, in following us up, were unable to move even as fast as our train. The rain was on Wednesday followed by a thick fog, through which the enemy's videttes were visible. Some slight skirmishing took place between his cavalry and ours, and the gunboat Galena threw a few shells among their ranks, which dispersed them, and for the night all was quiet; nor have the enemy made any signs of attacking us to-day, doubtless having heard of our reinforcements. All the prisoners taken by our men were intoxicated, and most of them had their canteens partially filled with bad whiskey. They say their losses, since the retreat to the James river commenced, amount to 30,000, our artillery having made sad havoc in their ranks, and that the firing of the gunboats was very accurate and destructive. They boast of taking General McCall prisoner when he was wounded, and speak of him as a skilful general. The rebels are, in their present position, far removed from their base of operations and supplies—their communication is difficult; while we are on the bank of James river, on which float our supplies, and able allies—the gunboats. These are some of the advantages gained by abandoning the Chickahominy intrenchments, and the White House as a depot. But the change has cost us terribly; and but for the valor and endurance of the men, the patience and promptitude of the officers, and the ability of the commanding general, the Army of the Potomac would have been annihilated by our indefatigable foe. As it is, our men are in good spirits and discipline, though much fatigued by the hardships of the retreat and battles of the past days. Their confidence in General McClellan is unshaken; this has borne them along, and encouraged them to surmount every trial, difficulty, and danger. Their fortitude, when foot-sore and weary, when suffering for water and from intense heat, want of sleep and rations, and, in short, when undergoing every privation, never forsook them; and their reliance was increased when they saw the foresight of General McClellan in providing so large a park of artillery, and proceeding so cautiously against the rebels. It was a shield and a safeguard to the retreating army at every step, and a terror to the enemy, who had to sacrifice their best and bravest troops in capturing one masked battery after another. We lost 25 of our guns, which must have been a rich prize to the rebels, as they stood in need of such war material. The wonder is, that with such a force, such an immense train, and during such a retreat, our loss was not even greater than it is. Had General McClellan received 50,000, or even 30,000 fresh troops, we would have whipped the rebels, and to-day, instead of bivouacking on the James river, would, in all probability, be resting in the hotels of Richmond.

CHAPTER XV.

INCIDENTS OF THE SEVEN DAYS' FIGHT.

Colonel Woodbury, of the 4th Michigan, fell at the head of his regiment, as he was cheering his men on; his command has been terribly cut up, having had fifty-three killed, and one hundred and fifty-eight wounded, besides thirty-three missing. Among the officers killed was Captain Rose, whom General McClellan complimented so highly at New Bridge. He was formerly principal of an academy, and eleven of his pupils, who were in his company, are either killed or wounded. Captain Pie, was also killed; he was a great favorite with his men. Captain Spalding and Adjutant Earle are wounded. The 9th Massachusetts has suffered the severest loss of any regiment in its division, amounting to one half the regiment. Colonel Cass, their leader, was wounded in the head, and for days we feared he would die. He is, however improving; he was on the sick-list when we went into action, but refused to allow any one to lead his boys but himself. The 62d Pennsylvania, of this brigade, also suffered heavily, and others of General Griffin's command. General Daniel Butterfield, of New York, behaved with great gallantry. He risked his life repeatedly; he rode close upon the enemy, and planted the colors of the 44th New York with his own hands. It had been twice stricken down; while doing so, two balls passed through his hat; one of his aids, young Fisher, of New York, was killed by a minié-ball while riding beside him. His brigade suffered terribly, and lost a third of its number. Colonels Stockton and McLean were both wounded. I learn that Prince de Joinville has to-day presented General Butterfield with his horse, in token of his admiration for the general's bravery. The prince, with the other French nobles on McClellan's staff, leave to-day for Europe. It is said they intend to return, but this is doubtful.

General Martindale's Brigade has also lost heavily. In fact all Morrell's division has been badly cut up. They did some of the hardest fighting. Captain Achmuty and Lieutenant Williams, of General Morrell's staff, had each a horse shot under him. Great praise is given to Lieutenant Batchelder for his defence of the ammunition-train, of which he had command; and which, but for his coolness and bravery, would have fallen into the enemy's hands. I have just had an interview with Professor Lowe, the aeronaut, who witnessed the battle of Friday from his balloon. He describes the evolutions of the battalions, the charges of the cavalry and infantry, the flashing of the artillery, and the carnage of the fight, as truly grand. He says the rebels also sent up a balloon, and that he and the occupant of the rebel balloon for some time viewed each other through their telescopes. The distance was too great to permit him to distinguish one division from another, but he could plainly discern the blue uniform of the Union troops from the butternut and many-colored clothing of the rebels. This enabled him to judge of the relative firmness and endurance of the contending forces; and he speaks highly of the rebels, for their unflinching bravery and obstinate resistance, which were at length overcome by our men. The information he gained by the ascent was of great importance to General McClellan in the disposition of his forces and the strengthening of our weakest points at the proper time.

Wounded from the Battle before Richmond.

A remarkable feature of the wounded I have received on board the transports from the seven days' fight is, that almost all of them are wounded in the limbs, principally in the left thigh. The number wounded in the head, abdomen, or side, is very few. One, Colonel Pratt, of the 31st New York, was wounded by a minié-ball in the left cheek, in Friday's battle. The ball entered the left cheek between the gum and upper jaw, passed through the nose, and lodged in the right cheek or malar-bone. He has gone to his home in Brooklyn, where he will have it extracted, as there was no pressing necessity for its being done here, and he was anxious to get to his home and family. Another poor fellow, named Sharp, of the 2d United States Infantry, was struck in the abdomen with a piece of shell, which lacerated the muscles and fractured the floating ribs on the left side. The wound left by the missile was the most jagged and extensive I have seen: the intestines, having lost their support, protruded. After returning them, and other proper surgical care, he is doing well, and, notwithstanding the extent of the wound, will probably recover. Lieutenant Freeman, of the same regiment, had his arm shattered, but it will be saved.

We dispatched, yesterday, the Vanderbilt and Louisiana to Washington with nearly 1300 wounded. Many of them are able to walk, having been but slightly wounded in the upper extremities, and some were sick. To-day we sent off the Arrowsmith with 700 wounded, the Elm City with 300; many on board of this vessel were very badly injured. We are now loading the steamer John Brooks, and will put 400 on her. A great many officers, some of them badly wounded, will go in her. The Kennebec and State of Maine will follow to-night, and will take nearly 600 more; many of them are but slightly wounded, and a large number are sick.

A number of prisoners will be sent down to-day to Fortress Monroe from this place. Among them are fifty-three officers. The men are fine-looking fellows, but miserably clothed, and terribly dirty. The Commodore took down nearly 500, mostly wounded, few very bad cases. This is a terrible scene, eclipsing that of the White House; but there is more assistance and less confusion, and the accommodations are more extensive than there.

As I before stated, when the order was given to abandon our old camp on the Chickahominy, the sick who were able were told to walk to the James river. Many of them gladly desired to do so who were unequal to the task, but as transportation had to be provided for a large number, they were not prevented. On being furnished plentifully with cooked rations, coffee, etc., off they started, a long and straggling line, on Saturday evening; some on crutches, some had canes. Most of them reached the James river Monday night, and bivouacked near Epping Island, in a beautiful, shady grove on the river's bank, where they received such attentions as we could bestow. On Monday morning they were sent to Harrison's Island, but soon after they started it began to rain in torrents, which so cut up the soft, clayey road, that it took them many hours to get there. Their suffering during the journey was very great, but unavoidable. On arriving, there was not any accommodations for them; but some of them soon erected shelter on the lawn in front of the Harrison mansion, and as I heard there was about a dozen wall-tents at hand, I got possession of them, and had them erected. In them all that could crowd took shelter; and on the lawn, the poor, weary fellows, with their blankets wrapped around them, lay down in the rain, and soon forgot, in sleep, the sorrow, privations, and dangers of the past week. We took possession of the dwelling-house for a hospital. As fast as each case was attended to, we sent them on the steamers. Nourishment was, with great difficulty, procured for them, but, after some delay, I had coffee and soup prepared for them; and in distributing it, the Rev. Mr. Fuller, chaplain of the 16th Massachusetts, was most efficient. He worked with untiring energy, and appeased the cravings of many a poor fellow who for days had not tasted any thing but hard crackers and muddy water, which he could not at all times procure. We hope by to-morrow to have matters in better preparation; but our labors are very onerous, and but few of the surgeons have as yet had any rest, and little, if any, food.

CHAPTER XVI.

VISIT OF THE PRESIDENT TO THE ARMY.

I STARTED yesterday for Fortress Monroe on the steamer John Brooks, with nearly four hundred wounded. It was not my intention to proceed further than the fort. My visit was for the purpose of obtaining supplies, and making other necessary arrangements. I found, this morning, that many of the hangers-on and sutlers, who have thronged the White House and Harrison's Landing, are about leaving for the North; it appears that General Dix, having had repeated complaints made to him of the frauds committed on the soldiers by the Jews and sutlers, has issued an order that they at once leave the fort. Yesterday Lieutenant Duval, of General Dix's staff, notified 200 of them that they should depart within twenty-four hours. All last night and this morning they have been on the move; the order is a just one, although it will bear heavily on some honest men, who have invested all their capital in the purchase of goods that are much needed by the soldiers and cannot be got elsewhere, for which they have charged a fair price, considering the cost of bringing the goods to this point; but others have been robbing the poor fellows by selling them worthless trash at enormous prices. I found that the steamer State of Maine, which I dispatched two days ago from Harrison's Landing, and which I hoped was now safe in New York or New Haven, has returned here, having broken her shaft. On going on board of her

I found the wounded doing well, but sadly disappointed at the delay in reaching their friends.

To-day (Tuesday) the President arrived here (Fortress Monroe). As I start back for Harrison's Landing he is going ashore to hold an interview with General Burnside, who is at the fort,—his division being on its way to reinforce General McClellan, but has been, as I am informed, countermanded. Yesterday the flag-of-truce boat which was sent up the York River on the 7th inst. returned: at Cumberland 105 sick and wounded of our boys were found and taken on board, the rebels consenting to their surrender, but afterwards changed their minds and obliged them to be brought back. They were terribly disappointed. They were under the care of Dr. Daniel Wersel, U. S. A. On my arrival at Harrison's Landing I learned that the refusal to give up the wounded at Cumberland, by the rebels, was owing to some mistake, and that another vessel will at once be sent for them. A grand review of all the troops is about taking place. The President, who has arrived from Fortress Monroe, is now in consultation with General McClellan, and the line will be formed at 6 P. M. It will necessarily be quite late before the review is over, as the line extends several miles; but it is moonlight, and this will afford the men an opportunity to see President Lincoln, of whom they have heard so much, even from the rebels, whose pickets daily taunt them with repeating the opprobrious names they have given the President.

Statements of Rebel Prisoners at Harrison's Landing.

On conversing, to-day, with some of the wounded rebels, I learned that the wounded we had been obliged to abandon, but whom we left in charge of surgeons, had been well taken care of by the enemy, who had treated them and the surgeons with great kindness. This is doubtless the effect of our good treatment to their wounded. The prisoners who arrived yesterday are being sent down the river to-day: *there are many officers among them*; I had some conversation with a colonel and a captain. They are gentlemen of education and refinement, and have been in the habit of making annual visits to the Northern cities, especially Baltimore and Philadelphia, where they are well known: they made the following statement, with every appearance of candor, and it seems worthy of credit. Before the evacuation of Corinth portions of Beauregard's army began to arrive in Richmond, and continued to do so until that event took place, by which time nearly 50,000 had arrived, and that, subsequent to the evacuation, half as many more arrived; that these 75,000 troops are the flower of Beauregard's army, the best of the old army of Manassas, and that, as a general thing, they have not been engaged in the late battles, nor in the pursuit of our army on its retreat, but are held in reserve; that the whole number of troops around Richmond amounts to 200,000; that General Lee has the chief command. Generals Beauregard, Jackson, and Joe Johnston, before receiving his wound at Fair Oaks, had the command of the *corps d'armée* under him. They speak of the report of Stonewall Jackson's death as if it were a *ruse*, and say that he will soon again turn up at some unexpected point. From what these officers say, I infer that the eight forts of earth-works north of Richmond, two or three miles from the city, are not very strong, nor are they mounted with heavy guns. They mainly rely on Fort Darling to defend the city, the obstructions and subaqueous batteries in the James river and on the fighting of their troops. They are greatly elated at our reverses before Richmond and Charleston, which they attribute more to the fighting quality than the number of their troops, but say they have plenty of reserves, and can place fresh men in any battle when those first engaged become weary.

They say it is utterly impossible for the Union army to take Richmond by land or water. By land, on account of the number and quality of their troops; and by water, on account of the defences of the James river. Of these, Fort Darling is but one, for besides it they have erected three iron batteries, mounted with heavy guns, and casemated for the protection of the gunners. That there are also submerged iron batteries, each containing five tons of gunpowder, connected with the land batteries by wires, and so arranged as to explode at any desired moment.

With regard to the obstructions in the river, they are such, that although it is possible to remove them, yet it will require such a vast amount of labor, and so much time, that it never can be done under the fire of the batteries, and no vessels can pass while they remain. During the whole of the seven days' contest our troops fought bravely, and drove the enemy back at many points: this was, they said, noticeable when General Heintzelman charged with his whole division. Yet in spite of this the general result is in their favor. The Chickahominy was no barrier to their pursuit of our wearied and decimated columns. General Woodbury's Engineer Corps remained behind till the last moment, destroying and blowing up the bridges. But the enemy has also engineers to reconstruct bridges; and from their intimate knowledge of the topography of the country, had a decided advantage over us, as they knew the position of many fords; so that while a portion of their army crossed on the bridges they rebuilt, others crossed at these fords. Thus they kept close on our rear. Our engineers obstructed all the roads through the White Oak Swamp so effectually, that they saved the Union army by delaying the advance of the enemy; but they toiled day and night to remove these obstructions, and found new paths, by which some of them were avoided. By Tuesday night they had cleared their way so that they could advance across the swamp in any number they pleased; but at that time our troops had reached the James river, and were comparatively safe. We are now encamped for five miles along its left bank. The rebels are in our rear, between us and the Chickahominy, their right resting on Richmond, where the main body of their army remains. Their left extends to the junction of the two rivers. If they had recovered from their fatigue they would attack us before they knew of our being reinforced; but the labor of the seven days' fight has told as heavily on them as it has on our men. Doubtless, before many days will have passed, we shall again hear from them. Our men are not unwilling, nor at all daunted at the prospect, though the enemy has two to our one. Yet our position is strong, our artillery well posted, and our able auxiliaries, the gunboats, prepared to meet them, but we look daily for reinforcements.

CHAPTER XVII.

SECOND BATTLE OF MALVERN HILL.

On Saturday last, an expedition under General Hooker set out for the purpose of recapturing Malvern Hill, where our troops fought so well, but lost so many, and the position. For some reason they returned without any engagement, but started again yesterday evening for the same purpose. The column was not all on the road until the moon had risen, which threw a flood of light on the men's brilliant bayonets through each opening in the woods. The roads were in good order; the artillery train went smoothly on, making but little noise. Precautions were taken not to give alarm to the enemy's pickets, one ot whom was arrested on the road. Guards were stationed around each dwelling-house they passed, to prevent the inmates giving the alarm to the enemy, whose camp was near. Our men having reached the place determined on to halt for the night, pickets were thrown out with the greatest quietude and caution, so as to prevent the enemy from being aware of our proximity. These precautions would have succeeded, but that some newly-fledged brigadier, to show his authority, gave the order to his brigade to halt, in a voice that could be heard for miles. It was heard by the enemy's pickets at 12 o'clock, and reinforcements were sent for. Our men bivouacked on the Quaker Church road, in the rear of the battle-ground at Glendale. Grover's Brigade was in the advance: their pickets saw none of the enemy, but three, who, on seeing the 2d New Hampshire, disappeared. At daylight the column moved, and passed through Nelson's farm, by the old battle-ground, and near the church, which on a former occasion had been riddled with shot and shell, and its pews torn up to make amputating tables. At half-past five the column reached Malvern Hill. The sky was clouded, the atmosphere damp and heavy, and not a breeze moved the leaves. The cavalry and artillery led the column into the field through the wooded gorge, in front of the hill occupied by General Hooker and his staff, who at once took a position, by posting his artillery and ordering the cavalry to the attack. The enemy had a battery in position on the right of the brick house which stands on the bluff towards the James river;—this was Stribling's Fauquier battery. The 8th and 17th Georgia regiments, and two cavalry regiments, were also on the field. Orders were given to the 8th Illinois cavalry to charge on the Fauquier battery, which received them with a storm of grape and canister that drove them back. It then fired shell and case-shot on the road leading to the Quaker church, to which Benson's artillery replied. The morning, as stated, was calm and cloudy, but the enemy, with great accuracy, continued to shell the road on which our troops were advancing. Grover's Brigade led the infantry, and stood the fire unflinchingly. The other brigades followed in good order. The men, by dropping down as a shell was heard, escaped unhurt, with the exception of two killed and fifteen wounded. Thus they marched upon the field and took their position. The smoke became so dense, from the absence of any wind, that General Hooker ordered the artillery to slacken their fire, and soon discovered that the rebels were retreating along the road that leads to Richmond, on the bank of the river. General Pleasanton, with cavalry and artillery, charged on them. They formed in line of battle to receive as they supposed, nothing but a cavalry charge, but a couple of rounds from the batteries undeceived them, when they again retreated, closely followed by our cavalry, which cut up their rear-guard and took fifty prisoners. Thus ended the second battle of Malvern Hill. The enemy were not prepared for us, and not receiving the expected reinforcements, retreated towards the river, where it would be unwise to pursue them, as a strong force was posted further up, near Richmond. We took over 100 prisoners. Lieutenant Hubbard captured ten prisoners and two horses. We lost Lieutenant-colonel Gamble, of the 8th Illinois cavalry, who was shot through the lung. Captain Benson lost a leg by the explosion of a shell near the muzzle of one of his guns. Before our men were all quietly settled down, General McClellan arrived, and, in company with General Hooker, rode over the field. It is reported that our troops will occupy this place permanently, but I think we will all soon leave the Peninsula. This opinion is based on the refusal to reinforce us, as our present force is inadequate for the capture of Richmond, and daily growing smaller by sickness.

CHAPTER XVIII.

INCIDENTS AT HARRISON'S LANDING.

For the last two days we have been occupied in sending off the sick and wounded, as soon as they were able to be moved, and we could procure steamers for the purpose. Every thing is unusually quiet since the enemy shelled our camp, from the opposite bank of the river, at night. I had a conversation to-day with a gentleman who has just returned from Richmond. He remained with our wounded at Savage's station, on the retreat of the Union army. He describes the scene as truly awful. The confusion and want of accommodation, caused by the retreat of the army, added to the sufferings of the wounded. It was many hours before they could secure a cot, shelter, or blanket, to lie down on. The dwelling-houses and negro-quarters were filled to overflowing. A few tents, and improvised coverings of boards and branches, were all the shelter that could be obtained. The surgeons were without instruments, bandages, stimulants, or the necessary appliances. The wounded from the battle of Peach Orchard were brought to Savage's, and during the battle in the afternoon, to the left of Savage's, shells were thrown into the hospital by the rebels. A flag of truce was sent to them, and a promise obtained to respect the hospital, signed by three colonels of the Confederate army. The wounded from this battle, which raged until nine or ten o'clock at night, were also brought to this hospital. At daylight, next morning, the rebels mounted a guard over the hospital, and sent out wagons to collect the wounded still left on the field. The burying of the dead, after these two battles, continued for three days. On Tuesday morning, the barricades and the smouldering ruins of the locomotives and cars burned by our forces having been removed, the truck-trains were run out from Richmond to Savage's station, and the Confederate wounded were taken to the city. Detachments of their troops were set to pick up the spoils of our camps,—old shoes and clothing. They also took our men's haversacks, belts, and even the fragments of shells that lay around. The rebel wounded were placed in hospitals and private houses. Our wounded were not removed until Tuesday week after the battle. In the mean time many of them had died of their wounds, and were buried near the station. When they were transferred to Richmond they were not treated as wounded men, but as prisoners, and placed in warehouses and prisons, where the air, from want of ventilation, was shocking. The rebels did not provide surgeons for them, except one in charge of each of the temporary hospitals. These took no means to relieve the wounded, save in one case, where a surgeon, with a rusty saw, performed an amputation, from which the patient soon died. The Richmond ladies attended to their own sick and wounded; but not one came near our men, among whom the mortality is increasing. Our surgeons were not kept in prison; and the gentleman who informed me of these facts, being a civilian, was allowed to come away to make arrangements for an exchange of prisoners, on giving his parole to return in twenty days, unless previously exchanged. He came by way of Petersburg to City Point. He says the rebels are exultant over our recent defeats, but that Richmond and Petersburg are filled with mourning for their relatives lost in the late battles. General Dix has arranged the exchange, which has commenced. Two hundred and fifty of the Union prisoners have been sent to the White House for this purpose. Generals McCall and Reynolds are in one of the prisons at Richmond which is used for officers. These officers and the wounded receive rations of bread and meat twice a day. The officers have bunks, but the sick lie on the floors of the warehouse, which has not been cleaned since last occupied as a prison. Until a day or two before he left, many lay in the same clothes they were taken from the battle-field. Before leaving, some of them had received clean drawers and coverlids. Their old clothing was collected, to be sent to a woollen mill, to be manufactured into clothing for the rebel soldiers. There are in prison, at Richmond, over a dozen sutlers of our army, many of whom have agreed to pay large sums for their release, if not exchanged. From some of these the rebels have received full particulars of our strength. Many of them are Jews: the rebels have made agreements with them to commence running the blockade, with contraband articles most needed in Richmond, on their return within our lines.

The steamer Louisiana was sent yesterday up the river to receive the sick and wounded Union prisoners who have been exchanged. She passed down the river to-day with a joyful load. These are the wounded taken at Savage's station. General Dix made the request for their release. They are on their way to Baltimore. Major Clitz, of the 12th Regulars, and Colonel Charles of the New York Tammany regiment, both of whom were reported as killed, are on board and are doing well. They give a much better account of the treatment they received than we received before. They say that, excepting the food, they were well cared for, and the rebels gave them the best food they had. All is quiet here. It is expected that General Beauregard, with 30,000 men, has taken possession of the south bank of the river down to City Point. This may cause a renewal of the firing on our steamers passing down the river. For the last week they have not been molested, and since the Juniata was fired into, but little injury has been done to any of them. We are busily engaged to-day, endeavoring to have the abuses existing on the Baltimore boat from Fortress Monroe remedied. Many of the sick sent down from here, who were able to go home on furloughs, and others discharged from the Old Point hospitals, have been kept lying on the floor of the boat and wharf, before they could procure berths. The consequence has been, in many cases, a relapse of their illness. These complaints have come from Baltimore, and I hope in future it will be prevented. The provost-marshal to-day seized a quantity of percussion caps at the express-office.

Matters and things here wear the usual quiet appearance. There has not any thing happened to break the monotony of drills, parades, &c., excepting the visit of Gen. Halleck to head-quarters. Some say we are going to make an advance on Richmond as soon as all our reinforcements arrive, and that Gen. Halleck's visit to Gen. McClellan was to decide on the number of troops he requires to secure the capture of the city. Others say we are about abandoning the Peninsula, and that Gen. Halleck refused to give Gen. McClellan any further reinforcements. Deaths in the hospitals are daily occurring. The weather is intensely hot. The fatigue parties are digging wells, but meet with but poor success. Our supply of water is miserable A terrible row took place last night on board the Adams'

Express Company's barge. The negroes employed by the Company, in the absence of the agent, Mr. Montgomery, getting intoxicated had a row, which broke the stillness of the night. Quite a number of absentees are daily returning to their regiment. This looks as if some change was near at hand. The surgeon of the 1st U. S. Sharp-shooters having died in the Richmond hospital, the account of his death and a eulogy was read last evening to the regiment. Dr. Marshall was an excellent surgeon and a favorite with his regiment. The occasion was peculiarly affecting: as the men, drawn up in a hollow square, heard of his death, their emotion was quite evident.

The thunder-storm of last week here, has given us some cool and refreshing weather. The army are daily engaged with reviews. The regimental bands are being mustered out of service, and in future but one will be allowed to a brigade. This, I am convinced, is mistaken economy, as the men fight much better with music, and remain in camp more satisfied if there is a band. Besides this, the band-men, if properly trained, carry the wounded to the rear, thus avoiding the necessity of reducing the ranks when most needed. The regiments most decimated are being filled up with recruits but slowly. Yesterday a cavalry picket was sent out in the direction of Richmond, and met the enemy's cavalry with an artillery escort. This was looked on as a sure forerunner of an attack, but as yet "all is quiet." General Marcy and General Butterfield returned to their duty to-day, and were (especially the latter) heartily welcomed by the men of their brigades. I see with satisfaction that our frequent requests for vegetables for the men has at last been heeded: a large cargo arrived to-day, and will be at once distributed to the commissaries. This change of diet will check the alarming spread of scurvy, and give great satisfaction to the men. A large force was sent across the river yesterday, to cut down the trees that gave shelter to the rebels during their midnight attack on us.

The firing on the mail-boats by the rebels, and the means taken to prevent it, have been the only topics here for a week. The list of sick is daily diminishing under the improved vegetable diet. One of the gunboats ran aground above City Point yesterday, and as yet is not got off, but it is expected that by to-morrow she will again be afloat. At twelve o'clock, last night, General Hooker's division fell back to its old encampment, leaving a strong guard at Haxall's; on perceiving which the rebels advanced by three roads from Richmond, under the impression that our forces were marching on the city, but on driving in our pickets for a mile or so, they discovered we had no such intentions, and fell back. While at Malvern Hill one or two of the soldiers set fire to an ice-house, the flames and smoke from which, on being seen by the enemy, made him suppose we were about to evacuate it, and a large force advanced by the Newmarket road, but on discovering their mistake returned. The remains of Lieutenant-colonel O'Conner, of the 81st Pennsylvania Volunteers, were discovered yesterday, buried near one of the barns used as a hospital after the battle at Nelson's farm. His money, compass, &c., were all found in his coat pocket, and were taken care of with his remains, which are now being forwarded to Pennsylvania.

Yesterday Gen. Butterfield's Brigade returned to their old camp, after having been on duty on the opposite bank of the James river. During their short campaign they saw but little of the enemy. Part of the time the brigade head-quarters were in the Ruffin house. Our ambulance corps is undergoing reorganization. Each division ambulance corps will be placed under command of a lieutenant, with a detail of ten men from each regiment. These men will be distinguished by a green cap-band. This arrangement, if properly carried out, will insure prompt attention to the wounded, and prevent straggling. On the mail-boat, this morning, a large number of officers and sergeants went down the river, on their way home for recruiting duty. We had an arrival from Richmond this afternoon. A small steamer came down with a flag of truce. On board of her are a number of British subjects, leaving Dixie. A Lieutenant Murphy, of the 67th New York Volunteers, arrived to-day, having, in company with three others, made his escape from Richmond. They were taken prisoners, with the other wounded, after the battle of Savage's station, and since then have been confined in one of the tobacco warehouses. They give a detailed description of their mode of escape—by pulling off a board from the back of the building, and getting into an alley-way. They are now with General McClellan, describing the Richmond fortifications. This morning orders were received to dispatch all the sick and wounded down to Fortress Monroe. This will occupy us for several days. The regimental, brigade, and division surgeons have also received orders to hold a general inspection, and to send to us every man unfit for active duty, so that they may be forwarded with the others. This indicates some great change; and, from the order issued in relation to the use of transports by the sick, I have but little doubt the whole army is about to evacuate the Peninsula. General McClellan has been very active, lately, in visiting the different camps, and their concentration towards the river would, if necessary, confirm this opinion. There is much dissatisfaction among the men at the failure to send reinforcements; and now that the engagements of General Banks' and Pope's commands have become known to them, they seem very desirous to leave here, as there is not any prospect of an attack on Richmond. The weather is becoming intensely hot, and the sick suffer much from the heat. Several of the generals commanding divisions and brigades, who have been away on leave of absence, have returned to their commands. These combined movements will, ere long, produce the usual result. The reports from the recruiting officers to their commandants are not encouraging to the men here, nor do the large bounties, now paid to recruits, please the troops. They argue that it is an injustice to those who have for so long a time borne the fatigue and dangers of the campaign.

Yesterday the news reached camp of the release of Colonel Corcoran, after a year's imprisonment in Richmond. The occasion was one of rejoicing in the 69th New York regiment; but they feel that the corps has passed through many scenes since his capture, which entitles every member to an equal amount of glory. The army, as a whole, is in good condition, though there are many who desire to return to their homes, and are sick of the war. This morning, about 10 o'clock, smoke was seen arising from the vicinity of City Point. The rebels had set the wharf on fire at that place: the smoke increased and soon the whole wharf was in flames. The flag-of-truce boat, which usually stops at this wharf, was consequently obliged to proceed further up the river and may not return to-night. The flames and smoke ascending from the fire could be seen for many miles. It is said that the gunboats could have prevented the destruction of the wharf, but feared they might fire on the flag-of-truce boat, then momentarily expected. The enemy's object in destroying it, is supposed to be to prevent our landing a large force on the other bank of the river. While the wharf was on fire, a report arrived that the enemy had appeared in force in the woods on the other side of the river. Two of the gunboats commenced shelling the woods in that direction, and kept it up for half an hour. These have been the only incidents that occurred here for many days; we daily look for the order to leave.

CHAPTER XIX.

EVACUATION OF HARRISON'S LANDING.

Early this morning the long looked-for order has been issued, and important movements are now being made: the gunboats were all ordered up to cover our march. The advance has started for Williamsburg: the rear-guard will probably start by midnight. The movement is not received with much favor, the bulk of the officers and men think that Richmond can be taken now if ever, as Gen. Pope has drawn off a large portion of the rebel force hitherto engaged in its defence; they also say that the present camping ground was gained at a terrible heavy loss to be abandoned without cause. For the past week, heavy ordnance and loads of ammunition have been shipped down the river. To-day the contrabands are being sent down on barges and the steamer Illinois. The 93d New York, which was doing provost-guard duty here, was sent down on the North America. About 10 o'clock, Col. Ingalls' tents and desks were sent on board the Long Branch, and he went to Gen. McClellan's head-quarters to march overland with the army. There has not been any loss but the burning of two barges that were worthless: all the stores were safely shipped. Thus the prolonged encampment of the Union army on the pleasant banks of the James river ends. Its future destination is not generally known, but we all first proceed to Fortress Monroe, where our fleet of transports are now lying, to the number of twelve or thirteen hundred.

March to Yorktown.

By Wednesday night all requisite arrangements were completed, and the army ready to march at short notice, at any time. Nearly all the sick had been embarked, and the rest could be disposed of in an hour's time. In the afternoon, it became known that General McClellan had gone down the river for some purpose connected with the anxiously expected movement; it was reported, and generally believed, that upon his return marching orders would be issued, and the line of march to be taken would be indicated, and the suspense relieved. The uncertainty which existed as to our destination was rather annoying to us who had to make the journey, as it might be, in the dark, not knowing what enemies we were to meet, or what battles had to be fought before we were extricated from our unpleasant situation. The weather continued to be quite cool and comfortable, and much better for marching than any which had prevailed for two or three weeks previously. Thursday morning was pleasant and comfortable, and nothing of particular interest transpired through the day, until in the afternoon, when General McClellan returned, and it was soon rumored about that the long looked-for time had arrived, and that the army would commence moving in a few hours, and that its destination was to be Williamsburg, in the first instance. It was believed that the army would move by three roads, in order to get through more rapidly, and to be better prepared to meet any attack which the rebels should make upon our columns. By some means the general plans intended to be pursued had become known (as events proved), probably it not being deemed necessary to maintain such perfect secrecy in regard to them as had hitherto been done. At about six o'clock in the evening, orders were issued to the regiments and batteries comprising General Porter's corps to prepare to move immediately. These orders were received with cheers by the soldiers, who were rejoiced at the termination of their suspense and the prospect of a change of locality. Many of them believed, up to the last, that it was an advance towards Richmond, to co-operate with General Pope in the reduction of the rebel capital. They could not, or would not believe, that after so many sacrifices, and the expenditure of so many lives, and so much time, labor, and money, the campaign was to be abandoned, and the Peninsula allowed to relapse to rebel rule again. They could not realize the fact, that the proud Army of the Potomac, which three months before had commenced its march with such high and noble hopes and aspirations, with full ranks and joyous hearts, to wipe out the record of Bull Run and Ball's Bluff, was now, with decimated ranks and disheartened spirits, about to retrace its steps and return, without having accomplished its purpose. True, too, that the army had fought well, and stood by their general through good and evil report. They had, at Yorktown, Williamsburg, Fair Oaks, Hanover Courthouse, Gaines' Mill, White Oak Swamp, and Malvern Hill, enshrined their name with a halo of glory by their dauntless courage and gallant bravery, so fearlessly displayed, often against superior, and sometimes overwhelming numbers;—and now, that all was to be abandoned, and a retrograde movement was to be made, they utterly refused to credit. Soon all was bustle and excitement in the camps, the tents struck, and wagons packed very rapidly. So perfectly had every thing been prepared, that it took but comparatively short time to have every thing in readiness. By nine o'clock most of the regiments were ready and waiting for marching orders, and by ten all the preparations were made. The division of General Sykes, which was to lead the advance, commenced its march at about that hour. This was followed by General Morrell and General McCall's divisions. It was nearly three o'clock on Friday morning before all were fairly started for the march. The sight was very romantic and interesting, as the long files of soldiers moved out of the intrenchments at the front and into the Charles City road, their bayonets glistening in the moonlight as they moved silently along. Suppressed congratulations were exchanged, that we were at length actually leaving the contracted lines within which, for more than six weeks, the army had lived, and suffered discomforts which must ever render the recollections of the place any thing but pleasant or satisfactory. We proceeded slowly along, and soon the signs of approaching day streaked the horizon, and in the light of early dawn we bid, at last, farewell to the scene of our recent uncomfortable experiences. The air was cool and healthful, and the men generally cheerful and good-natured. The incidents and descriptions of the scenes connected with the beginning of marches have become so familiar, it is sufficient to say, that at last we were fairly started on our journey, and prepared to meet whatever fortune or adventures were in store for us. We reached Charles City Court-house at about eight, A. M.,—this is about five miles from Harrison's Landing,—and from it a road which leads to Barrett ferry, on the Chickahominy river, near where it empties into the James. To this point our day's march was intended to reach, and it was said to be twelve miles distant, but my subsequent experience would seem to indicate that it was nearer fifteen. The Charles City Court-house, which is the seat of government of Charles City county, is a very ancient and venerable-looking one-story brick building with two wings. The main building was used as a court-house, and the wings contain the jury-rooms, &c., &c. Adjoining the court-house is another smaller building, which contained the various county offices, and where were kept the public records of the county. These buildings have for some time past been used as a sort of head-quarters for one of our cavalry regiments on duty in that vicinity. The records and public documents which were kept in these buildings, extended back for nearly two hundred years, and must have been of very great importance to the inhabitants and property-owners of the county. These had been pulled about and torn to pieces and scattered all about the building and adjoining grounds. Great confusion must arise from this wanton destruction of valuable papers, and litigation in the future be largely increased thereby. By such conduct friends and foes are injured indiscriminately, and without any accompanying advantage to compensate for the injury inflicted. Here also is the county jail; and these, with three or four other buildings, appear to constitute the city. It does not take much to make a city South. The dwelling-houses appeared to have been generally deserted by their inhabitants. Leaving this place, we moved along slowly and cautiously, as it was thought beyond here we might possibly meet with some trouble from the enemy Previous cavalry reconnoissances had shown no rebel force between us and the Chickahominy river, but yet there was a possibility that they might attempt to annoy us, even if not in force to attack seriously. The moving column of soldiers, artillery, army wagons, and horses filled the road for miles, as it moved along. There were not many residences along the road, and some of them had been abandoned by their former occupants. The few inhabitants who remained were astonished to see us moving along in such force. They pretended to have had no communication with their rebel friends, or with Richmond, for a long time, and to be in complete ignorance of what had lately transpired in the outside world. They were very curious to know if it was a movement of our whole army, or if only a portion of it, for some particular purpose. Their rebel proclivities caused, what their caution could not entirely disguise, the exhibition of their rejoicing at the thought that we were going away, although they, generally, made professions of neutrality, and denied having any part in the war, &c., &c. One fact is generally noticeable in this State, and I have found it almost invariably wherever we have been, that is, the absence of all young or middle-aged men. A persevering inquiry will usually disclose the fact that they are with the rebel army, although most generally their friends claim that they have been forced away under the conscription, or volunteered to save the disgrace of being drafted. There are to be found on the plantations only women, old men, and children. The negroes who are able to be of any service are also mostly gone. Some having been removed down South by their masters for safety, and the balance having sought refuge within the lines of our army, where they, of course, cannot be pursued, and are thenceforth free.

This portion of the State is fertile and productive, and has been styled the Garden of Virginia, but owing to these causes and the disturbing influence of war, is largely lying waste and overgrown with weeds and brambles at present. The crops gathered this year will be but small, and with the destruction caused by the presence of contending armies, the inhabitants must suffer greatly, and will find difficulty in obtaining a subsistence until next year's harvest is gathered. In every household there is mourning for near and dear ones, whose lives have been sacrificed to the wicked and pestilent delusions to which, for the time being, the Southerners seem to be given over. All along the line of our march the houses were visited by stragglers from our army, of whom there will always be many, in spite of every exertion made to prevent it. The occupants of these houses appeared highly indignant because guards were not stationed, as formerly, to guard their property and prevent intrusion. They thought it extremely hard that they should be compelled to contribute towards the support of the army in any way. Poultry and fruit rapidly disappeared, and many a soldier's mess that night could boast of a *fowl* addition. In some instances, what was taken was paid for, but in more they were in too great a hurry to rejoin their regiments to settle. The sufferers acknowledged, however, that their friends, of the rebel army, treated them with no more regard for their vested rights; but what seemed to afflict them most was, that the hated Yankees should have the benefit of secesh property. Of course this pillaging by soldiers as they pass through an enemy's country must be condemned, and when detected and proved, should be punished for the good of the army itself, which such practices tend to demoralize; but still it is a great temptation to one, who has for weeks lived on salt pork and hard bread, to see a young and fat fowl within close proximity to him. The march was conducted in an orderly manner, and the absence of any attack or attempted opposition to our passage, must of course detract from the interest of the story. It however gratified both officers and men, who, as nothing could have been gained by fighting, more than was better attained without it—a passage through the country—desired that we might get peaceably through it. They were all ready to fight, if required, but preferred, if possible, to be spared the necessity. Without any incidents worthy of note, the river was reached by the advance early in the afternoon, and by night the divisions of General Morrell and General Sykes were crossed over to the opposite bank. General McCall's division having taken another road, and having left the old camp subsequently to the others, did not reach there until the next forenoon. A splendid pontoon bridge, of nearly a third of a mile in length and about thirty feet wide, had been built across the Chickahominy by the engineer brigade, and upon this marched the weary soldiers, followed by the artillery, and encamped upon the opposite shore for the night. Near this bridge were lying the gunboats Delaware and Yankee, to protect it against any attempt the enemy might make to destroy it. The day's march had been long and tiresome, but the men stood it very well. The weather throughout the day was cool, and until about one P. M. was overcast; so that, except for the dust, the march had been pursued in comparative comfort. In fact, up to this time, the weather had been most favorable. Had it been ordered expressly it could not have been bettered; except, perhaps, a little rain, to lay the dust, would have been an acceptable improvement. The intense heat under which we have been sweltering for weeks past, has been succeeded by a cool and comfortable temperature, which has enabled us to march through the day and encamp at night, to the manifest advantage of the army, as regards its health and strength. Night marches have not been resorted to, except upon the first night, but the men have been allowed to rest and refresh themselves after the day's march, and prepare for the labors and fatigues of the succeeding day. Saturday morning the march was resumed, and the columns moved on towards Williamsburg, at which place the advance arrived about eight A. M. General Morrell's division arrived there about one P. M., and passed on to the vicinity of the old battle-field, where they remained encamped until Sunday morning. Every thing passed peaceably.

It was now evident that the rebels were either unaware of the time when and the direction in which we were going, or that they had other business for their army than following us. Their experience at White Oak Swamp and Malvern Hill may have taught them a lesson which they do not care to repeat at present. If any attack is intended by them, it must be upon our rear-guard, but it is not thought that they will now disturb us at all. This day's march witnessed a repetition of the previous onslaught upon the poultry and orchards of the secesh inhabitants by the stragglers. As a general thing they were civil, however, and willing to pay for what was taken (when requested to do so). Large quantities of unripe fruit and melons were devoured, which will most probably cause a material increase of cases of diarrhea and dysentery, and refill the regimental hospitals, which had been cleared of their occupants preparatory to this movement. There was, also, some disappearance of fowls and poultry of all kinds, which had become a very common article of diet in the camps. Many of the soldiers were seen to carry, in addition to their arms and accoutrements, extra rations in the shape of turkeys, geese, chickens, and ducks, which, by the noise *they* made, had evidently been recently served out to them (?), and were yet, in many instances, alive and kicking. Just before entering Williamsburg, there was noticed an enterprising private by the side of the road, under the shade of a large tree, with some half-dozen unripe water-melons spread out before him, which he was disposing of to his less fortunate comrades at the moderate rate of fifty cents each. How he became possessor of this valuable merchandise is unknown, but that his profits equalled the total of his receipts there is no doubt. He was not a native Yankee, but an Hibernian, and one who evidently, with the reckless generosity and profusion characteristic of his countrymen, combined the thrift and shrewdness which is supposed to belong to the natives of the land of his adoption. The secessionists of Williamsburg, as elsewhere along the route, were much rejoiced to see our army making a retrograde movement, anticipating that soon this part of the Peninsula, also, would be surrendered to the rebel rule again. The colored population had taken the alarm, and were very anxious to learn what the future had in store for them. Some of the more indiscreet of the rebel sympathizers, upon learning that we were evacuating our position upon the James river, indulged in threats of what should be done to the negroes when the Yankees were gone. This increased their alarm and agitation, and the exodus of this class of the population, most of whom had been the slaves of rebel fugitive masters, has already commenced, and probably a few days will see the town relieved of nearly all of them, but a very few will remain to experience the tender mercies of their secesh friends. Between the action of the rebels in carrying their slaves down South, and the operation of military rule, the Peninsula has been cleared of the more valuable portion of the slave property, those who are left being generally either of an ancient or very tender and juvenile age, neither of which are of much profit. Practical emancipation has taken place; and those who have not availed themselves of its benefits, are of the class who are either too old, too young, or too shiftless to do so. This morning, one of the rebel sympathizers of this place, named Robert Coles, was arrested, by order of the provost-marshal; at his residence a quantity of ammunition and some arms were found. It is said that he was busily engaged, yesterday, in running bullets, while our troops were passing through the town. The avowed purpose was, to stop the departure of the contrabands after the expected withdrawal of our troops. At an early hour, this morning, the march was resumed, and continued in an orderly manner until Yorktown was reached. There was now no danger of an attack, and there did not exist the necessity for any special care in making the advance. Nothing worthy of note occurred, and Yorktown was reached soon after noon, and the weary soldiers encamped in the old camp, made familiar to most of them by a four weeks' residence, during the famous siege of the rebel fortifications. Here they remained and rested. The marching was beginning to tell upon the men, and there were a good many stragglers, who had fallen out of the ranks. The provost-guard was constantly employed in riding to and fro upon the road, hurrying them up, but in spite of their exertions they came in slowly, by twos and threes, and sometimes in squads. Most of them rejoined their commands in the course of the day and evening. The scenes of the previous two days were repeated along the route, although not to so great an extent. It was, however, highly dangerous for poultry to show itself in any close proximity with the soldiers.

Upon my arrival at Yorktown I called upon General Van Alen, the military governor of the place, who received me kindly and courteously; and to him am I indebted for kind favors and attentions received. Since the occupation of the place by the Union troops, it has been much improved, and its general appearance and clean and orderly condition is highly creditable to him and to Captain Revere of the 44th regiment, New York Volunteers, the provost-marshal. When the "Union" troops first took possession of the place, it was in a filthy condition. Under the direction of Captain Revere it has been thoroughly cleaned, and large quantities of filth, offal, and decaying carcasses of animals have been removed and buried. The main street has been filled and raised two feet, and every thing possible has been done to make the village a healthy and respectable place of residence. The earthworks and intrenchments built both by the Union and the rebels remain intact, and by their extent and massiveness show with what perseverance and energy both parties contended for the locality. The first buildings erected in Yorktown for twenty-seven years, is a row of five one-story buildings, built under Captain Revere's direction for the use of the officers, etc., connected with head-quarters. The place is fully prepared for defence against any attack which might be made upon it by the rebels, who cannot safely or successfully enter upon any operation of this nature. A single gunboat would command Gloucester Point opposite, and prevent the erection of batteries there, and any hostile demonstrations from the other side must result in a speedy repulse of any force which might be brought down for that purpose. Upon the plain, outside the rebel works, quite an extensive burial-ground has been laid out, which already contains about three hundred graves, mostly of our soldiers who have been buried there. When the army advanced from this point, a large number of sick were left here, of whom many died. Some bodies were also brought here from Williamsburg and other points up the Peninsula, and here, after "life's fitful fever, they slept well." A headboard at each grave records the name, regiment, and company of its occupant; so that their friends can, at any time, find the place of their sepulture. A neat rail-fence incloses the whole and protects it from intrusion.

The avant-courier of the army of the Potomac arrived at Hampton Roads this morning, in the shape of Hunt's artillery reserve, and immediately went into camp for two or three days' rest. Fitz-John Porter's corps is now at Newport News, or rapidly arriving there, and by to-morrow morning the entire army of the Potomac will be at Yorktown, Newport News, and Hampton. Up to the present time I have heard nothing but rumors of fighting; they were based on the firing of gunboats, as they shelled the woods on the banks of the James river, to keep them clear of the rebels who might use their cover to hang on our flanks and rear to annoy us, and perhaps do us considerable damage. So far as can be learned, not a single rebel has been seen on the entire march. In short, the change of base has been effected without the loss of a man, the necessary firing of a shot, or the destruction of a hundred dollars' worth of stores, commissariat or quartermasters', and the army will soon be in a position to speedily embark for other points, where the enemy and Richmond are more accessible and success more certain. Most assuredly, to effect such an important change in the relative position of contending forces, without a severe and disastrous conflict, must have called forth the highest powers of a great general, or it must have resulted from the weakness of the enemy. One or the other cause gave to our arms this fortunate escape from disaster, and perhaps destruction. Old Point Comfort will be quite lively of course for a little time. Storekeepers and sutlers are hauling in sail and making ready for a long calm.

CHAPTER XX.

SECOND BATTLE OF BULL RUN.

PART of the Army of the Potomac, after fatiguing marches, have formed a junction with the Army of Virginia, now commanded by General Pope. For the last four days a heavy firing has been heard, and I learn that another battle has been fought on the identical battle-ground of Bull Run. On the 26th, General Pope discovered that the enemy was turning his right towards Manassas, and as the division ordered to take post there had not arrived from our forces at Alexandria, he broke up camp at Warrenton and the Junction, and marched back towards Washington by three columns. General McDowell's and General Sigel's corps, with part of Reno's division, marched upon Gainesville by the Warrenton and Alexandria turnpike; General Heintzelman, with the remainder of Reno's division, marched on Gainesville; and Pope, with Porter's and Hooker's divisions, marched back to Manassas Junction. General McDowell's corps interposed between the enemy's force that reached Manassas through Gainesville, and his main body, that was moving from White Plains through Thoroughfare Gap, and drove Longstreet's corps back through the Gap to the west side of the mountain. Gen. Hooker's forces came upon the enemy at Kettle Run on Wednesday afternoon, the 27th, and had a sharp engagement with them, killing and wounding a large number, and capturing some baggage and small-arms. On Thursday morning the command moved forward rapidly to Manassas Junction, which General Jackson had evacuated some hours before. Returning by Centreville, on the Warrenton Pike, six miles west of the village, he met the forces of McDowell and Sigel, late in the afternoon. A severe fight followed, which ended when darkness came on. Next morning Heintzelman's corps advanced on the enemy at daylight from Centreville, and at the old battle-field of Bull Run the combined forces of our army and the enemy fought with fury until after dark: the result was in favor of the Union troops. The enemy acted on the defensive, and remained within sight of our camp during the night. The fight was renewed on the two following days, with heavy loss to both sides, but no decided advantage to either. On the 30th, General Pope again attacked the enemy. The Union forces are suffering very heavily, and hundreds are arriving from Washington to witness the battle and attend to the wounded, among the latter a great many clerks in the Departments are constantly arriving to attend to our men. The response by them to a call issued for the purpose, has been most prompt. Among them is Vincent R. Jackson, of the city post-office in Washington, and I learn he and twenty others have been taken prisoners by the rebels, though acting as nurses and entirely unarmed.

The battle which was raging yesterday (the 30th August) was one of the bloodiest of the war. The Confederates were reinforced, and drove General Pope back to Centreville with heavy loss. The excitement was intense at Pope's defeat, and from his dispatches was entirely unexpected. It is feared that the supplies for his army may be cut off, as the rebels are marching for the Chain Bridge, but this is doubtless mere rumor.

From all indications for the past week, it was clear that

a severe battle would come off at Manassas or Bull Run. The first sign of this was the rebel raid on Catlett's station, on the Alexandria railroad, on Sunday, the 24th August; and next their appearance at Bristow station, on the 27th, and the destruction of our army stores. This was followed by an attack on our troops at Manassas, and the continued arrival of reinforcements, with the evident intention of turning Pope's right. On Wednesday morning Taylor's Brigade of Slocum's division of the Army of the Potomac left Camp Ellsworth near Alexandria by rail for Manassas, and arrived at Bull Run bridge at seven, the next evening. They landed and crossed it without delay and marched for Manassas; but on ascending the hill over the valley of Bull Run, they met the enemy's skirmishers, who fell back. The brigade proceeded to Manassas, and as soon as they came within range of the circular fortifications around the Junction, they were opened on by a heavy fire of artillery. Having no artillery or cavalry, they were obliged to fall back to the shelter of a hill. Here they were attacked by a brigade of rebel infantry, and a sharp fire of musketry was kept up for half an hour, when a force of rebel cavalry was seen advancing in the rear of the brigade, which obliged the general to retreat across the run at Blackburn Ford; while doing so, they were followed by horse-artillery, and badly cut up.

The enemy seized on the advantage, or rather disadvantage, of our troops being so far separated, and actively endeavored to fall upon and whip each division, in detail. On Tuesday, the 22d, Stonewall Jackson arrived at Bristow station, four miles south of Manassas, burned the station and two railroad trains, tore up the track, cut the telegraph wires, and took all the Union guards on the railroad prisoners. He and General Ewell had started on Sunday from near Warrenton, with their divisions; crossed the Rappahannock, six miles south of the Blue Ridge, and arrived by way of Orleans and Salem, making the distance in less than three days. His first attack after was arrival, on the dwelling-house of a Mr. Lipscombe, in which were a dozen Union officers, all of whom, with the exception of one, were taken prisoners. The next attack was upon a company of 105th Pennsylvania Volunteers and about twenty cavalry, left to guard the road. Two or three of them were killed and the remainder were taken prisoners. A train of empty cars then came along, from Warrenton, and was fired into, but escaped. Jackson then issued orders to tear up the track. It was done, and a second train coming along, ran off the track and was also fired into. A third one, in like manner, followed, and was also run off the track and into the last train. All the persons on board were made prisoners. The cars were then set fire and destroyed. Proceeding down the track, about a mile, they burned the bridge at Cattle Run, tore up the track, and cut the telegraph wires, and, subsequently, burned the bridge at Broad Run, near Bristow. On Wednesday morning Ewell's division, with the batteries, took up a position near the railroad, one on each side, the other quite near the track, with infantry and cavalry between. This entire force of the rebels was encamped behind brushwood and the railroad bank, with an open field in front. General Hooker's division left Warrenton to attack, with a portion of Kearney's; but these did not have an opportunity of getting into the fight. General Hooker, being in command, gave orders to charge through a piece of woods and into the open space, not expecting to meet the enemy in great force; but no sooner had they entered the woods than a murderous fire was opened on his men, from the entire line of the rebels,—three batteries throwing grape and canister. The most of it, however, passed harmlessly over their heads; but the fire from the infantry was very destructive, compelling some of Hooker's regiments to fall back to the woods; but, on being supported by others, they repeated the charge, and fired several volleys, when the enemy broke and retreated. Hooker's boys pursued them, yelling. The 3d New Jersey Brigade, commanded by Colonel Carr, sustained a loss of over six hundred, killed and wounded, in this action. Colonel Carr had his horse shot under him. This was plain evidence that the rebels were in force at Manassas, and that it was his intention to turn Pope's right. The battle of Saturday, the 30th of August, was continued by the army corps of Heintzelman, McDowell, and Sigel, against a force of fifty thousand of the rebels, under Jackson and Lee. The location of the battle was in the vicinity of Haymarket, towards Sudley church, but a few miles northwest of the old and famous Bull Run. Heintzelman's corps came up with the enemy's rear at ten o'clock, A. M., seven miles from Centreville. He there found Jackson fighting with McDowell and Sigel's forces, in the direction of Haymarket, the position they took, by going north from Centreville, to command Thoroughfare Gap. It was supposed that the reserve of Lee's army, thirty thousand strong, might suddenly appear near the field. Fitz-John Porter was so posted that he could, with equal facility, march on Lee, whether attacking McDowell, Sigel, or Heintzelman. The enemy was reinforced early on Saturday, and attacked Pope's army before the arrival of Sumner and Franklin, a severe battle followed, in which Pope was badly beaten and forced to fall back on Centreville.

This second battle of Bull Run was a long and bloody

one. General Pope had concentrated the greater portion of the army under his command, and commenced the attack. He supposed, at first, that the rebel forces engaged were only those which had been met on the previous day under Generals Jackson, Ewell, and A. P. Hill, but they had received reinforcements in the morning. The line of battle was formed with the left resting on that portion of the Bull Run battle-field which, on the 21st of July, 1861, was occupied by the main body of the rebel troops. The line was extended in the direction of Manassas Junction. The battle began at noon, and success appeared to be on the Union side until about four in the afternoon. General Heintzelman's corps was on the right and McDowell on the left. The army corps of Fitz-John Porter and Sigel, with Reno's division, were in the centre. The enemy's artillery was advantageously posted, and at once opened a brisk fire on our line from right to left. The ground in that vicinity is broken and uneven, and for the most part covered with woods. The fighting on both sides was desperate and destructive—the artillery of both armies firing shrapnell and grape. The Union troops were, to some extent, protected by the unevenness of the ground from the enemy's most destructive fire. Yet they suffered terribly, and many of their best officers were killed or wounded. Our artillery was well and accurately served. About four o'clock the whole of General Pope's troops, excepting those under Banks, were closely engaged with the enemy. The whole army, from generals down, behaved well and fought with heroic valor. At this time the result was very doubtful; but soon reinforcements of the flower and full strength of the rebel Army of Virginia were brought up to the front of the engagement. The estimated number of the rebels was between 150,000 and 200,000, under the command of

Gens. Lee and Johnson, who brought their men forward in dense masses, and hurled them with irresistible violence against every part of our lines, which turned the tide of battle against us. In addition to this furious onslaught on our right and centre, and without any diminution of the enemy's force at these points, an overwhelming number of reinforcements were precipitated on our left wing, under General McDowell, which compelled him to fall back, not only on account of the violence of the attack, as the fear of all our forces being outflanked by the superior forces of the enemy. Our left wing kept retreating, until at nightfall it formed an acute angle with the line of battle formed in the morning. The severe losses our troops were sustaining, and the evident superiority of numbers, compelled the retreat of the whole army to this side of Bull Run and the heights of Centreville, where General Pope established his head-quarters. Our loss in this second unfortunate battle of Bull Run is over 6000. The enemy's is not as much.

The division and brigade generals behaved with great bravery and coolness, and our men fought with their usual valor; but the number pitted against them, and the dispiriting results of the previous days' fights, added to the lack of enthusiastic confidence in their leader, produced its inevitable effects—a disastrous defeat. The wounded taken to the rear during the fight are in our possession, but all those who lay on the battle-field are in the hands of the enemy. During the battle General Schenck was wounded in the arm, which has been amputated. General Towers was wounded in the thigh. General Hatch was slightly wounded in the head. While General Pope was writing a dispatch he had a narrow escape, as a shell from one of the enemy's batteries struck and killed two horses belonging to his staff, standing quite near him.

General Franklin's corps did not reach the battle-field in time to be engaged. The brigades which suffered most are being sent to the rear of Centreville to protect the roads to the capital against any attack or raid that might be made in the rear of the army. The men are much dispirited and demoralized. The heavy rain of Saturday night prevented a renewal of attack by the enemy on Sunday morning. Both armies rested during the day, with the exception of movements of baggage trains, and a flank movement by the enemy to cut them off on the road to Fairfax Court-house. On Monday morning the scene was beautifully striking from the heights of Centreville. The weather was clear and balmy. The panorama splendid, full of life and bustle, spread out before the beholder. In the direction of Bull Run you could see the mountains rising in the distance, with the splendid surrounding scenery. There was also to be seen, not only the large bodies of troops moving up steadily to their assigned positions in the front, but hundreds of wagons and ambulances hurrying to the rear, so that, as far as the eye could reach, the road was crowded with moving troops and trains. The flashes of the enemy's guns could be seen in the distance, and the curling smoke of exploded shells was seen sailing in the air. The non-arrival of Franklin's corps in time for the battle is much talked about. It reached here yesterday, and took up a position in the front.

During the fight of Saturday, General Buford's brigade of cavalry, comprising the 1st Michigan, the 1st Virginia, and the 1st Vermont regiments, was ordered to reconnoitre on the left to prevent the enemy turning our flank; riding beyond the left where our infantry were found close behind the batteries, which were playing on the enemy while the men were loudly cheering, the cavalry reached an eminence, and were about to send out a detachment to explore, when a large force of the enemy were seen coming along the line of the adjacent woods. A rebel battery wheeled into position, which soon threw shell, canister, and grape, into the midst of our cavalry. Long lines of rebel infantry could be plainly seen hurrying to take up position, and soon other batteries opened on our left.

Our cavalry, forced to return, retreated behind a low ridge; but the clouds of dust revealing their place of retreat, the rebels continued to shell them, and obliged them again to change their position. Soon a cavalry force was observed riding towards them. The order was given to draw sabres and prepare for a charge, when it was discovered that the squadron were friends, of the 4th New York Volunteer Cavalry, which now fell in behind General Buford's Brigade. The bugle sounded the advance, and over the hills galloped our men to meet the enemy. As they appeared, the rebel cavalry discharged double shot-guns at them, and then both met in full charge. Our men broke their line; they rallied in fine style and dashed forward again; but again their line was broken,—seeing which the rebels opened on our boys with a battery, and compelled them to return. By this time our left had given way, and on the retreat passed the cavalry, which now safely carried off a battery that was short of ammunition and came near being captured. Our troops then fell back on Franklin's division which had just come up, and were formed in line to prevent straggling and quell the panic which now existed. Franklin's arrival a few hours earlier would, probably, have altered the result of the fight. In this cavalry charge, Colonel Broadhead of the 1st Michigan, a brave and gallant officer, fell mortally wounded, Lieutenant Morse was killed, and Lieutenant Merriam was wounded and taken prisoner. Franklin's division after rallying our panic-stricken men, retired to Centreville. General Martindale's Brigade made a charge and drove a body of the enemy concealed in the woods, who were harassing our forces by their rifle-shooting. General Hartsall's Brigade made a similar charge, but with a different result. They penetrated the woods, when a deadly fire of grape and canister opened on them; at the same time a murderous volley of rifle-balls came from one side, and a dashing charge of the enemy from another. Our men fought well, but were forced to retreat. The enemy remained on the battle-field all night.

The road, from Centreville to Alexandria, is crowded densely with wagon trains, ambulances, and carriages. Some of the wounded have been sent to Washington, but a larger portion of them are being sent to Alexandria. The court-house, city-hall, and churches there are being converted into hospitals, and confusion reigns supreme, distrust and disaster is painted on every one's face along the road.

On Monday evening following the disastrous battle of Bull Run, a severe engagement with the enemy took place at Chantilly, two miles north of Fairfax Court-house, between a portion of our army and Jackson's forces. Our loss was very heavy, including General Stevens, who was shot in the head, while he was leading his brigade into action, bearing the colors, the color-sergeant having been previously shot. His son, also, who was acting on his staff, was wounded. General Philip Kearney was also killed the same evening. He was shot through the back, while wheeling his horse around to cheer on his men. His loss is deeply deplored by the whole army. He was considered one of the bravest generals in the service, and the enemy made repeated efforts to kill, wound, or capture him. His dashing and fearless bearing, and his conspicuous figure, with but one arm, made him an easily distinguished and coveted aim. Up to the night of his death he was, on every occasion, to be found in the thickest of the fight, and seemed to lead a charmed life. The Union army has not lost an officer who will be as much regretted as General Kearney. The operations of the contending armies, on the south side of the Potomac, completely absorb the attention and interest of everybody, citizens and soldiers. The excitement that would naturally be awakened by the knowledge of the fact that bloody battles were being fought within cannon sound of the national capital, was considerably increased, because no full and authentic information respecting the results, or losses, had been received from the scene of action.

The authorities at Washington called for volunteers from the citizens to proceed to the battle-fields to pick up and attend to the wounded and bury the dead. Thousands are strewn, for miles, all over the sanguinary field. The reason for this call on the citizens, is so as not to weaken the strength of the forces by detailing the weary soldiers for the duty. Hundreds of citizens promptly responded to the call,—each one supplied with two days rations, a bucket, and tin cup, to supply water to the wounded, and also a bottle of brandy. Transportation was, as speedily as possible, provided for them. Orders were also issued for the immediate removal of all the sick and wounded, that were able to be moved, from the hospitals in Washington, to make room for those expected to arrive from the battle-field of Bull Run. Soon the streets were crowded with ambulances, conveying them to the cars for Baltimore, Philadelphia, and other places. In the afternoon the War Department impressed into the service of the government, all the stages, hacks, and wagons, which soon swelled the long ambulance train that was on its way to bring in the wounded. Some of the citizens tendered their private carriages for the purpose, and, by nightfall, the turnpike from Alexandria to Fairfax Court-house was crowded with this long procession. The experiment utterly and shamefully failed,—the drivers and many of the volunteer nurses, who drank freely of the brandy, mistaking the road, travelled all night, and at two in the morning, instead of reaching the battle-field, found themselves entering Alexandria. They were at once ordered to return to Washington, which most of them gladly obeyed. Others went in a train of cars from the capital, but, by some mismanagement, it was four hours behind time in starting, and by this time half of the volunteer nurses had gone home to their beds. When the train did start, it slowly proceeded to Fairfax station, where it stopped. Some of the nurses, determined to be of some use, proceeded from this place on foot, in a heavy falling rain, to Centreville, where they were stopped by the guards and sent back. Some went, by way of Fall's Church to Ball's Cross-roads, but were here informed that the pickets were driven in by the rebel cavalry. They then crossed to Fairfax Court house, from which place to Centreville the road was completely blocked by trains of wagons, gun-carriages, and ambulances, going in different directions. All this time the rain was pouring in torrents, and, to add to their discomfort and confusion, they were met by seven hundred Union prisoners, taken by Jackson but paroled immediately. Behind them were twelve hundred rebel prisoners, who were captured during Friday's battle. They were proceeding under guard to Washington.

At Fairfax Court-house, the hotel and other buildings were converted into hospitals. It was here that the news was received of the tide turning against the Union troops, which obliged them to abandon the field during the night. At Centreville, the whole of Pope's army, with the exception of Banks' corps, were found bivouacking: some drawn up in line of battle on the heights. Some of the brigades which had been badly cut up were in a demoralized state, and their generals were exerting themselves to restore order and discipline among them. The confusion was terrible, and arose from many regiments and parts of regiments getting separated from their commands, and now were unable to find the brigade or division to which they were attached. So great was the uproar, it was impossible to ascertain the number killed or wounded. During the past fortnight over a dozen battles had been fought, some of them little more than skirmishes, but the battles of Thursday, Friday, and Saturday were the most bloody of Pope's campaign, though not equal to many fought on the Peninsula under McClellan.

Among the Union losses, besides Generals Kearney and Stevens, General Taylor was mortally wounded, and died last night in one of the hospitals at Alexandria. Colonel Fletcher Webster, son of Daniel Webster, was also mortally wounded on Saturday, and has since died. The scenes in the hospitals at Alexandria are heart-rending. The churches are crowded with the wounded. In the Baptist church, under the care of Acting Assistant-surgeon Hammond, I performed in two hours several operations; the beds are filled with the poor fellows, many of whom are mortally wounded, all of them suffering from the worst horrors of the battle-field. The dwelling-houses on an adjoining street, and all the public buildings, are in like manner filled. The surgeons are working continually. The old Lyceum is now being prepared to receive patients, as every other available place is full. The wounds are chiefly from minié-balls. Many of them are wounded in the lungs, and all of them have suffered by the tedious journey from the battle-field over the rough roads, and the utter impossibility of obtaining any refreshment. Even water was difficult to procure, and the teamsters, in many cases, were so panic-stricken that they forsook their teams.

CHAPTER XXI.

GENERAL M'CLELLAN RESUMES COMMAND.

To-day, by order of the President, General McClellan has again resumed the supreme command of the army. Immediately after accepting the chief command of all the Union forces in the neighborhood of Washington, General McClellan proceeded to inspect the troops and fortifications on the south side of the river. This occupied him until after midnight. His reception by the officers and soldiers was marked by the most unbounded enthusiasm. In every camp his arrival was greeted by hearty and prolonged cheering, and manifestations of the wildest delight. Many of the soldiers who fought under him in the hardest battles of the war, wept with joy at having again for their commander one upon whom they could place implicit reliance. Already his hurried visit to our camps has wrought a remarkable change in the soldiers. His presence seemed to act magically upon them, despondency is replaced by confidence, and all are glad that McClellan will hereafter direct them. He has been busy in perfecting the organization of the army, and preparing it for the duties to be assigned; and has easily resumed his old habits, and spends most of his time among the camps and forts.

Yesterday General Halleck was at General McClellan's quarters for a long time, and subsequently the latter proceeded to join the army. This, now, consists of veterans for the most part; and a little time for reorganization, and for the designation of some new general officers, will make it so formidable a force, in conjunction with the new regiments now here, as to render it doubtful whether the rebels will dare to advance into Maryland. Fresh excitement multiplies upon us with each incoming day; and this has been the most painfully exciting period in the history of our national capital. What with the pouring in of the wounded from the field, the rushing hither and thither of ambulance carriages, wagons, and vehicles of every description; the movements of troops through the city towards the scene of war; the queryings and button-holeings of every person coming from across the river; the heralding and bulletining of every rumor however vague and unreliable, the whole town is kept in confusion worse confounded.

The scenes in the street, at the hotels and newspaper offices, and at the various departments, beggar description. Early this morning, long before the denizens of the capital are usually alive, the whole population was out, and then commenced the manufacture of rumors and reports, each relator vieing with the others in extravagance and color. The Washington morning papers set the ball rolling with the story that "our army was safe at Centreville;" but this story was soon spoiled by another, that the enemy had succeeded in moving quietly down near the railroad, towards Alexandria, and is turning our left wing, and that they were now on this side of Fairfax Court-house, and between that place and Falls Church.

This latter story gained credence from the fact that at 10 A. M. a long line of army wagons, loaded with camp paraphernalia, came moving up Fourteenth-street, from the Long Bridge, and defiled out towards the outskirts of the town in the direction of the springs. Then an officer of General Pope's staff came in, confirming the report. Yesterday there was brought into General Halleck's head-quarters, from Virginia, as prisoner of war, Captain Ashe, of North Carolina, acting adjutant-general in Gen. Jackson's army, from whom much has been learned of the state of affairs in the rebel army, and at the South. It is learned from other sources, entitled to credit, that the enemy have no fears or doubts of their ability to take Washington, and that very soon. Their force they deem amply sufficient for the purpose, numbering, as it does, under the five generals, Jackson, Longstreet, Ewell, Hill, and Smith, not less than two hundred and fifteen thousand men at the present time. Jackson, Longstreet, Ewell, and Hill are now consolidated at Manassas, while Smith (our own Gustavus) is marching, with a column thirty thousand strong, on Fredericksburg. The gentleman from whom these facts were learned left the rebel camp at four A. M. yesterday. He also states that the rebels now there were quite destitute of rations, they having expected to subsist on those captured from our men at and near Manassas. They were in this disappointed, as their supply trains had not come up when my informant left; and as they had not been heard from, it is to be presumed that the rebel troops are fully as badly cared for in the commissary line as our own. The rebels appear to look upon this movement as their last hope, and I am confidently told will never turn their backs upon Washington, but are determined to do or die there, and now. Their mortality has been enormous, and their own captured officers and surgeons admit a loss of from ten thousand to twelve thousand in killed and wounded up to Saturday night last.

Generals Jackson and Longstreet had a quarrel one day last week, growing out of the question of rank, but it was settled in favor of the former by General Lee, who commands the whole rebel force in person. The Bull Run bridge, on the Orange and Alexandria railroad, has its ups and downs as well as every thing else. When the rebels left Manassas last spring, they burned the structure, but it was rebuilt by our people, and held by them until yesterday week. The first structure built by the Union forces was merely a temporary one, but over it was thrown a beautiful trestle frame afterwards, and the temporary one was thrown down. On the night of Tuesday, the 26th of August, the rebels made a dash upon it, drove in our guards, and burned it the second time. Nothing daunted, however, Colonel McCollum got his men at work again, and on Monday night of this week had it rebuilt and ready for the cars to cross. But alas for all human calculations, about midnight of the same night a body of rebel cavalry dashed down to the bridge, drove away the sentries, and burned it for the third time. General Pope's head-quarter trains have arrived at Alexandria. General McClellan has arrived from Alexandria, and established his head-quarters in this city. The sick, wounded, and missing continue to arrive, by all possible means of conveyance, from the field, and are being cared for at the several hospitals. The following statement was made by a gentleman who has every appearance of being reliable. He left Washington yesterday to go to Centreville to look for his brother, who was wounded on Saturday. He went out on the cars as far as Fairfax station (seventeen miles), then walked across to Fairfax Court-house, arriving there at 4 P. M. Here he met, as he judges, about four miles of army wagons, loaded with the army luggage and sick and wounded men, coming this way. There was also some artillery, some cavalry, and a large number of skulkers

10

interspersed, all belonging to McDowell's corps. They brought the news that Pope's entire army had fallen back, and were *en route* for the forts around Washington. My informant pushed on about a mile the other side of Fairfax, and as he reached the summit of a hill, he saw in the plain before him a large number of our troops drawn up in line-of-battle order. Here he met an officer, who told him that Jackson had succeeded in turning our left wing, and our troops were momentarily expecting an engagement. Just then the rain commenced falling, and my informant went back to Fairfax. He had not more than reached the village before the action became general, and continued until night, in the midst of a terrible thunder-storm. General Pope's assistant adjutant-general, Selfridge, who had left the scene at six o'clock last night, confirmed the above report. There is great dissatisfaction against Pope and McDowell, made continually manifest by imprecations and execrations, which are loud and deep. General Pope may claim that he has obeyed orders, no matter what the result may have been, but I find no one inclined to do McDowell honor. To-night the Union army will all be concentrated in the works around this city, and General McClellan has already assumed the position of commander-in-chief of all the forces in the field in this part of the country. The announcement of this latter fact has been hailed with acclamations of infinite delight by nearly the whole population. Those who were before trembling with apprehension, and preparing to evacuate the city, are now assured of safety, and feel confident that the splendid army concentrated in the vicinity will be able, under the administration of a general in whom it has confidence, not only to repel the assault of the whole rebel army, advancing with rapid strides upon the defensive works around the city, but to drive them back and utterly defeat and rout them, and thus within a few weeks end the present campaign. After a desperate struggle upon the twice-trodden field of Bull Run on Saturday last, the forces under General Pope withdrew to the other side, of the heights of Centreville. It appears the enemy immediately began to execute another of those manœuvres by which they have accomplished every success they have gained.

As was reported, on Sunday morning intelligence was brought to the head-quarters of General Pope that a large force of rebel cavalry and artillery was moving around his right. The general, apparently regarding the movement as a simple reconnoissance in force, to ascertain definitely his position, paid little attention to the information; but subsequent events have demonstrated that it was the beginning of a general movement of the rebel army to the right and rear of the forces of General Pope, in position at Centreville. Fortunately, as a protection to the immense supply trains, moving in the direction of Fairfax Court-house, a considerable force had been detached from Pope's army and thrown in that direction. The remnant of McDowell's *corps d'armée* had been sent to the rear, and was located upon the Warrenton turnpike, leading from Fairfax Court-house through Centreville, about a mile beyond its junction with the Little River turnpike, leading to Leesburg. Gen. Couch's division was located near Germantown, about two miles from Fairfax Court-house, upon the Little River turnpike. During yesterday information was received that a large rebel force was approaching Fairfax Court-house by the latter route, and a portion of Heintzelman's corps, under Generals Kearney and Grover, was moved in that direction; and General Hooker was specially detailed, by orders from head-quarters here, to take command of all the forces at that point. Just before dark an attack was commenced by a strong rebel force, comprising the divisions of Generals Ewell, A. P. Hill, and Longstreet, upon the position occupied by General Couch. Generals Kearney and Grover were marched rapidly through the woods to his support. A few discharges of artillery were made by one of our batteries, but the battle, which was brief and fierce, was almost exclusively an infantry engagement. The charge of our gallant troops was desperate and irresistible, and the enemy were almost immediately repulsed. It was here that General Grover's Brigade, of Hooker's division, had one of the fiercest bayonet fights that has occurred during the war. The brigade charged into the woods, where the enemy were posted, in three lines, behind a breastwork four or five feet high, and in about twenty minutes five hundred and seventeen of their number fell. Formed in one line, the brigade broke through two lines of the enemy, but, being unsupported, they were obliged to fall back. The 2d New Hampshire regiment, Colonel Marston, actually crossed bayonets with the rebels, and had a desperate encounter, in which they lost severely, although they drove the foe from their position. Among the killed was Lieutenant Hiram Banks, of the 16th Massachusetts regiment, brother of Major-general Banks. He was a true soldier, and was rapidly winning his way to distinction. Major Gardiner Banks, another brother of General Banks, is in command of the 16th Massachusetts, Colonel Lannatt and Lieutenant-colonel Lawson being in hospital. General Butterfield commanded a division in General Fitz-John Porter's corps, in the battle, and in his division twenty-two color-bearers were shot. The victory was achieved with the loss of two of our most gallant, brave, and accomplished generals,—Isaac J. Stevens and

Philip Kearney. The former fell at the head of his brigade, and the latter while leading one of his regiments into position.

The object of this rebel movement upon Fairfax Courthouse was, unquestionably, to obtain possession of some portion of the vast amount of supplies which were parked in that vicinity. It was known here yesterday, from information derived from Wm. S. Ashe, formerly representative in Congress from North Carolina, but lately assistant adjutant-general to Stonewall Jackson, who was captured by our troops on Monday morning, while making a reconnoissance, that the rebel army was greatly in want of provisions. Their raid upon Catlett's station and Manassas Junction, and this last movement, were all intended to obtain supplies. Their movement towards Maryland is supposed to be actuated, not so much by the hope of thereby capturing this city, as to obtain food for their army. They fought, last night, like desperate and starving men, but they failed in their object. The supply trains, which had all been moved from Centreville to Fairfax Court-house, were immediately put in motion: and without the destruction of any public property, except the loss of a wagon here and there overturned on the road, all the thousands of wagons have been brought into Alexandria, or within the circuit of the forts around this city. As soon as it was ascertained that the whole rebel army had moved to the right and rear of Centreville, the rest of General Pope's forces were marched towards Fairfax Court-house, General Fitz-John Porter bringing up the rear; and by midnight to-night the whole army will have arrived within the shadow of our fortifications. There was no object in holding Centreville after the departure of the rebel army from before it, and now new plans are to be formed and new positions taken. During last night a small force of rebel cavalry came in as far as Fairfax Court-house, about three miles from Upton's Hill. This morning a large force of rebels was reported at Leesburg, and it is stated that a considerable portion of the rebel army will attempt to cross the Potomac, between that point and Harper's Ferry. Reports have also reached here that another rebel force, under the command of General Gustavus Smith, has arrived at Fredericksburg, and designs crossing the Potomac into lower Maryland, somewhere about the Rappahannock river. This is the present position. There was no lack of courage in our troops, nor faltering on the part of their officers, to which may be charged this retrograde movement; but there was, and is, sad complaint of mismanagement by commanding generals, and a deplorable want of confidence in their capacity. Mr. Dennis, military agent here for the State of Indiana, has received a letter from Colonel Meredith, of the 19th Indiana, which, with the 2d, 6th, and 7th Wisconsin regiments, form General Gibbons' Brigade. On Thursday evening they encountered Hill's rebel division, from whom they took a battery, which they are reported as still possessing. They held the battle-field, but Col. Meredith was the only field-officer who was not hurt. He had three horses shot under him. Our entire loss in this brigade, killed, wounded, and missing, was seven hundred and seventy-eight. The Indiana 19th lost two hundred and twenty-seven. The brigade was not in the fight on Friday, but was on Saturday, and held out to the close of the day. Their loss has not been ascertained. A New York battery came in this morning to exchange their damaged guns and appurtenances for new ones. It went off in the direction of the arsenal. I did not learn the name of the commanding officer. It is stated that the New Hampshire battery lost three of its guns. Baltimoreans, of secession sympathies, state here, to-day, that the rebels will cross into Maryland, below Harper's Ferry. It is stated that General Wool has gone to Harper's Ferry, to concert measures for the protection of the Baltimore and Ohio railroad. A gentleman from the immediate neighborhood of Leesburg states that a force of rebels is there.

Washington, September 2, P. M.—The city to-night was in a state of great excitement, and not without most substantial cause. Crowds were gathered at all the hotels, and on the streets, discussing and speculating on the future. It may here be said, that while the more timid of our fellow-citizens apprehend danger from the rebel movements, there are stout hearts that are not intimidated. Last night there was a series of skirmishes along the whole front, during which we lost two or three of our best generals, and other valuable officers. According to prevalent reports, it was Hooker's division which was mainly, if not altogether, engaged in driving back the rebels, but the one mile of skirmishing was attended with much loss of life. At about four o'clock this morning, a train of one hundred wagons, with commissary stores, was intercepted by the enemy between Fairfax and Centreville, and driven off towards Manassas, before the party could be overtaken. They secured the entire train. So soon as this raid in the rear of our army at Centreville was known, the necessity of guarding that direction became apparent, and at noon the whole army of Virginia had abandoned Centreville, and was massed this side of Fairfax Court-house. This noon they again took up a line of march, and this evening the advance was in sight of Munson's Hill. The enemy's cavalry followed them in the distance, but made no attack, and the entire movement was being accomplished in excellent order. At noon to-day, General McClellan rode out to meet the returning column, and was received with great demonstrations of gratification and pleasure by the army. The works for the defence of Washington are all in excellent condition, and are strongly manned by experienced artillerists. The gunboats lining the Potomac are doubtless designed to prevent any attempt to interrupt the navigation on that river.

The Retreat of the Left Wing in the Bull Run Battle, September 3d, 1862.

When General Franklin's corps arrived at the battle-ground on Saturday afternoon, the fortunes of the day had been decided, and the command was halted near Cub Run. Major-general Slocum, seeing that General Pope's left wing was falling back towards Centreville, formed his division in line of battle across the road, and deployed a squadron of cavalry attached to the corps, as skirmishers. General Smith's division was also drawn up in line of battle half a mile in the rear. When the troops came back they were brought to a halt, and not allowed to pass this point, and numbers of stragglers and skedaddlers were collected. General Hooker's division, and General Kearney's division came back in order, the regiments marching with well-closed ranks. Many of the stragglers attempted to fall in with those regiments and march off the field with them, but they were repulsed and kept out of the ranks of the steady veterans, who did not desire the companionship of men on the retreat who would not face the enemy by their sides in the front of the battle.

As incidents of the battle, I will mention that over eleven hundred paroled prisoners, some of whom were taken by the enemy as far back as Thursday at Manassas, arrived late this evening at Aqueduct Bridge, Georgetown, and report that General Lee has established his headquarters three miles beyond Bull Run, on the Warrenton turnpike. The only force at Fairfax was Stuart's cavalry, he being there in person. The rebels assisted the men in the burial of our dead last night, whom they stripped of their clothing, except their pantaloons. Our men say that the rebels were so hungry, they rushed for the haversacks of our killed and wounded. They saw the soldiers of the enemy marching to the rear, on the Warrenton turnpike, towards Thoroughfare Gap. Washington is comparatively quiet, the excitement of the last two days having subsided. Such disposition has been made of the troops within the last twenty-four hours as to restore confidence. Reports have reached here, from time to time, of certain regiments having been annihilated, when after the lapse of a few days the rumors prove groundless, the appearance of numerous stragglers being the best refutation of the exaggeration. Brigadier-general Butterfield, in the battle of Saturday, commanded that portion of General Morrell's division taking part in the engagement. General Morrell was with General Griffin's Brigade, which took no part in the fight. Colonel Henry A. Weeks, of the 12th New York, who commanded General Butterfield's Brigade, was shot through both legs. His coolness and bravery on the field, and the able manner in which he manœuvred his command is worthy of the highest praise. The officers, one and all, and the men of the 12th regiment, fully sustained their reputation. Captain Ryder, who was temporarily attached to General Butterfield's staff, was shot in the head, but not mortally wounded. Captain Fowler, also of the Twelfth, was wounded in the foot: his conduct here, as well as at Malvern Hill, elicited the warmest commendation of the whole brigade; when unable longer to lead his company he was unwillingly mounted on a horse, which was captured from the enemy, on which he proceeded to Fairfax Court-house: while resting there during Monday night the enemy shelled the town, and he again narrowly escaped with his life. On Tuesday he was sent forward, *via* Alexandria, to Washington. Some of the best officers were not present during the engagement; Captain Boyle was acting brigade provost-marshal, and Captain Cromie, who had been severely wounded during the Seven Days' fight and taken prisoner at Savage's station, was not sufficiently recovered to rejoin his regiment. Lieutenant Oliver distinguished himself during the fight; he is a well-deserved favorite with officers and men. Colonel Roberts, of the 2d Maine, who commanded General Martindale's Brigade, had his horse shot under him. All the regiments engaged fought gallantly, and none better than the 17th New York and 18th Massachusetts regiments, never before under fire. The 5th New York sustained severe loss.

General Duryea's Brigade, which is composed of the 97th, 194th, and 105th New York, and 107th Pennsylvania regiments, was ordered, during the battle on Saturday, to advance into a piece of woods near the old Bull Run battle-field. Here they found the 57th New York, which had been obliged to fall back from the advanced position which had been previously occupied. They were ordered to relieve them, and did so. This was about one o'clock, P. M. The brigade was then ordered to advance to the position originally held, and from which the 57th had retreated. Soon after reaching this advanced position, the rebels made their appearance in considerable force and with four pieces of artillery, with which they opened fire; but fortunately their guns were too much elevated to do serious mischief. This continued for half an hour without material advantage to either side. While thus engaged, General Duryea received a wound in the right hand from a piece of shell, while dismounted and cheering on his men. He had the hand bandaged up, and remained on the field in command of his brigade through the day. The brigade was then ordered to fall back and occupy a position in the woods, about 400 yards in the rear. They remained in this position two or three hours, engaged in skirmishing and bush-fighting, and until an order was received to fall back further; but before this could be done the order was countermanded, and they were ordered to advance to their original position. Here they remained until between five and six o'clock, P. M., constantly under fire of the rebel artillery.

Captain Thomas Hight, of the 2d regular cavalry, was taken prisoner by the rebels near Manassas, and the first question asked him by his captors was, whether he belonged to Pope's army. Colonel Fitzhugh Lee took him in charge, and told him that he could not be paroled until Stonewall Jackson should come up or fall in with them. He was put upon a horse and rode with Lee, except, whenever they came in collision with our own troops he was sent to the rear, so that he might be out of danger. When Stonewall Jackson came up, the next day, Captain Hight was paroled. He was given to understand, that if he had been under General Pope's command he would have been sent to Richmond. On Sunday morning, as the rebels neared our provision trains of cars at Manassas, Captain D. L. Smith gave orders to save all that could be saved and to burn the balance, which was done. To carry out this, he directed two young clerks in the commissary department, named Rollis C. Gink and James Paul, to stay to the last, which order they cheerfully obeyed. They succeeded in saving over one thousand dollars' worth of coffee and bacon, and other articles of value, when the rebels again appearing, they began to think it was time to leave. Looking for their clothes, they came across the army mail-bags; and dropping their own property, they shouldered the mail-bags, and carried them a distance of twelve miles, through heavy rain and mud, to Bull Run, where they got the cars, and delivered the mail safe in the post-office. One of these brave young men has been quite ill since from fatigue.

CHAPTER XXII.

INCIDENTS AFTER THE BATTLE OF BULL RUN.

THE excitement existing for the news of the expected great battle has been partially gratified by the intelligence, received to-night, that a skirmish occurred last night, in the vicinity of Poolesville, between about 140 Union cavalry under Captains Means and Cole, of eastern Virginia, and a large force of rebel cavalry, and that a battle has been going on to-day on the Virginia side of the river, opposite Poolesville, 28 miles from Washington. General Sumner's corps has been sent forward to intercept the rebel troops, who are said to be concentrating near Poolesville with the intention of crossing into Maryland. Reports from Falls Church state that brisk cannonading, in the direction of Poolesville, was distinctly heard this morning, about nine o'clock. A large number of ambulances and an immense train of wagons are proceeding towards Poolesville, and three batteries are now on their way. The provost-guard is again impressing all the hack-carriages found in the streets, and sending them to join the ambulance-train. These preparations indicate a severe engagement, and a large number of wounded to be cared for, but nothing beyond this is certainly known. When the restoration of General McClellan to the supreme command of the army was made known in the hospitals, the men who had been wounded at Bull Run and Chantilly, under General Pope, though suffering agony from their wounds, sent forth shouts of gladness, and endeavored to risè from their cots to hurrah for him. Nor is the effect of General McClellan's reappointment confined to the army in the field or the wounded in the hospitals, it has actually allayed a panic, already begun, among citizens of all classes, who are now loud in their expressions of congratulation, whatever their former opinions may have been.

Since the accession of General McClellan, the recruits are arriving in great numbers to fill up the decimated ranks. They will add much to the efficiency of the several divisions, now so much reduced in numbers, especially that of General King, which left Cedar Mountain on the 19th of August, and arrived at the Rappahannock next day. The following morning the enemy opened their batteries on the division, and kept up the fire till Friday night, during which the division lost a very large number of men and some officers, among whom was Lieutenant Jordan, acting aid to General Hatch. On Saturday the division moved to Warrenton, preceded by Buford's cavalry, which drove out a considerable force of the enemy. On Tuesday morning the command reached the Sulphur Springs, where they were again shelled by the rebels from the south bank of the Rappahannock. The enemy also sent down to the river, and stationed in the bushes a body of infantry, who attempted to pick off our men. A detachment of the 2d Berdan Sharp-shooters were sent down the river and stationed behind trees. From this position they soon checked the enemy's fire, and held them in their own ambush until after dark, when a flag of truce was sent by the rebels, under pretext of returning a woman found in man's clothing, but really for the purpose of withdrawing their men. On Wednesday the division was ordered to fall back to Centreville, and reached Groveton that night, where it joined General Reynolds with a division of Pennsylvania troops. Early on Thursday, signs of the enemy were discovered, and the brigade of General Hatch was sent forward to reconnoitre; but finding nothing, save indications of a small cavalry force, the command moved on. Hardly a mile had been made before a heavy fire of artillery was opened upon General Hatch's brigade from the left. Campbell's battery, 4th artillery, immediately galloped up to the front, got into position upon a ridge, and opened upon the enemy, posted just across a valley upon the crest of another hill, but a short distance off. Gibbons' Brigade was then ordered up; the 2d Wisconsin taking the left of the line, then the 6th Wisconsin, next the 19th Indiana, and lastly the 7th Wisconsin.

Scarcely had our lines been formed before the rebel infantry began to advance, pouring a terrible fire of musketry into our ranks, and repeatedly attempting to charge on our battery. It was a hotly contested fight; for over an hour these four regiments were under a storm of ball and buckshot, fired by a whole division of the enemy, and never yielded an inch. Colonel Conner fell, mortally wounded; others dropped fast, and the ranks seemed to melt away under the fire. The rebels repeatedly advanced in overwhelming numbers, and were as often driven back by the steady fire of these Western regiments, until night closed the scene and both parties retired from the field. As the fight was about to close, Doubleday's Brigade came up to the support of Gibbons'; it consequently lost but a few of its numbers. All night the surgeons worked hard and earnestly, attending to the wounded. Amputations succeeded each other in rapid succession, until the gray dawn of the morning broke in through the windows of the temporary hospitals. Among the few benefits derived from the war, is the marked improvement in military surgery. Some of the surgeons, who now skilfully perform the necessary operations, and judiciously decline to amputate where a hope of saving the limb exists, were at the commencement of the rebellion inadequate to the positions they occupied. On Friday morning the weary men of this division started for Manassas, having fought an entire division, under Ewell, who had been wounded in the leg. In the afternoon the division returned to the field of yesterday, and found Sigel's and Reynolds' divisions shelling the enemy. As the brigades of Hatch, Doubleday, and Patrick moved off to the left to the aid of Sigel and Reynolds, an order arrived from McDowell for the division to proceed to the right, and pursue the enemy, said to be retreating. Although this was known to be an error, the order was promptly obeyed, and the brigade of General Hatch hastened up the road until it approached a ridge, where the regiments were deployed in line of battle, and moved rapidly up the slope to the left. Suddenly a sheet of fire burst on them from the right and left, at close range, checking their advance and causing a momentary panic. At this juncture General Hatch rode along the line and restored order. It was now getting dark, and the field presented a view of unequalled grandeur. The fire of the enemy kept up incessantly a steady sheet of flame, blazing away from the ridge—now advancing and then receding—enveloping our troops completely, and mowing down the men by scores. General Hatch's horse was shot under him; his assistant adjutant-general, Captain Judson, was captured; one of his aids, Lieutenant Lyon, was dismounted. It being found impossible to carry the enemy's position, and the regiments having been terribly thinned, orders were given to retire, and the division gradually fell back for the night, leaving many of the killed and wounded on the field. Saturday morning the enemy had disappeared, every thing was perfectly quiet, and not the least indication of another engagement was to be seen. Suddenly the rebels were discovered upon our right; and in a few moments it was found that they had moved around to a position at right-angles with that held by them on Friday. Our line immediately swung round, and the engagement commenced. After some hard fighting, the enemy succeeded in turning our left: bringing his batteries rapidly, one by one, still further around, near our rear, he compelled us to withdraw from the fight, though we retained a portion of the field. During those three days' fight, our loss in killed, wounded, and missing was unusually heavy, though our troops fought well against superior numbers. Every effort was made to remove our wounded, but many had to be left on the field. Our paroled prisoners say they were well treated by the rebel officers, but that their men treated them shamefully. General Jackson sent within our lines the hat, sword, watch, spurs, and other personal effects of Major Barny of the 24th New York, and issued an order permitting our paroled prisoners to bring back with them the private effects of their comrades killed on the field. The enemy captured several hundred new uniforms of the Brooklyn 14th, and distributed them among their artillery.

The Rebels cross the Potomac.

It is believed the rebels have crossed the Potomac in force, this side of Point of Rocks. Jackson has entered Leesburg with his troops, and is pushing on for Harper's Ferry. Longstreet with his corps is marching in the same direction. They are well supported with artillery. Many of the inhabitants along the route are escaping to Maryland. Others have, while attempting to do so, been arrested by the Confederates and imprisoned. Night before last, a rebel battery arrived at Edwards' Ferry and fired on the boats on the river. The rebels announce their intention of crossing the river at three points and marching into Pennsylvania, with the intention of capturing Harrisburg. All our wounded that were in the hospitals at Warrenton have arrived at Alexandria, after a perilous and tedious journey of four days, part by railroad, and part by wagons; and passed close to where the battle was raging for miles. They came in charge of Dr. Haynes, and escaped molestation.

Visit to the Bull Run Battle-field.

We had some interesting experience within the enemy's lines since the recent battles. Several of us surgeons went in buggies to the field after the long train of ambulances had started, under a flag of truce, on Monday morning, for the purpose of bringing in our wounded. When we had gone about a mile beyond the stone house which had been used as a hospital during the first battle of Bull Run, and which stands on the Warrenton turnpike beyond the stone bridge, we established a depot on the hill, and sent out the ambulances all over the field. The rebel pickets, on meeting with them and learning their business, passed them without hesitation. Half of the day was spent in examining the battle-field of Saturday, and caring for the wounded we found. After passing the rebel pickets we met a whole brigade of cavalry stationed on the Warrenton road, and large parties of their infantry, all of whom passed us in silence. The part of the field which most claimed our attention was upon the right of our lines, where General

Hatch's Brigade, of Kearney's division, had been engaged. During the battle this brigade had lain behind a piece of woods, having skirmishers thrown forward to its edge. In front there is a plain about a quarter of a mile wide, and an ascending slope, crowned by a rail-fence; behind it is an excavation, through which the Manassas Gap railroad passes. Behind this fence, and within the excavation, there had been posted a large force of the enemy, to attack whom Hatch's brigade had been moved over this extensive plain and up the ascending slope. From the point where they emerged out of the woods and moved up the hill, the ground was thickly strewn with the dead. When our line had been formed, it was open to a destructive fire from the rebel artillery and infantry, which mowed down our ranks, so that the dead lay in one continuous line where they fell. Here and there, under a tree, or the shadow of a rock, we saw groups of men who had been wounded, most of whom died unsuccored, while an occasional one was living still. The rail-fence, in front of which our line of battle had been formed, was blown to pieces and scattered by the enemy's grape and canister—the rails being perforated by bullets. On the other side of the railroad-cut a group of rebels were employed burying their own dead, with whom we had some conversation. They treated us politely, and offered to accompany us through the woods in search of our wounded, many of whom said they had been well treated by the enemy. In passing along the railroad excavation to a point where it was followed by an embankment, we found eighty-five of our dead; these we had covered by the levelling of the embankment over them, as the most expeditious mode of burial. We came up with a party of our wounded under the shade of some trees and a negro cabin, in which a number were being cared for. There were about sixty, officers and men, all badly wounded, in these places; among them was a lieutenant of the 30th New York, whose spinal column had been seriously injured by a rifle-ball; he was completely paralyzed, and could not be removed. The rebels who accompanied us during our search were quite communicative; they seemed to know all about our army, its strength, and condition. They said their marches to reach the battle were long and harassing, their food, though often indifferent, was plentiful, and their confidence in Generals Jackson, Lee, and Longstreet, unbounded. They stated they had no doubt of soon clearing Virginia of the Union army, and carrying the war into Maryland and Pennsylvania. After going over a large portion of the ground, and making complete arrangements for the discovery of all the wounded and the burial of the dead, we returned to the depot, and performed some of the necessary operations. With the aid of the other surgeons, all that had been brought to the depot were cared for. Next morning we did not see any of the enemy but a few cavalry videttes on commanding points.

The medical director of the rebel forces informed our ambulance drivers this forenoon that the place must be cleared as soon as practicable, and those of the wounded who had not been sent away should be brought down to the stone house to be paroled. As this would necessarily occupy several hours, I drove down the road across Bull Run by the ford, below the stone bridge, meeting occasionally two or three of the rebel soldiers. In a meadow, near the Run, I saw another hospital depot, and our men engaged in burying a number of the dead. All over the identical battle-ground of the first Bull Run, our dead lay thickly scattered, after the second fight, as far as the eye could reach, side by side with the fast-decomposing carcasses of horses and mules, broken caissons and fragments of shells, and but one cannon. Further on, I met some of the enemy's pickets, who were now inquisitive as to my objects, and closely scrutinized my dress. I had on a linen blouse over my uniform, which they wished to see, evidently doubting my being a surgeon; but I soon satisfied them on this point, and proceeded on for half a mile, when I again met another hospital containing about sixty more of our wounded, under the charge of Dr. Berryville, who informed me that our troops had evacuated Centreville and that the rebels had taken possession of it. I proceeded, however, passing many dead artillery horses, and a quantity of rifle ammunition. On reaching Centreville, I was met by a rebel officer, who inquired my name and business, and told me to consider myself a prisoner; but on claiming the exemption of surgeons from arrest, I was, after a few hours' delay, permitted to proceed by the provost-marshal, who was busily engaged in placing guards over the medical stores left by our surgeons for the use of the sick. He stated it as his intention of protecting them for the Confederate government, whose property he declared they had become, expressing his willingness to issue whatever medicines were absolutely required for our wounded, but said "he wanted none of our d——d Federal extravagance!" At two o'clock, on Tuesday, we left Centreville for Fairfax Court-house. On the road we met several of the enemy's pickets, who allowed us to proceed, on presenting their provost-marshal's pass; but, on reaching our own cavalry pickets, we had considerable difficulty to get through, and had to wait their sending back to headquarters, at Fairfax Court-house, for instructions for our admission within our lines. We noticed that the enemy had but a small force at Centreville. We met on the road the colonel of a Massachusetts regiment and over twenty of his men, all unarmed. They said they had got separated from their regiment in the battle of Monday, and had been since lying out in the woods, without food, endeavoring to evade the rebel pickets. They were on their way to Centreville, and would soon have been arrested; but, on learning their mistake, they again took to the woods, and reached our lines in safety.

On arrival at Fairfax Court-house, we found General Couch with his division, and some cavalry regiments, covering the rear of our army. From Fairfax to Alexandria the road was filled with our men, marching in good order to Alexandria, at which place we arrived that night.

CHAPTER XXIII.

REBEL ADVANCE ON FREDERICK, MARYLAND.

THE rebels having crossed the Potomac, their forces occupy the north bank of Seneca Creek, their line extending to Middlebrook, on the road between Washington and Frederick, the capital of Maryland. The Union forces that had occupied Frederick have fallen back to Harper's Ferry. Friday afternoon the rebel pickets extended as far as New Market, eight miles southeast of Frederick, the Union pickets having been withdrawn to sixteen miles from that place. The rebels got possession of several cars loaded with pontoon bridges. Many of the Southern sympathizers of Baltimore, and other places, are joining the rebels, but there is no general uprising of the people, as they evidently expected. On Saturday morning the rebel cavalry arrived at the Frederick junction of the Baltimore and Ohio railroad, cut the telegraph, and carried away the operator and his instruments. They did not molest any one else, nor was there a shot exchanged between them and the Federal guard at the bridge over the Monocacy, which retired on their approach. Later in the day their infantry arrived and took possession of the bridge, throwing out pickets in all directions. Another body of the rebels, 5000 strong, crossed the Potomac yesterday afternoon. Gen. McClellan sent forward some cavalry, under Colonel Pleasanton, to Poolesville, to reconnoitre from that point back to Frederick, and ascertained that the enemy is not in force. Last night our forces occupied six miles further out, and continue to-day to advance. The rebel force that passed through Frederick on their way west, is variously estimated from fifteen to fifty thousand. It is thought this raid is not alone for the purpose of obtaining supplies, but to induce General McClellan to draw his forces from the defence of Washington to pursue them, and thus give their army in Virginia an opportunity of advancing on the capital. Our force at Harper's Ferry is large enough to hold at bay an army of twenty thousand until the arrival of McClellan. The intelligence of this morning indicates that a division of the rebel army has taken a western course towards Hagerstown, the inhabitants of which have fled to Chambersburg, though that town has not as yet been occupied by the rebels. By moving on Hagerstown from Frederick, the enemy virtually turns his back on Baltimore and Washington, but will then be within seven miles of the Potomac at Williamsport. The enemy's cavalry is scouring on the borders of York county, Pennsylvania. No further movements have been made by the enemy, with the exception of scouting parties being sent out in the direction of Hagerstown. A body of rebels have also crossed the Potomac at Noland's ford, and marched on Buckeyston, five miles from Point of Rocks. They are sadly in want of clothing and shoes, a greater part of their cavalry and infantry being barefooted. Their advance-guard, during the night, camped at White Oak Springs, three miles from Frederick. During their march they seized all the cattle and provisions they could find, but paid for it in Virginia and South Carolina money, or United States treasury notes, and generally treated the people well, declaring they came as friends and not as enemies. They destroyed the culvert of the Chesapeake and Ohio canal, thus cutting off navigation with Washington. Another division of their forces crossed the Potomac on Friday night, near Berlin, consisting of cavalry, infantry, and artillery, and made a junction with the other forces at White Oak Springs. On Friday evening the people of Frederick heard that this force was collecting cattle and sheep from the farmers. This caused great excitement, as the whole military force left in the city consisted of one company, under command of the provost-marshal, who, on learning these facts, at once commenced to have the wagons loaded with the most valuable of the stores, leaving sufficient for the use of the six hundred patients in the hospitals there—the balance were set fire to, to prevent their falling into the enemy's hands. This conflagration, as might be expected, increased the excitement, and many of the citizens at once left the city, by every mode of conveyance, and during the night thousands departed, blocking up the roads to Baltimore and Pennsylvania. Many of the convalescent patients in the hospitals also left, and becoming exhausted on the way, were afforded shelter by the farmers. The rebels entered Frederick at ten in the morning, to the number of twenty thousand, and marched quietly into Market-street, where they were halted, and a proclamation issued, of which I subjoin a copy. The people were informed that their persons and property would be respected, and that any supplies taken for their troops would be paid for. They appointed a provost-marshal, with a strong guard to preserve order. During the afternoon the streets were thronged with the rebel soldiers, visiting the stores, that had been closed, but which their provost-marshal ordered to be opened. They made large purchases, for which they promptly paid, and preserved the strictest order. In the evening a meeting was called, at which Bradley Johnson delivered a most conciliatory speech: he asserted the ability of the Confederates to take Washington and Baltimore, and dictate terms of peace in Independence Hall at Philadelphia. The following is the proclamation:

TO THE PEOPLE OF MARYLAND.

Head-quarters Army of Northern Virginia,
near Frederick, September 8, 1863.

It is right you should know the purpose that has brought the army under my command within the limits of your State, so far as that purpose concerns yourselves. The people of the Confederate States have long watched, with the deepest sympathy, the wrongs and outrages that have been inflicted upon the citizens of a commonwealth allied to the States of the South by the strongest social, political, and commercial ties, and reduced to the condition of a conquered province. Under the pretence of supporting the Constitution, but in violation of its most valuable provision, your citizens have been arrested and imprisoned, upon no charge, and contrary to all the forms of law. A faithful and manly protest against this outrage, made by a venerable and illustrious Marylander, to whom in better days no citizen appealed for right in vain, was treated with scorn and contempt. The government of your chief city has been usurped by armed strangers, your Legislature has been dissolved by the unlawful arrest of its members, freedom of the press and of speech has been suppressed, words have been declared offences by an arbitrary decree of the Federal Executive, and citizens ordered to be tried by military commission for what they may dare to speak. Believing that the people of Maryland possess a spirit too lofty to submit to such a government, the people of the

South have long wished to aid you in throwing off this foreign yoke, to enable you again to enjoy the inalienable rights of freemen, and restore the independence and the sovereignty of your State. In obedience to this wish, our army has come among you, and is prepared to assist you with the power of its arms in regaining the rights of which you have been so unjustly despoiled. This, citizens of Maryland, is our mission so far as you are concerned. No restraint upon your free will is intended—no intimidation will be allowed, within the limits of this army at least. Marylanders shall once more enjoy their ancient freedom of thought and speech. We know no enemies among you, and will protect all of you in every opinion. It is for you to decide your destiny, freely and without constraint. This army will respect your choice, whatever it may be, and while the Southern people will rejoice to welcome you to your natural position among them, they will only welcome you when you come of your own free will.

R. E. LEE, *General Commanding.*

Many of the citizens of Frederick, who sympathized with the South, attended this meeting, but the Unionists who remained in the city kept to their houses. At ten o'clock all the Confederate soldiers were ordered to their camps on the outskirts of the town, and soon all was again quiet. The Federal flags were lowered, and the Confederate stars and bars were hoisted in their stead. Most of their officers were quartered at the hotels and private houses. All the cattle seized by the rebels in the surrounding country, were immediately driven towards the Potomac.

There is now but little doubt that the whole of the Confederate army are crossing the Potomac. They have extended their pickets for twenty miles on the roads leading east and west from Frederick. Their main column is moving direct for Pennsylvania, through Hagerstown and Chambersburg, to Harrisburg. The inhabitants of the two former places are fleeing, there being no Union forces to protect them. General McClellan has advanced his headquarters beyond Rockville. His army is approaching the Monocacy river, some of the bridges over which have been destroyed by the enemy. At half-past seven o'clock last evening, the rebels made a raid into Westminster, about five hundred strong, with two pieces of artillery, but abandoned it this forenoon, marching towards Uniontown. While at Westminster, they destroyed the books of the provost-marshal, and those that contained the names of persons enrolled as liable to do military duty. They took possession of the post-office, and carried away all the postage-stamps. They treated the inhabitants with respect and consideration. They made large purchases, and paid promptly, even for the food for their horses. Colonel Rosser, who was in command of their cavalry, rode a horse which had belonged to General Pope. Many recruits joined them, but none were accepted unless armed and equipped.

Loss of Harper's Ferry.

This morning, at daylight, General Pleasanton, with the 8th Illinois cavalry, and Captain Fitchall's battery, started after the enemy. At Boonesboro' he came up with the 9th Virginia cavalry, with a battery acting as a rear-guard. The Illinois cavalry charged after them through the town, and two miles out, on the Hagerstown turnpike, capturing two of their guns, and killed, wounded, or took prisoners about thirty of them. General Richardson's division, being in advance, took the road from this place towards Sharpsburg, two miles and a half from which town he came up with the enemy, in large force, who occupied a long range of hills. They showed a line of battle a mile and a half long. The afternoon was spent in ascertaining the position and force of the rebels, not a sufficient number of our troops having come up to bring on an engagement. During last night the larger part of the army arrived on the ground. It is now nine o'clock, and no engagement has taken place. The rebels are rapidly moving across the river. The receipt of intelligence confirming the loss of Harper's Ferry, and the absence of dispatches from General McClellan, throughout the early part of the day, cast a gloom upon the community, which was relieved at a late hour to-night, by the news of the hasty evacuation of Harper's Ferry by the rebels. This is considered to be sufficient evidence that General McClellan is progressing successfully, and that the whole of the rebel army, including the captors of Harper's Ferry, are involved in the rout. Up to late this evening few of the wounded, in Sunday's battle, had arrived at Frederick. They have, probably, been provided for at Middletown and Boonesboro. A hundred and eight prisoners, captured along with General Longstreet's baggage train, by the cavalry that cut their way through from Harper's Ferry, arrived here this morning, and fifty more have reached Chambersburg.

CHAPTER XXIV.

BATTLE OF SOUTH MOUNTAIN.

There is a report to-day, September 13th, that a battle is raging south of Hagerstown, between the Union forces and the rebels, under Stonewall Jackson. The cannonading was heard at Hanover and Chambersburg, this morning, proceeding, evidently, from an action between McClellan's forces and the rebels, at South Mountain. The heaviest part of the fighting was done by the 9th army corps, under General Reno, who was shot dead. General Burnside was also on the field, and assisted in the direction and command of the troops. The fight commenced early in the morning, and lasted until nine at night. The Union loss is over twelve hundred, killed and wounded. The enemy's loss is much heavier, and differently stated. The forces, on both sides, fought with great bravery. The position of the rebels was very strong, and required repeated efforts to dislodge them. Their artillery was advantageously posted and did great execution on our ranks; but the determined charges of our men triumphed. We took a large number of prisoners. Among the enemy's loss, there are many officers. The rebel General Lee is reported wounded, and General Garland killed. They are hurriedly retreating for the river. The right wing of the Union army was opposed by Hill and Longstreet. The left, commanded by Franklin, was equally victorious.

The Field of Battle.

From Middletown the road runs in a westerly direction through a rather rough country, and strikes the abrupt rise of the mountain, at about three miles from the town. It here becomes very steep and stony; in some places the hill rises considerably above the road, on either side, forming a gulch rather than a road. High and rough as the country is at this point, it is fenced, and near the summit of the mountain, at a point where the sides of the road are considerably higher than the road itself, a good stone wall runs around from the road to the right at right-angles, and crosses the field to the wood. A short distance beyond, a lane leaves the road from the left at a right-angle, and on either side of this lane there is a low stone wall with one rail above it. This spot, intersected by the road and the three stone walls, was the scene of action.

From an early hour in the day two 20-pounders on a ridge below the mountain had shelled the various parts of the mountain's side, where the rebels were supposed to be, and at 9 A.M. a portion of General Cox's division went forward as skirmishers, and drove the rebels from the lower part of the mountain. This was followed by artillery firing on both sides, which ended in many of the enemy's guns being silenced. Early in the afternoon, General Scammon's Brigade—the 12th, 23d, and 36th Ohio regiments —was sent forward up the mountain, and deployed in the rough ground to the right of the road, while the 45th Pennsylvania was deployed to the left of it; on its left the 48th Pennsylvania was formed. All this time the rebels lay concealed behind the two stone walls to the left of the road, where they had posted a battery, which played upon our men, as they advanced, with terrible effect. Notwithstanding this, our men pushed up the hill and over the difficult ground to the left of the road. On one side the 45th Pennsylvania carried the position, but with terrible loss; on the other, the Ohio boys were repulsed in their first advance, and were driven back. They, however, soon rallied, returned to the charge and carried the position. All around this point the dead lay thickly strewn, and also down the lane where the Pennsylvanians fought. At nightfall the Ohio boys were relieved by the 51st New York, 51st Pennsylvania, 21st and 35th Massachusetts, under command of Colonel Ferrero, who held the summit of the mountain. Soon after dark the rebels made a determined attempt to regain their position, but were driven back by these regiments, who held the field during the night. On the other side of the hill, the 17th Michigan, a new regiment, was engaged with a part of the enemy's force in the woods. They employed the stone-wall tactics, and delivered their fire from behind this barrier with telling effect, cutting up a regiment of the rebels so severely they could not be rallied. The rebel force engaged, during this fight, was part of the division of General D. H. Hill, and part of Longstreet's,—these latter were brought eight miles on the double-quick to the battle. On the following day, at Clayton's Pass, five miles south of this engagement, and near the town of Burkittsville, a portion of Franklin's corps—Slocum's division—not over 6000, engaged the rebels under General McLaws. It was a brief and decisive action. The enemy was driven from the town on the eastern slope of the Catocin mountain, across the hill, and lost over 400 killed and wounded, and 500 taken prisoners. The Union loss was under 300. The town of Burkittsville is situated about four miles southwest of Middletown. It is a pleasant village of neat brick houses, with one or two handsome churches.

General Franklin arrived near the town with his corps on Sunday afternoon, and at one sent forward General Slocum's division: two regiments of Bartlett's Brigade, the 5th Maine, and 96th Pennsylvania, were sent out as skirmishers through the village and up the lower slopes of the mountain, driving the enemy's pickets before them. On the slopes they were supported by the 16th and 27th New York, which steadily advanced, fighting all the way, until the enemy's main body was found, which was admirably posted on the eastern slope of the Catocin mountain, at Clayton's Gap. The road here is narrow, and winds up the mountain in long reaches, which could be so swept by grape-shot that nothing on it could live. Apart from this road, the side of the mountain is so steep and rocky that it is only with great difficulty one can climb it. The enemy had availed himself of every advantage of his position. At the foot of the steep part of this hill his infantry was posted, behind stone walls, and also on other parts of the mountain; and the only part where an attempt could be made to scale the place was swept by eight pieces of artillery.

Notwithstanding the desperate nature of the undertaking, it was determined to attack without delay, and Newton's Brigade, of Slocum's division, was ordered up to strike the main blow; while Kearney's old brigade, composed of the 1st, 2d, 3d, and 4th New Jersey regiments, under command of Colonel Talbot, was ordered to support General Newton. Simultaneously with this movement, General Brook's Brigade of Smith's division was sent to skirmish the mountain, and advance upon the extreme right flank of the enemy. It had a long way to go, and thus the battle was a single straight-forward attack, by Slocum's division, with a contingency on the rebel flank in case they met with great difficulty. As Newton's Brigade moved forward there was not a straggler to be seen. All seemed equally eager for the fray, and intent on victory. Men never went into an action with better spirit, which was shown through the whole battle. The obstructions in the line of advance were of great advantage to the enemy, and consisted of six-rail fences and two stone walls, all of which had to be crossed, the enemy playing fearfully with their artillery all the time. The stone walls were all held by the enemy's infantry, who were ultimately driven from them by our troops at the point of the bayonet. Soon after this advance began, General Newton, seeing that the rebels were started, ordered forward the other two brigades of Slocum's division, to advance with his own. Onward they pushed, the enemy flying and fighting, until they reached the foot of the steep declivity, where they, apparently, expected to make their best defence. It is hardly possible to conceive how this position could have been carried; but it was, with little delay and loss by our men. After the battle, it was found that it was a work of no small difficulty to climb the precipitous side of the hill. Yet our boys struggled up, with courage, while the foe above poured down upon them a perfect storm of balls, and drove him from the very summit of the hill, flying down the further side in one wild and confused mass. A large number of prisoners were taken, especially from the brigades of Howell Cobb and Semmes. Nearly the whole of the Cobb Legion were captured, with their colors, on which is inscribed, "Cobb Legion—in the name of the Lord." The colors of the 16th Virginia regiment were also taken. The field of battle presented a much less torn-up appearance than usual, which can be accounted for by the fact that artillery was not much used on either side. The stony and steep slope of the hill was thickly strewn with the dead. The rebels had to abandon one of their guns, which fell into the hands of the Union troops; and such was the suddenness and boldness of the charge, that it was with difficulty they saved their remaining pieces. The removal of the wounded from the field, after the close of the action, was one of the most impressive pictures of the day. The road leading to the Gap was filled with long and winding lines of ambulances, going and returning. As fast as the men could be placed in the ambulances, they were removed to the principal private-houses in Burkittsville, and their wounds dressed. Many had to remain where they fell all night, and the impossibility of attending to them promptly, cost many a life.

The inhabitants of Burkittsville opened their houses with alacrity for the reception of the wounded, and offered the kindest attentions to the sufferers. The surgeons were busy all night, and the most painful operations were submitted to without a murmur. As soon as they are able to bear removal they will be sent to Frederick, where arrangements are made for the reception of 1000 patients. The rebel wounded were nearly all taken to the Baptist church in Burkittsville, which has been converted into a temporary hospital, where they receive the same attention as our men, at which they express their surprise and gratitude. On the battle-field, bodies of the dead lay about in every direction, and in every imaginable position. Here fell an officer, sword in hand, urging on his men; one was drinking from his canteen as the fatal bullet pierced his brain; another, in the act of discharging his piece; and others, while loading their muskets. Most of the killed were shot in the head, which is owing to the elevated position on which the enemy was posted. General Howell

Cobb commanded a brigade in McLaws' division, and led his brigade into action. He was wounded in the leg.

The Cobb Legion, commanded by his brother, was terribly cut up: but few of its number came out of the action alive. Seeing our men advancing upon them up the mountain's side, the order was given to push down from their position and repel us. Instead of remaining behind the stone wall, and taking advantage of it as a protection against our fire, they madly leaped the wall, and, with a yell, rushed on our advance column. It was a madness that led them to death. Besides the fire of our advance column, they suffered from an enfilading fire on both sides. Several rebel officers were killed, and many taken prisoners. General Newton and his brigade acted with coolness and bravery. He was in the thickest of the fight, and his men climbed up the steep rocky sides of the mountain with unflinching bravery. The loss of the brigade, considering the severity of the action, is very small. The 2d brigade of Stevens' division, under Colonel Bartlett, was alike conspicuous for its courage and steadiness. Colonel Matthewson and Major Lawson were both wounded. The latter had reached the top of the mountain before being disabled.

General Smith's division pushed on after the enemy, who retreated for some distance, and shelled their rear; but as no stand was made they returned, on account of the news having reached them of the fall of Harper's Ferry. On the right, at some distance, heavy cannonading has been heard, which probably proceeds from Sumner's corps, engaged with the enemy. As no effort was made by the rebels to recover their dead after the battle, orders were issued for their interment. The wounded in the houses at Burkittsville are all doing well; but few deaths have occurred since their removal from the field. The rebel wounded are chiefly injured in the lower extremities, and one or two of them positively refused to submit to the necessary operation, preferring death, the inevitable consequence of their obstinacy, to the supposed suffering of an amputation. One very remarkable case, of a gunshot wound through the loins, came under my notice. The patient, though quite sensible, was entirely free from pain, notwithstanding the wound would prove mortal, and produced total paralysis of both legs.

Operations of the 9th Army Corps.

The scene of the reception of our troops in Frederick was one of exciting joyfulness, but, if possible, was excelled when they started in pursuit of the rebels on the following day. For hours the long lines of men, horses, and artillery, kept passing through the town, and it was not until near midnight that the monster military procession had drawn to a close. The citizens hailed them as performing, or about to perform, the double task of preserving the country and driving from the soil of Maryland the rebels who had come to conquer and despoil them, or to tamper with their loyalty; but they were not easily to be moved. The brief stay of the Southerners in Frederick is the reason they assign for the failure of its citizens to join their army. The 9th army corps proceeded to Middletown, a small village, beautifully situated in a valley about eight miles from Frederick, where they learned that the enemy occupied the Catocin mountain in force (a description of which is given in the previous chapter), and that they were strengthening their position, with the avowed intention of resisting any attack that might be made upon them by our forces. It was known that they had a large body of men, but the idea prevailed that they would not make any decided stand until they reached Boonesboro' or Hagerstown. On the night of the 13th September, the troops removed a little distance from the town, where they encamped for the night, ready and willing for any work they would be called on to do on the following day. The new regiments were all anxiety, the old ones confident that success would be theirs, while fighting under McClellan and Burnside, even though opposed by Jackson, Lee, and Longstreet, with their daring and desperate troops: their night's rest was not broken or disturbed by any forebodings of defeat, and the morning found them eager for the contest. The day broke fine, but with the appearance of coming rain, which rendered the air cool and pleasant, and well suited for an engagement. At an early hour, the booming of guns told that the artillery had resumed the contest begun the previous evening, but which was now destined to be attended with far more important results than before. The men were soon marching to the scene of action. It was a splendid pageant—the long lines of infantry, unattended by wagons, and consequently unbroken, passing over the hills in a steady and solid column. On approaching nearer, the reports of the artillery became more distinct, and the wreaths of smoke that rose after each discharge, showed at a glance the relative positions of our own and the enemy's batteries. The rebels were apparently holding back their fire, so as to use it with effect against our infantry when they were attacked by it: this, their usual wise plan, told severely upon some of our poor fellows. The position was well chosen, and with all possible reference to military advantages. Situated on the slope of the mountain, covered with woods, it was splendidly calculated for masked batteries, and those surprises, for which the rebels have become so famous. The road ascending the side of the mountain was steep and narrow, and so filled with large stones that quick locomotion was impossible, and a charge a difficult thing to execute. The enemy also had a series of breast-high stone fences, that had been built by the farmers. Behind these they could fortify themselves, and pour volley after volley into any opposing force, while they were comparatively free from danger, being able to drop and load as soon as they fired. They had also cut down the trees in the immediate vicinity of these fences, to as to leave an open space, that must be crossed by the attacking force before they were dislodged. In these natural fortifications they possessed great odds; and without good officers and men, it would have taken a much larger force than that we employed to dislodge them. But our men went there that morning determined not to fail.

The fight, properly speaking, began on Sunday morning, our troops forcing their way to the top of the mountain known as South or Seared mountain, one of the Catocin group, by a road situated a little to the left of what is known as the National road, and thus drove the rebels back, step by step. At three o'clock the greater part of the corps was fully engaged, and fought desperately until seven, when the enemy was fairly driven back, leaving their dead and wounded on the field. By nine o'clock the summit of the hill was entirely in our possession, and the rebels, under cover of the darkness, left for parts unknown, and all firing ceased in that quarter. They were not closely pursued, for fear of mistaking our own men for them. The most daring fighting was done by Cox's division, as before described,—their splendid bayonet charge, made upon the rebel intrenchments, behind the stone walls, though warmly received by a shower of bullets, was irresistible. They continued to push on; and though many fell dead and wounded, still the rest heeded it not, but kept on their avenging course, like a destroying avalanche, and, with a yell, rushed on to surmount the obstacles, killing the enemy right and left, who could not stand the cold steel. After making a feeble resistance, they broke and retreated as fast as possible, leaving a number of wounded and some prisoners in their victors' hands, which were at once sent to the rear. The regiments that achieved this gallant exploit were the 11th, 12th, and 30th Ohio. The officers and men of these corps acted with unflinching bravery, and reflected credit on the whole division to which they belong. About noon, General Wilcox's division, composed of the brigades commanded by Acting Brigadiers Welch and Christ, was ordered to the support of Cox's division. They went forward to the ridge, where they found him, slowly, but surely, advancing on the left of the Sharpsburg road. The 50th Pennsylvania was sent to support him, and the balance of the division was formed on the right of the road, with Cook's battery planted opposite to a rebel battery that was stationed on the ridge. It opened with good effect; but there were other rebel batteries that had not, as yet, exposed their positions, but which now opened an enfilading fire on the left, from this central point of defence, commanding the road. Their first discharge disabled one of Cook's guns, killing and wounding four men, on which the battery retired. At this point the enemy appeared and threatened to charge, intending to capture Cook's battery. A rumor was now started among the men of Wilcox's division, that a large rebel cavalry force was coming down on them, which almost created a panic in the ranks. All this time they were under a heavy fire from the enemy's guns; grape and canister were flying about them in a most lively manner. The 79th New York was now sent to repel the expected charge, and the 17th Michigan was dispatched to their support. The division then changed front to left, and advanced again to the ridge. At about four o'clock the pickets reported that there was a battery, and two regiments supporting it, some little distance ahead, in the woods, when an order was received from General Reno to take it, if possible. A fitting reply was made to the order, and General Sturgis's command was sent to support General Wilcox. The enemy appeared to divine our intention, and also prepared to make a charge. It was now about five o'clock, and the charge was met by the 45th Pennsylvania, under Major Curtin, and the 17th Michigan, under Colonel Whittington. A desperate fight followed, both sides doing bravely, but the determined will of the Union soldiers prevailed, and the rebels were driven back with great loss. The charge was a splendid one, and cost the Union forces nearly four hundred, in killed and wounded. The two brigades under Ferrero and Nagle, of Sturgis's division, which had been ordered to the support of Wilcox, advanced on the left of the road, Ferrero's in advance. They met with determined opposition, and some hard fighting was done by them; but the rebels were again obliged to fall back, leaving their wounded, and some prisoners, in our hands. During this the division of General Rodman was sent to scour the adjacent woods, around the base of the hill, on which Ferrero held his position under the most trying circumstances. The 51st New York and 51st Pennsylvania contended, in the most heroic manner, against superior numbers. All of this brigade, from Colonel Ferrero down, fully sustained the reputation they had earned through the Virginia campaign.

The brigade of General Nagle was not actively engaged, but discharged the duty allotted to them with coolness and steady obedience. General Rodman's division did some hard fighting in the woods, and lost a number of men. Our victory, though complete, has been dearly won, as we have lost many brave fellows, as well as Major-general Reno, who commanded the 9th army corps, formerly under Gen. Burnside. All day General Reno had been most active, fearing no danger, and apparently at several places at one time. Up to seven o'clock he was safe, standing, with his staff, back of the woods in a field, in front of which were the rebels; a body of his troops were before him, and at this point the enemy's fire was directed. A minié-ball struck him, and went through his body; he fell, and from that moment seemed to have a knowledge that he could not survive. He was at once carried to the rear and attended by his surgeon, Dr. Cutter. At the foot of the hill he was laid under a tree, where he died in a few minutes. The officers of his staff exhibited the most sincere grief at his loss. Many wept over him, and vowed to avenge his death. He was one of the bravest generals in the service, respected and loved by all, and warmly attached to General Burnside, who will deeply deplore his loss and mourn his untimely end. The country can ill afford to lose such men as Kearney, Stevens, and Reno. The command at once devolved on General Cox, who ably directed the movements of the corps. It is difficult to determine the exact loss in the different divisions, brigades, and regiments, as to each; but our total loss is fully 1200. The enemy's loss is still greater. The roads and woods are thickly covered with their dead. Colonel Wild, of the 35th New York, was severely wounded in the arm; Lieutenant Williams, 51st New York, wounded in the chest, and Lieutenant Springweller, of the same regiment, was shot dead. The wounded were cared for in the temporary hospitals, the surgeons working all night at their onerous tasks, doing all in their power to make them comfortable, which they seemed fully to appreciate, and but little complaint was heard, the poor fellows bearing their sufferings like martyrs. Some expressed their regret for loss of legs and arms, as it would disable them from duty. When all the wounded were dressed and cared for, they were sent further back in ambulances, where they could be better provided for. The proportion of killed is unusually small to the number wounded—the rebels must have had two for one of our killed, as from their position behind the stone walls, when struck it was mortal, being chiefly in the head or chest. The appearance of the field the morning after the fight was a terrible sight. In some places the dead were lying two or three deep. On the road or pass along which ran the stone walls, the dead lay thickly strewn. The death of many was so instantaneous that their arms were in position of firing their pieces, while others still retained the bitten cartridge in their hands. They appeared to be mostly young men, many of them mere boys. The difference between the clothing of the Union and the rebel dead was very marked. The Union troops were all well clad, while the rebels were in rags: in many instances without any pretence at uniform. Their garments were of all colors and styles. There firearms, however, were all good, and they used them well. A number of farmers came on the field to witness the sight, of which they had so often heard but never seen. They collected as relics every thing portable: cartridge-boxes, bayonet scabbards, old muskets, and even cannon-balls were carried away by them.

A party of men were detailed as soon as possible to

bury the dead. When this sad and painful office was performed, and the men rested from the fatigues of the battle, orders were given to prepare for another march and another fight. General Burnside rode by, this morning, and is again to take command of the corps in person. He was welcomed by the men with shouts of delight. It is expected that the rebels, disappointed at their reception in Maryland, will attempt to recross the Potomac, and reoccupy Virginia. But it is hoped that before doing so, General McClellan will force them to another fight, and, if possible, cut off their retreat.

CHAPTER XXV.

THE BATTLE OF ANTIETAM.

On Wednesday, September 17, the Union and rebel forces in Maryland met in the Blue Ridge, and fought a battle which, when its full extent is known, will probably dwarf all other battles yet fought in the present war. General McClellan commanded the National troops in person, and had on the field the whole command of General Burnside, recently augmented by the addition of several new regiments,—the army corps lately under General McDowell (now under command of General Hooker), General Sumner's corps, General Franklin's corps, General Banks' corps, commanded by General Williams, and Sykes' division of Fitz-John Porter's corps. On the other side, the rebels undoubtedly had present the whole force which they originally brought into Maryland. They were commanded by General Lee. The battle was fought in the valley immediately west of that portion of the Blue Ridge known as the South mountain, and to the east and north of Sharpsburg, almost in a semicircle, the concave side of which is towards the town. Unlike most of the valleys in this Blue Ridge country, this valley has not a level spot in it, but rolls with eminences of all dimensions, from the little knoll that your horse gallops easily over, to the rather high hill, that makes him tug like a mule. Many of the depressions between these hills are dry, and afford ample cover for infantry against artillery. Others are watered by the deep, narrow, and crooked Antietam, a stream that seems to observe no decorum in respect to its course, but has to be crossed every ten minutes, ride which way you will. Sharpsburg lies on the western side of the valley, and a little to the south from our point of view. Right across the valley, from the northeast, runs the turnpike from Boonesboro' to Sharpsburg. Two little villages, Porterstown and Keetersville, or Keedyville, lie on the eastern side of the valley, at the foot of South mountain. Numerous fine farm-houses dot the valley in every direction, some standing out plainly and boldly on the hill-tops, others half-hidden down the little slopes; and, with the large, comfortable barns about them, and their orchards of fruit-trees, these hitherto happy and quiet homes greatly enrich the view. Nearly every part of the valley is under cultivation, and the scenes are thus varied into squares of the light green of nearly-ripened corn, the deep-green of clover, and the dull-brown of newly-ploughed fields. Towards the north, where our right lay, are some dense woods. Imagine this scene, spread in the hollow of an amphitheatre of hills, that rise in terraces around it, and you have the field of last Wednesday's battle.

Our position had been taken in outline, as it were, on Tuesday, and was filled up to its proper strength as fast as the troops arrived and streamed down the mountain by the road from Middletown. This they continued to do for the greater part of Tuesday and Tuesday night. It was a magnificent sight to see our men thus poured forward across the field to different points, in long shining lines. Burnside's men turned short to the south, passing across the foot of the Elk Ridge mountain, and took a position on our extreme left. Porter held a commanding eminence to the right of Burnside, though Warren's Brigade of Porter's corps was subsequently posted in the woods on our left, in support of Burnside's men. Sumner's corps was on an eminence next to the right, or north from Porter, and General Hooker had the extreme right, in and behind the woods before mentioned, and on the Antietam. Our left was on Elk Ridge mountain, and our line of battle stretched to the northeast, across the Sharpsburg road. The line was between four and five miles long. The rebel left was in the woods, directly in front of General Hooker, and their force was posted across the valley between us and Sharpsburg, in a line nearly parallel with our own. Though the men have been spoken of as on eminences, it must be understood that they were carefully covered in every case just below the crest of the hills they held. Our artillery was also carefully posted behind the crests of the hills, ready to be run up and to blaze away at a moment's notice. Nearly every hill had a battery on it, and the greater number of batteries looked over fields that extended to the limit of the range.

General Hooker had the honor to open this great combat. He commanded the corps formerly under General McDowell, composed of Ricketts' division, Meade's (formerly McCall's), and King's division. Many of these men came up in the night, and there was perhaps a little confusion in posting them. Meade's men say that they slept among the rebels. Owing to this over-near neighborhood, the pickets got at it in the night, and kept up a scattering fire until the battle began. General Meade, who was thus nearest the rebels, was relieved at daylight by General Ricketts' division, which also immediately advanced against the enemy, supported by the division of General King, which eventually became engaged on the right of General

Ricketts', and also by the division of General Meade. The line advanced through a piece of woods, a corn-field, and a piece of ploughed land, and into another piece of woods, where it found the enemy in line of battle, and was received with a hot file-fire, which told very severely on our men. But they steadily advanced into the fierce fire, giving back one equally destructive; while our batteries, particularly a Pennsylvania battery under Captain Matthews, and Captain Thompson's 1st Maryland battery, played splendidly upon the enemy's line. Thus pressed, the rebel forces gave way, though they certainly did not "skedaddle." Slowly, and in fair order, they fell back, disputing every foot that they gave up with the greatest obstinacy. Still our boys pushed on with great courage and determination, every man, from Hooker down, intent only on victory. Occasionally a more determined resistance at some point in the line, or some difficulty in the ground, would check our advance for a few moments; but, with these exceptions, it was almost steady from its commencement until about ten o'clock in the morning, when General Hooker was wounded and carried from the field. General Ricketts at once assumed command of the corps, but our victorious movement had lost its impulse. At that time our right had advanced and swept across the field so far, that its front, originally almost in a line with the front of the centre and left, formed almost a right-angle with them. While our advance rather faltered, the rebels, greatly reinforced, made a sudden and impetuous onset, and drove our gallant fellows back over a portion of the hard-won field. What we had won, however, was not relinquished without a desperate struggle; up the hills, and down through the woods and the standing corn, over the ploughed land and the clover, the line of fire swept to and fro, as one side or the other gained a temporary advantage.

Thus the battle raged, till Sumner's corps came up to support the worn-out heroes who had maintained the fight so long against very evident odds. How gloriously they went at it, those Peninsula boys—Burns's old brigade, led by gallant young Howard, who lost an arm at Fair Oaks, and Meagher's Irish Brigade, led by the gallant Meagher himself, and many other heroes tried in the fire! As the Irish Brigade charged the enemy's line, their cheers arose in one great surge of sound, over the noise of battle, over the roar of a multitude of artillery, and was heard far down the lines to the left, where Burnside's boys were just getting at it. Thus met, the rebel advance was checked and broken, and they were driven with awful slaughter. It is beyond all wonder how such men as the rebel troops are, can fight as they do. That, ragged and filthy, sick, hungry, and in all ways miserable, they should prove such heroes in fight, is past explanation—men never fought better. There was one regiment that stood up before the fire of two or three of our long-range batteries and of two regiments of infantry, and though the air around them was vocal with the whistle of bullets and screams of shells, there they stood, and delivered their fire in perfect order; and there they continued to stand, until a battery of six light twelves was brought to bear on them, and before that they broke. Nothing mortal can bear a battery of six light Napoleon guns, if there is plenty of grape and canister in the ammunition chests. Thus Sumner effectually stayed what at one time threatened to be a fearfully dangerous onslaught. But all the ground Hooker had gained was lost, and we were as we had been before the misty daylight had dawned upon us. But there is a stir and a murmur around us different from the noise of battle. There are troops in motion behind, and here comes Franklin's corps. When the battle began at daylight, this corps was in camp eight miles away, on the mountain over which it had driven the rebels on Sunday last. There it was, in all the seemingly inextricable camp confusion ; and in the valley, at the foot of the same mountain, was Couch's division, temporarily attached to Franklin's command. All these troops had had orders on Tuesday night to be in readiness to march at a moment's notice, and so they lay down. But the night passed, and no orders came to move; and the morning hours went by, till it seemed that they could not be wanted. But at eight o'clock the orders came, and here they are, at one. It was a good march, and, unlike most troops that make those hasty marches, they are not too late, nor are they used up. Heralded only by the jingle of their own canteens, and their regular tramp, they move into the field. No slogan announces them; no music note tells that the Campbells are coming. But hardy, brave, and comparatively fresh, here they are. The two fresh divisions at once moved forward, for it was rightly reasoned that the enemy must be fully as much shaken as we were. Onward went Slocum, with the three brigades that carried Crampton's Gap so handsomely on Sunday; and onward went Smith, with the brigades of Hancock, Brooks, and Davidson, who first made the enemy's acquaintance on Warwick Creek. Exhausted, no doubt, by his last desperate endeavor, the enemy gave way. Easily, and without the great outlay of life that it at first cost us, the ground was once more won.

Hitherto we have spoken only of what transpired on our right. There, after desperate struggles, we had won what, considered in itself alone, was a glorious battle, and our enemy was there fairly beaten. When the batteries that participated in Hooker's attack at daylight first opened their fire, and were severely felt, several rebel batteries opened upon them, and also on our advancing line. Some of these batteries were on points quite out of the battle that raged on the right. As they opened their fire, one by one, our batteries, posted on various eminences, opened on them, and, in their turn, were opened upon by still other rebel batteries; and thus was begun a stupendous artillery fight, which soon became quite independent of the battle on the right. From every little hill a battery thundered, until the mountains around seemed to be shaken with the roar, and the tracks of shells and shot were woven across the valley like net-work. So numerous were the batteries, and so constant their fire, that it was impossible to keep up with it. However much this or that beautiful shot might excite your admiration, you could not decide who made it, or what battery was entitled to the credit. It is probable that the artillerists were frequently deceived themselves, and assumed, as their own, those shots that luckier gunners had made. The effect of the artillery can hardly be estimated, save where the effect of its fire can be seen ploughing through the masses. When, as in this battle, batteries fire at batteries, no result is perceptible; and even if a battery ceases to fire, you are not sure that it is damaged. The whole artillery fire of Wednesday looked very like a waste of ammunition, though, doubtless, many a badly injured gun was the result. Whether any one "blundered" on the left, it is impossible to state now; but the battle, there, got started late, and went on slowly. It was noon when the fire of musketry first announced an engagement at close quarters in that direction; and then the firing was not heavy and continuous, but desultory and light in its character. Our first advance was made there down the slope of a hill, to a bridge which crosses the Antietam river. Beyond the river the enemy had so posted his men, as to sweep the bridge with a severe musketry fire: their own advance was checked, and General Burnside seemed to hesitate. The peculiar brass pieces handled by the Hawkins' Zouaves—one of the many recent experiments in artillery—were then tried on the rebels beyond, as the position was one in which regular artillery could not work; but the peculiar brass pieces achieved but little, and the enemy remained in position beyond, and kept up a severe and well-directed fire upon our men. Finally, at about two o'clock, P. M., after much time had been lost, the bridge was carried by a brilliant charge, in which the 11th Ohio and 11th Connecticut participated very conspicuously and lost many men. If the greater obstacles constitute the post of honor on a field of battle, General Burnside may justly claim to have had that post in Wednesday's fight. Once more across the river, he found the enemy in force before him, and in a new position of great strength, on a hill. Against this position he advanced at once, and the old valor of the divisions of Generals Cox, Wilcox, and Sturgis was once more triumphant, and the hill was taken. No sooner was its summit reached, than a heavy battery of artillery at once opened upon his ranks, with a fire which must have annihilated them if permitted to continue. It was at once clear that the hill was untenable, unless the battery was taken. At the same time the enemy, in front, began to receive heavy reinforcements, and General Burnside's position became critical.

To go forward, with that heavy battery mowing his flank, and with an equal number of the enemy on his front, and overwhelming numbers coming up, would seem like madness. To stand still would only be destruction; and then came the alternative to retreat. Bitter as this alternative was, it had to be taken, and steadily the line swept back, relinquishing the hard-won hill; but it was now so fully under the fire of newly posted batteries, that no enemy could occupy it.

As Burnside's line withdrew, the word was passed along the hill for Sykes's men to "fall in;" and the tough old soldiers of the regular regiments, who had been lounging on the hill, quiet spectators of the battle, hurried gladly into line, joyful at the prospect that their turn had come; there they stood, ready to check the progress of any sudden disaster. Night prevented further operations. Let it be understood that we were only not entirely successful on the left. We suffered no disaster · nor could we suffer any; for it is the glory of General McClellan's plan of battle, that if the rebels had even routed Burnside and driven him in confusion from the field, our left would still have been safe, for there, close in hand, was Porter's corps, fresh and ready for the emergency. General McClellan had his headquarters during the day at a commanding point of the field; he did not remain there all the time, but rode over the field from point to point, as the battle raged here or there, watching vigilantly its progress, and sharing the dangers of the nameless heroes who fought so bravely to win the glorious day. As we rode from the field at nightfall, and passed Porterstown, near to where our wagons were parked, we noted one circumstance which alone ought to establish the superiority of our men. There was beef cooking on the fire. All about the camp, kettles stood in rows on blazing rails; and while the battle raged furiously, at half a mile distant, rations were being prepared as quietly as if all were in camp. Thus our tired boys were sure of a supper ere they slept, while if the rebel soldiers had any thing at all to eat that night, it must have been a scanty bite all around.

The smoke of the battle of yesterday is now dispelled, and we can see more clearly what has been done. Our victory is an undeniable and glorious one. Our soldiers have done what was expected of them. They have come upon the rebels, who, showing fight, were met and whipped at every point along the line by our invincible army. In every concerted movement yesterday we were successful, while every movement against us was handsomely repulsed. General McClellan's head-quarters for the day were at a large house on the hill on the north side of the Porterstown valley, about one mile from Keedysville, and in a position overlooking the entire field of action. To the wide field of vision opened before him, may be imputed a large measure of the success which attended our arms during the day.

At nine o'clock in the morning the severest fighting commenced, when Sumner's full corps became engaged with the enemy. These veterans of the Peninsula pitched into the seething tide of the battle with a right good-will, their old and plucky general leading them. It is said, indeed, that his undaunted courage carried a division, Sedgwick's, into the enemy's line, where they fought superior numbers successfully for an hour, though at times their situation was critical indeed. Nothing but the most daring and determined courage saved this noble body of men from annihilation. The rebels here made a bold push to capture the 1st Rhode Island and Kirby's, formerly Ricketts', batteries, against which they have the old grudge of Fair Oaks and Savage's station to settle. Ricketts' light brass twelve-pounder battery poured grape and canister with destructive effect, and with the aid of its support of infantry from the 15th Massachusetts, effectually checked the enemy's advance in the direction of the battery: the fire of the combined infantry and artillery literally mowed down the rebels. The 15th Massachusetts followed the enemy, who by this time rallied their forces and received assistance. Nobly did this regiment sustain itself against the increased and increasing numbers of the rebels, bringing down scores of them at every discharge. They were finally obliged to fall back to the original line, which they did in good order, fighting the mean time under cover of Kirby's well-directed grape and canister. The 15th Massachusetts went into action with six hundred men, and came out with about two hundred uninjured, the rest killed, wounded, and missing. The 1st Rhode Island battery was well served, and ably supported by the 34th New York and the Baxter Zouaves, and finally drove off the rebels. The 34th and 2d New York Militia, and Baxter's Zouaves, suffered terribly. One of the severest struggles occurred near Numas's house and barn, where a large force of rebel infantry was posted, with some artillery. The scene described is, that the ground is covered with the rebel dead and wounded. Fire from several of our batteries was directed there with terrible effect, as the hecatomb of victims attest. Numas's house and barn were destroyed by fire, making a splendid spectacle after the night began to darken. Colonel Pratt, of New York, was wounded in four places, at different times during the day. After he had received the second wound, and was bleeding profusely, he led his men into a most gallant and successful charge, receiving his death wounds. The colonel of the 17th Michigan was killed while advancing his men to a bayonet charge, after they had exhausted their ammunition. The Washington artillery, of New Orleans, was the last battery of the enemy to cease firing last evening, all the rest having previously become silent. It is supposed that the want of ammunition was one cause of the slacking of the rebel fire in the latter part of the day. Our well-served and numerous batteries did the most towards silencing those of the enemy. In the afternoon the rebels were using the ammunition captured at Harper's Ferry, with more effect than their own ammunition used in the morning. The enemy used, in this engagement, railroad iron, slugs, and smooth stones, as missiles of destruction. The New York troops which suffered most severely were the 82d, 34th, 59th, 69th, 53d, 9th, and 42d.

This morning, September 18th, a few shells were thrown into the enemy's lines, to ascertain their whereabouts. Shortly after a flag of truce came out from the rebels to solicit permission to bury their dead. This was granted by General McClellan, and until four o'clock this afternoon was given in which to do the work. Our forces are in a condition to renew the engagement, begun so gloriously yesterday, with increased vigor. About three o'clock a heavy rain began, which would prevent further hostilities. The pickets, on the outer posts, have been firing at intervals to-day. Six regiments from General Cox's division are engaged at South Mountain, to-day, in burying the dead from the battle-field of Sunday last. On Tuesday night, the 16th instant, the enemy massed his forces under Lee, Jackson, and Longstreet, with the intention of turning McClellan's right-flank. At daylight artillery skirmishing was commenced on the right, and continued until about a quarter of eight o'clock, when musketry firing commenced —the opposing forces having got within the musket range of each other. This was near Sharpsburg, and about five or six miles northeast of Boonesboro'. Sumner's corps was mainly engaged. Sedgwick's and French's divisions were formed in line of battle, and so advanced in two lines across the fields and through the woods. The brigade of General Max Weber formed the first line of French's division. As they came on the brow of the hill they found the rebels in rifle-pits and behind stone walls, who immediately opened a withering fire, which our men stood bravely. The enemy had also planted two batteries in a position to give us a galling flanking fire. This was replied to by our batteries, and a terrible cannonading ensued. The Irish Brigade—Meagher's—which is in French's division, made a gallant and effective charge upon the enemy, who retired slowly, disputing the ground as they went. The enemy were driven beyond Sharpsburg, towards the Virginia line. General Sumner was in his element, and encouraged his men by calling upon them to "go in boys," wavng his hat enthusiastically in the air, &c., &c. He has every reason to feel increased pride in his command after the work they did yesterday. General Max Weber was shot, and severely wounded, while ordering a bayonet charge. His assistant adjutant-general, Captain H. M. Burleigh, was also wounded in the shoulder. The rebels were driven three miles beyond the position they occupied at the begining of the fight in the morning. Brigadier-general Crawford, while leading up his division in an attack upon the enemy's centre, was severely wounded in the thigh, but refused to leave the field. Jackson's forces are now so backed up against the river, that unless he can get off towards Hagerstown, where there is a ford by which he might cross the river, or receives aid from the vicinity of Harper's Ferry, he must experience great difficulty in extricating himself from his present position. The usual report, that General Jackson has been killed, is, of course, circulated. The battle-ground covered a large area, composed of mountain, wood, field of grain, and marsh near the Antietam river, which had to be, and was, forded by our soldiers, although the water was from three to four feet deep. The loss on both sides was very heavy, but the enemy's loss was largely in excess of our own. Three barns, besides all the dwelling-houses in the vicinity, are filled with the wounded. About three thousand prisoners were captured. The firing was kept up until half-past seven P. M.

Further Particulars of the Battle of Antietam.

The battle of Antietam, in western Maryland, fought on Wednesday, the 17th September, between the main bodies of the rebel and Union armies, was the fiercest and bloodiest battle of the war. The close pursuit of the rebel forces by McClellan's army, the several skirmishes with the rear-guard of the enemy, and the positions assumed by the contending armies on Tuesday, rendered it apparent that a tremendous battle would speedily be fought in that vicinity. Accordingly, on Tuesday afternoon and during the night, both parties were busily engaged in marshalling their men and making judicious disposition of their troops, preliminary to the commencement of the battle. McClellan had pushed forward his several army corps with great alacrity, and on Tuesday evening our advance, composed of Hooker's corps, drove back the enemy on the right, and secured a favorable position for the opening of the great battle at the coming dawn. It was with great reluctance that the enemy surrendered that favorable point on the right, and on several separate occasions during the night he appeared to be attempting to regain it before morning came, as he kept up a sharp picket-fire from dark till daylight. But whenever the pickets of the enemy endeavored to advance, under cover of the darkness, they were promptly repulsed by our own. General Lee, the commander-in-chief of the Confederate forces, and his principal generals, were also actively employed forming their lines to meet and resist the anticipated attack, and placing their columns in position, ready to be hurled against our infantry or sent to storm our batteries, as opportunities, during the shifting scenes of the battle, might afford, or their minds suggest. The enemy received heavy reinforcements from the Virginia side of the Potomac. Jackson's, Hill's, and McLaws' divisions, which had participated in the attack on Harper's Ferry, were among the troops that had left that place on Tuesday. They recrossed the river, marched all night, and arrived in time to participate in the battle of the valley of Antietam. All the available forces of the enemy were concentrated to resist this grand assault. It was believed that, with the exception of some detachments, the whole Army of Virginia, under the command of its ablest generals, confronted McClellan's army on this battle-field. General McClellan planned the battle, and gave instructions to the different corps commanders what part their troops were expected to perform in the conflict; while he himself was on the field all day, visiting different portions of the lines, and directing all the operations, from the commencement of the contest to its close. The battle-field is one of the most magnificent that could be selected for a contest of such magnitude. The valley of Antietam is a luxurious part of Maryland; the ground admirably adapted to the successful massing of troops in reserve, as they could be shielded behind the numerous knolls from the artillery fire on either side,—as well as to the free and fair engagement of the contending infantry, when the lines came in close proximity. The undulating nature of the ground furnished fine positions to both parties for artillery, while the beauty of the surrounding scenery—the trees beginning to show their rich autumnal tinges—threw a halo of enchantment over what was now, at once, the garden and the battle-ground of Maryland. On our left, heavily-wooded mountains rose to a considerable height, inclosing the valley on that side, and Antietam creek wound its way through the gorge and along the verdant valley beneath. Away, in every direction, hills covered with splendid corn and clover fields, vales rich with the summer's harvest, and orchards laden with ripening fruit, spread out before our view. It almost seemed at times, during the cessation of the firing, that many engaged in the bloody fray would turn from the scene of carnage to contemplate the lovely valley and its surrounding scenery.

The position of the Union forces, as ordered by General McClellan, was splendid. Hooker's corps, formerly McDowell's, which had made the advance, occupied the extreme right of the Union line. Here the battle began. Mansfield's corps, formerly under Banks, acted in concert with Hooker's. Franklin's corps came up in that vicinity during the afternoon, and acted as a reserve at first, but was pushed to the front later in the day. Sumner's corps had the centre of the line, where some of the hardest fighting took place. Fitz-John Porter's corps, which was only slightly engaged, followed next in order; while Burnside's corps acted as a flanking column on the left. It was here that our loss was heaviest, by reason of the determined opposition of the enemy to the repeated, and finally successful attempt at storming the stone bridge over the Antietam. On the centre and right, as well as on the left, the fighting was furious and the losses severe. Along the crests of the chain of hills our batteries were posted, in opposition to those of the enemy planted in similar positions beyond. The smooth-bore short-range guns were placed on the little knolls in front, and the rifled artillery, for longer range, on the higher hills behind. Supporting their several batteries, regiments of infantry were lying down, or moving into line, just taking their positions to begin the battle, while whole brigades and divisions could be seen from the commanding summits, also hidden by the elevations of the ground, marching away to support these attacking lines. On various prominent points small groups could be distinguished. These were corps, division, and brigade commanders, surrounded by their staff officers, who had, for the most part, chosen positions where they could direct the operations of their own commands, and at the same time perceive how the battle was progressing in other sections of the field. The cavalry, with four batteries of flying horse-artillery, under General Pleasanton, were posted in the centre, to the rear, whence they could descend swiftly to any portion of the field. On a higher hill, still further behind, General McClellan established his head-quarters. From this commanding eminence he could view the whole scene of action, watch the execution of his plans, and speedily proceed to any portion of the field, where his personal presence in the front might be required.

As General Hooker captured the position where the battle commenced, it is proper to state, for the sake of continuity in the narrative, that after the enemy had been driven from his position at South Mountain on Sunday, Hooker's corps, preceded by artillery, with skirmishers and supports in front, moved forward to Valley Mills, on Monday, where a slight artillery engagement took place. Later in the afternoon, the corps pushed forward on the road which stretched away to the left, for the purpose of obtaining a position in which it could engage the enemy's flank with the hope of turning it. The corps consisted of Meade's, Doubleday's, and Ricketts' divisions. Meade's division (formerly McCall's), composed of the Pennsylvania Reserves, led the march, the other two divisions following. Thus the corps moved forward in solid column. The advance-guard came upon the enemy's pickets about five o'clock, on Tuesday afternoon. Meade's division was deployed in line of battle, his skirmishers in front driving in the rebel pickets. The rebel line of battle was encountered in a piece of woods, with ploughed fields and cornfields to the right and left. It is only necessary, in view of the description already given of the fight, to say, that the opposing forces were hotly engaged with artillery and infantry till dark. Both fought in splendid style, our men determined to take the position, and the rebels apparently as determined to defend it; but at last our men drove them from the ground, secured the important position, and slept on their arms all night. There was an opening in the woods, thus forming two separate belts of trees: General Seymour's Brigade occupied that on the left; the 2d Brigade, Colonel Magilton commanding, covering the opening; while the 3d Brigade, Colonel Anderson commanding, occupied the belt of woods upon the right. This was the position of the division at dark, the pickets of the opposing lines being, in some instances, within a dozen yards of each other during the night, and sharp picket-firing was continued until morning. The battle began at the first dawn of day. General McClellan's order of battle provided that the attack should be commenced on the right, continued along the centre, and in turn pressed forward by Burnside on the left,—Franklin's corps, constituting the reserves for the right and centre; and Porter's corps for the left of the line, and its flanking column. The arrangements for the battle were complete, and the battle was won almost without the necessity of a shot being fired by the troops in reserve. The moment it was light enough for the pickets to perceive each other, they blazed away. The men in line on either side sprung to arms. The skirmishers on either side were thrown out in front; but as soon as the troops advanced, these, of course, retired, and the two battle lines were immediately engaged. In these operations, our front line, formed as on the preceding evening, steadily advanced, supported by two other lines, composed of the two remaining divisions of Hooker's corps. The enemy had placed heavy pieces of artillery to defend this point; but as our lines advanced the rebel artillery retired, while, on the contrary, our batteries, advancing with the infantry, took up new positions as they went. Ricketts' division pushed forward to the left of Seymour's Brigade, while Doubleday's advanced in front of the position which had been occupied by Magilton and Anderson on the previous evening. Thus Seymour's Brigade was detached on the right, and the other two brigades of Meade's division were led forward by their commanders between Ricketts' and Doubleday's divisions. Our troops fought with determined bravery for several hours, drove the enemy from the ground he occupied at first, advanced through the thin belts of woods over the ploughed, corn, and clover fields beyond, slaughtered the rebel regiments in a fearful style, and captured a large number of their colors. Ricketts' division advanced to the support of Seymour's Brigade, and fought with vigor. After the men had been hotly engaged, and expended their ammunition, they returned to replen-plenish their cartridge-boxes, and while doing so Ricketts' division pushed forward and delivered a fresh volley in the enemy's front. Duryea's Brigade was on its right, Hartsuff's a little in advance, on the left, and Christian's, consisting of Jones's Brigade, was placed in the rear as a reserve: Thompson's and Matthews' batteries of rifled guns wheeled into position between Duryea and Hartsuff.

The sun had scarcely risen before the whole division was participating in the bloody fight—the enemy returning our fire with considerable effect. Through the corn-field the enemy advanced in considerable force, with eight or nine colors flying, in line of battle. It was a splendid sight to see their long and steady line, the men moving among the high stalks of corn, the bayonets glistening above the ears, and the battle-flags floating over all. The whole division fought in gallant style, and equal bravery and valor were displayed by the rebel troops. The firing was terrific at this time, and the ground (especially the corn-field), after the battle, told how severe the contest had been. The rebels succeeded in killing a number of gunners at one of the batteries. The remnant of Duryea's Brigade, which was still fighting in the corn-field on the right, took up a new position, a little in the rear of a ledge of rocks, and kept up a continuous cross-fire, preventing the enemy from carrying off the guns. Early in the engagement, both Hartsuff's and Christian's brigades were under fire, and poured destructive volleys into the enemy's ranks. General Hartsuff was wounded in the side by a rebel sharpshooter. The command of his brigade devolved on Colonel Coulter, of the 11th Pennsylvania Volunteers. Our wounded, as fast as they fell, were carried to the rear, and without delay put into an ambulance, to be carried to the hospitals we had established, and were promptly cared for. The fight was raging furiously all this time, with great destruction to both sides. As the right flank could be easier turned by the enemy, it was the most important point to hold. It was consequently of much importance to General McClellan and General Hooker to provide for its protection and defence by our troops. The enemy was observed to be massing large bodies in that direction, and he subsequently tried to drive us from our position at that point; but the attempt was gallantly repelled, and proved entirely ineffectual. All the brigades in each of the divisions here engaged suffered severely. General Ricketts' had his horse shot under him, but himself escaped injury. A similar accident happened to General Duryea. His brother, Captain Duryea, was severely wounded. Many of the other staff-officers had their horses shot. But one field-officer of this brigade escaped injury; and of the four regiments which went into the fight, two hundred men could not he mustered on the following morning. Other brigades of this division suffered in like manner, which will give the reader some idea of the fierceness of the conflict at this point. When the rebel battery suddenly opened in the morning, at the commencement of the action, Doubleday's division, composed of Patrick's, Phelps', and Gibbons' brigades, was within a few hundred yards of it, and suffered severely. The rebels appeared to be short of ammunition, as they threw solid shot where shell would have been more destructive. One of their shells, thrown as Gibbons' Brigade was getting into motion, exploded among the 6th Wisconsin regiment, killing and wounding several of Company A. This brigade preceded the other two, all of which went into action in regular line of battle, supported by Doubleday's old brigade, under

Lieutenant-colonel Hoffman. As General Hatch had been wounded at South Mountain, Colonel Phelps commanded his brigade.

The ground was obstinately contested by the enemy. The rebels in large force, supported by strong reserves, were driven nearly a mile beyond their original position, by the right wing, in which Doubleday's division participated. At the close of the action, not more than sixty men out of one of the brigades could be mustered, but many have come in since. Among the regiments especially commended for their splendid conduct, was the Brooklyn 14th, which behaved in the most gallant manner, and suffered severely. General Gibbons' Brigade moved up in column, and deployed in line into the woods. General Patrick's Brigade came up immediately, and formed on the right, in support of Gibbons'. The brigade commanded by Colonel Phelps formed partly on the left and partly on the right, as reserves. The fire in front of Gibbons' Brigade was fearful, but the troops held their ground until more than half the officers and men were killed and wounded. They were then relieved by General Patrick, and retired to the foot of the hill, where they re-formed for future action. After getting into the woods, at the commencement of the fight, where the action was severest, in moving to the front, an enfilading fire of the enemy did considerable execution among Col. Phelps' men. They returned it with vigor and effect; but in order to escape the dreadful consequences of a flanking fire, the brigade changed its front, and filed off under a ledge of rocks on the right of the wood, and fought in that position, near where the troops who had come from the front were reorganizing, until all the ammunition was expended but nine or ten rounds. At the same time the fire of the enemy was tremendous, and other troops were wavering in front. General Hooker had given instructions to hold that position, at whatever cost. General Hatch's Brigade was pushed forward to the front, and became engaged, and a fresh line of reinforcements sweeping up, poured a regular fire into the rebels, who soon retired, and left us master of that portion of the field. For a moment it seemed as if we must entirely relinquish the ground which had been taken so bravely on the right the night before; but, just at that critical moment, reinforcements came to our relief. This had the effect to reanimate the troops, whose ranks had become so terribly decimated, and several regiments which were reorganizing, although they had not been replenished with ammunition, dashed into the fight behind the reinforcements, and fought until they had expended every round. In this encounter on the right, a large number of flags were taken. General Patrick's Brigade has five of the battle-flags, one for each of his regiments, and a spare one for a battery of artillery. As our victorious troops crossed over a hill, they suddenly came upon a mass of rebels five or six thousand strong, in the hollow. This rebel force had been quietly awaiting just such an opportunity as was now presented. They immediately arose, and poured in some murderous volleys, and, with flashing guns and fixed bayonets, stood like a wall of fire and steel before our men, whom they drove back a considerable distance, to the corn-field, where such fearful execution had been done among the rebels at an earlier stage of the contest.

At this important moment Captain Campbell's battery opened on the rebels with double-case and canister, at close range, and mowed them down in heaps in that fatal corn-field. At the same time a portion of the division came upon the enemy's flank, and the enfilading fire from our artillery and infantry was more than they could stand. They fled in considerable confusion, and although they had driven us back from the ground which we had taken, we still held the position where the fighting had commenced in the morning. Captain Campbell was severely wounded in the shoulder. After this encounter, the command was relieved by General Sumner's corps. Lieutenant Haskell, of General Gibbons' staff, while riding in the corn-field, returning from delivering an order, came across a corporal in the 2d Wisconsin regiment. The corporal was badly wounded. The lieutenant asked him how he came by such an ugly wound in his breast, "was it a piece of shell that hit you?" The dying corporal feebly replied, "No, I was wounded first by a musket-ball, and afterwards a rebel thrust a bayonet into my breast."

It is impossible to estimate, with any degree of accuracy, the number of our losses or those of the enemy. It is certain that no harder fighting was ever seen on this continent—not even in the bloody battles of the Peninsula. One or two instances, in this connection, will be sufficient to illustrate the fearful character of the contest. That of General Duryea's Brigade, as previously mentioned, is one. The 2d regiment of the United States Sharp-shooters, which had been reduced by death and sickness to one hundred and twenty men, lost over one half their number, among them Colonel Post and Adjutant Parmalee. The regiment is now reduced to a number less than a single company, and is commanded by Captain Stoughton, the only captain remaining on the field after the fight. Five captains are now on the sick-list, and were absent in the hospital. The ranks of the Brooklyn 14th were also greatly thinned.

Rather early in the action Gen. Hooker was wounded in the foot by a musket-ball. It was a matter of sincere regret to this gallant general that he was compelled to relinquish his seat in the saddle,—and was not vouchsafed the privilege of leading his men in the consummation of the great work which had been assigned him in the morning. Gen. Hooker is a soldier in the fullest sense of that military term. Of commanding form, and pleasing features, he presents a fine appearance on the field. He has with him nearly all of his excellent staff-officers, and has retained Major Myers, Captains Sanderson and Houston, and Dr. Magruder, of McDowell's staff; and, as an additional aid, has appointed Captain Moore, of the Italian army, who is here on leave of absence from Victor Emanuel, and who served with the lamented General Kearney in European battles, and in all the battles of Virginia, up to the moment of the death of that regretted general. General Hooker's wound is painful, though not dangerous. He says he would have been willing to have compromised with a mortal wound at night, and died a soldier's death at the conclusion of the action, could he have remained with his command all day. He had eight orderlies shot during the progress of the battle.

The army corps which had been under General Banks before he was directed to take charge of the defences about Washington, was assigned to the venerable General Mansfield. It consists of two divisions commanded by Generals Williams and Green. The corps advanced to the scene of action in close columns of companies, arriving on the field about a couple of hours after the battle was begun. General Williams' division occupied the right, and General Green's the left, when the command was formed in line. The battle was raging fiercely on the right, when this corps came up. With commendable alacrity the divisions were placed in positions ready to push into the contest. Hooker's men were fighting bravely and losing heavily, and assistance was required. Rapidly the regiments wheeled into position and deployed into line. General Mansfield was mortally wounded while directing their formation. A rebel sharp-shooter seeing him mounted in front, within range of an excellent rifle, and evidently perceiving also, from his venerable appearance, that he was a general officer, took deliberate aim and shot him down. The general fell, mortally wounded in the breast, and was carried from the field before his command became engaged in the important operations of the day, in which the corps bore no inconsiderable part. General Williams being senior officer, assumed command of the corps, and General Gordon, till then commanding a brigade, took charge of his division. The corps was formed in battle order in the rear of General Hooker, and relieved a portion of that officer's brave, but decimated regiments. General Williams' division was deployed with Crawford's Brigade on the right, and Gordon's on the left and centre. This is a small command, there being only two brigades in the division. These two brigades went right into the contest, pushed through the woods and met the enemy, still fighting furiously and in full force. The division, though small, bore not a little of the brunt of the enemy's retaliatory attack upon Hooker, and in turn helped to fill the corn-field and the surrounding fields with dead and wounded rebels, which were subsequently found there. Changing position, rendered desirable by the movements of the enemy, this division fought with distinguished valor, and held the position they had taken up, until subsequently relieved by some of the fresh troops, who were led by General Sumner. They were warmly engaged on the left of the hard-fighting previously described, and shared a portion of it. They fought side by side with other victorious troops under the command of Hooker.

General Green's division, which is better known as General Augur's, was divided before going into action. It is composed of General Geary's old brigade, commanded by Lieutenant-colonel Tyndale of the 28th Pennsylvania regiment; General Prince's old brigade (General Prince who was taken prisoner at Cedar Mountain), commanded by Colonel Steinrook of the 109th Pennsylvania; and General Green's Brigade, commanded, after Mansfield fell (and the other changes in consequence), by Colonel Goodrich. This brave and gallant colonel, however, was, like the venerable General Mansfield, killed at his post by a musket-ball, at the commencement of the fight, and the command of the brigade devolved upon a subordinate officer. The division was brought into the thickest of the battle, on the left of General Williams; the 3d brigade, under the lamented Colonel Goodrich, having been placed by General Williams on the right. The other two brigades at first were posted as supports to the 3d Rhode Island battery. The battery was placed in position in front of a small (Dunkard's) church. The guns, apparently without much infantry support, at first presented a tempting offer as trophies to the enemy, and consequently a large force of the rebels soon advanced in splendid style, firing on the gunners as they came, apparently determined to capture them. But as they came within convenient distance, they soon found, to their sorrow, that these two brigades of General Green's division had, in the mean time, been getting into position, and had formed on a line to the right and left of the Rhode Island battery. The rebels came from the woods in splendid style, as mentioned, and were met not only by the galling fire of the artillery itself, but by a simultaneous fire of the infantry, which until then was unperceived by them. It is comparatively an easy undertaking for a large body of soldiers to capture a battery of artillery, however quick its fire, if undefended by infantry, because the advancing line soon shoot down the horses and the gunners; but it is quite another thing to capture guns, and carry them from the field, when they are well supported by infantry. And so, in the present instance, were these Rhode Island guns defended. The rebels were driven back into the woods, when our infantry then advanced, drove them out of it, and occupied the woods themselves. The battery then wheeled to the left, and poured in a most destructive fire upon their retreating lines, and upon other rebel troops appearing on the left. The 27th Indiana regiment, which had been sent to participate in the last-mentioned operation, fired fast, and was compelled to retire before some of the other regiments because the men had expended all their ammunition.

The 13th New Jersey regiment, which was present on a similar service, did excellent execution, and remained in the woods till the command retired. The rebel battery had been compelled to retreat—the gunners leaving limbers behind. This position was held for a full hour, until, at nearly noon, the rebels came out in tremendous force in front of Gen. Howard's command, of Sumner's corps, which had already got into action further to the left; and General Green's being partially outflanked, and subjected to a disastrous enfilading fire, was compelled to withdraw from the woods about a quarter of a mile, and did not actively participate in the action during the remainder of the afternoon. Six flags were captured by this division, which are held by the regiment that took them. Indeed there is scarcely a brigade, which was actively engaged, along the lines, that did not capture some of the enemy's colors, and wear them in triumph from the field. I have stated that Colonel Goodrich, commanding a brigade, was killed early in the action. It is also my painful duty to state that among many other noble fellows who fell during the battle, Lieutenant-colonel Tyndale, who was likewise commanding a brigade, was wounded near the close of the engagement. The corps was fiercely engaged for four or five hours, and lost a number of its best officers and men; in return for which, the satisfaction to be mentioned is, that more than corresponding numbers of the enemy were stricken to the ground. The corps, shattered but not disorganized, remained in front until relieved by a portion of General Franklin's command in the afternoon. A considerable portion of the hard fighting of the day was done by the troops under the command of General Sumner. Before coming on the field of action, he had under his command, as senior officer, his own and General Mansfield's corps,—two veteran commanders, and who fought near the same portion of the field whereon the latter fell with a mortal wound. Previous to the present engagement, as will have been perceived, General Mansfield's corps had been detached for temporary service with General Hooker, who had command of the right wing of our army, while Sumner had the centre. Hooker, who had opened the battle early in the morning, had been fighting some hours, with his whole command, before General Sumner received his orders to bring his troops to the front. It was nearly eight o'clock when he was directed to cross the Antietam with his corps and push forward into the engagement. The order was obeyed with promptitude. General Sumner himself, by his personal presence keeping his columns well closed up, and after his lines were formed urging them forward to the front. The corps came upon the field in three lines, Sedgwick's division on the right, French's on the left, Richardson's considerably in the rear, and went into action on the left of General Hooker's. General Sumner on arriving on the field found General Hooker wounded, and his command being pressed back by superior numbers. As the corps advanced—in three division lines—so the first division (General Sedgwick's) went into the battle, in three brigade lines, General Gorman's Brigade constituting the first, General Dana's the second, and General Howard's the third. They formed in rear of the position occupied by Hooker on the evening previous, and then marched up to about a hundred paces apart, where they were brought under the enemy's fire. When these troops had been placed in position, it was perceived that the enemy had been fast extending his line of battle to his right—our left; and a gap existed, where he was coming in heavy force to flank General Hooker's left, while we had no troops there to oppose him. When General Sedgwick became acquainted with the position of matters in his immediate front, he ordered the 34th New York regiment to march, by the left flank, to meet this flanking force of the enemy. During this movement the regiment was exposed to a double fire, receiving it both on the flank and front. This unexpected greeting, before it had formed into position, had a very disastrous effect. The regiment immediately broke, and the consequence was, that the first line retired in confusion to the rear, carrying the second line away with it. The mass of fugitive soldiers, falling on the third line, had almost the effect of breaking it also, and scattering the whole division in confusion over the field. A portion of Baxter's Zouaves, in the third line, did break; but the remainder of the regiment, and of the brigade, held its ground and met the onslaught of the enemy. The officers did all that mortal men could do to reorganize the terrified troops and put them forward in their positions, but the force of the enemy was tremendous. Captain Howe and Lieutenant Whittier, of General Sedgwick's staff, were prominent among those who attempted to rally them. They succeeded in rallying a portion of the 34th, and re-establishing it in action; but it had already lost many of its choicest officers. The remnant of the 34th was rallied around its colors and conducted to the front, on the left of Howard's Brigade. General Sedgwick was wounded while gallantly urging the men in his division to fearlessly face the foe—no matter though the rebels came with such superior numbers. At the time he was shot he was far in the advance—right in the thickest of the battle—close by his forward line. He was wounded in two places, one striking his wrist, the other his neck. Reluctant to leave the field, he remained two hours after he was wounded, when he was taken off, and the gallant General Howard, who lost an arm in the battle of Fair Oaks, assumed command of the division. Major Sedgwick, assistant adjutant-general, and nephew of Gen. Sedgwick, was seriously, and it is believed, mortally wounded. Gen. Sumner was one of the prominent personages on the field. Though he is a veteran commander, the weight of years seems to rest lightly upon him. The vicissitudes of a campaign do not inconvenience him, and he came upon the field, apparently, with all the vigor of more youthful generals. Accompanied by his staff officers, he was in the hottest of the fight, conducting himself in the most commendable manner, and succeeded in rallying those who had become disorganized.

General Dana was slightly wounded at the head of his brigade, when the fearful front and enfilading fire of the enemy caused our lines to waver. The wound, however, is not dangerous. It is a flesh wound in the leg by a musket-ball, and the general hopes to assume command of his brigade again before the present campaign is ended. The command was ordered to retire to the piece of woods in front of which it had been fighting.

In obedience to the order of General Sumner, General Sedgwick's division fell back and reorganized in the woods, about three hundred yards to the rear, where the line of battle was formed again. The division, however, performed little efficient service after that. While it was re-forming in the edge of the woods, Capt. Kirby's battery came up, and Gen. Sedgwick, after he was wounded, placed it in position. The battery opened a sharp fire with spherical case-shot, effectually driving back a force of the enemy which was seen advancing. Kirby's battery was supported by the 125th Pennsylvania Volunteers; so that the enemy did not attempt to take it. Simpson's and Hooper's batteries, which were in position on the brow of an adjacent hill, opened on a brigade of rebels that was fast bearing down towards General Sumner's right. The nature of the country gave full sweep to the artillery, and the rebels retired before its raking fire. These troops were subsequently relieved by General Franklin's corps. The loss was heavy,—as it is a fixed principle, that when troops falter before a fire, though ever so fearful, their loss is greater than if they stood by their colors and fought bravely, no matter how numerous the foe, until support arrives. Colonel Wistar, who lost the use of his right arm at Ball's Bluff, was wounded in the other yesterday; amputation will, probably, be necessary. In the Fifteenth

Massachusetts regiment nine officers were killed and wounded, out of seventeen on duty. Company E went into the battle with forty-three men, out of which number five were killed and twenty-three were wounded. The colors are always tenaciously guarded by their bearers; and when one color-bearer is shot down and the colors fall, another man immediately grasps them, lifts them to the breeze, and carries them either till he is stricken down to the earth himself, or bears them triumphantly from the field. An interesting instance of this kind occurred in the battle of yesterday. The color-sergeant of the 15th Massachusetts regiment was shot dead; he fell with the colors in his hand. The flag was instantly caught by his comrade, who, sad to say, had scarcely raised them in the line, when a bullet killed him also, and again the colors fell. A third time they were raised; and were carried from the field when the regiment retired.

One interesting incident was quite observable on the rebel side. Our troops had broken the enemy's line, stricken down the rebel flag, and were steadily advancing over the disputed ground. The rebel color-bearer had fallen mortally wounded. As he fell, he caught the colors which were falling from his hands, and grasped them tightly with his fast-failing strength to his bosom. Another rebel took them from the dying man, and bore them off. Numerous instances of similar devotion and bravery were found on either side. General French's division, which had just been organized as a part of General Sumner's corps, is composed of General Kimball's veterans, a brigade of raw recruits under Colonel Morris, and Max Weber's splendid command. When the heavy firing had been heard in front, Sedgwick's and French's divisions marched in parallel columns across the Antietam creek,—

Richardson's division not crossing for nearly an hour afterwards. French formed his division in three lines on the left of Sedgwick's. General Max Weber's fine brigade formed the first line; the new troops under Colonel Morris, the middle line; and General Kimball's command, the last. Thus the new troops were placed between two brigades of splendid disciplined soldiers. The right of this division's line rested on a fine plantation, with its group of houses in the hollow. Each line was over half a mile in length, and about fifty yards from the other. The lines of the two divisions moved forward almost simultaneously, until they encountered the vast force of the enemy, which immediately opened with artillery and infantry. None of our artillery in front of this division had got into position, and the infantry performed alone the important service which followed. Our troops moved forward from the ravine or hollow, up the rising ground, for the purpose of carrying the crest of the hill upon which the enemy was posted. They moved rapidly at first; but the fire was so fearful in front of General Sedgwick, that the left of his line retired (it will be remembered), leaving a wide gap on the right of General French's.

He pushed forward a regiment from Kimball's Brigade, to prevent the left flank being turned. Changing front towards the right, General French met the enemy, who was advancing through the gap, and engaged him, while Richardson's division went into action. The Irish Brigade was sent forward, and, with an impetuosity which cost many lives, gained the crest. Colonel Burk's Brigade now assisted in driving the enemy away. General Max Weber was wounded in this encounter. General Richardson's division, as before stated, got into action, and bore the brunt of the enemy's attempt to cut our line. The divi sion deployed into line of battle by brigades. Meagher's took the lead to the right, Caldwell's followed, and Burk's came last. When they arrived on the ground, the enemy were engaged with French's division, in the ploughed field in the hollow. General Richardson was wounded while personally directing the movements of the division. The Irish Brigade was ordered to charge up the hill, the 69th and 29th New York to charge the enemy's column on the right, and the 88th and 63d New York to charge on the left. The two former regiments obeyed in gallant style, but Lieutenant-colonel Kelly, of the 69th, being wounded in the face, they faltered, but continued an unbroken fire on the enemy from the ascending ground on which they halted. The other brigades of this division participated in this attack, driving in the enemy's column. General Meagher's horse was shot under him. General Richardson was wounded, while near one of the batteries, by a piece of shell, in the shoulder. He was taken to the same house where General Hooker lay. General Hancock, by order of General McClellan, assumed the command of the division until the close of the battle. General Franklin's corps, as stated, marched from Crampton's Gap, and arrived while the battle was raging, and went into action without delay, doing good service, and slept on the battle-field. General Fitz-John Porter's corps was but slightly engaged. The corps of General Burnside performed an important part in the battle, having had to encounter the most determined opposition in successfully executing that part of General McClellan's plan to which it was assigned. Being distant from that part of the field, I can give but a general outline of its operations. Antietam creek lay between General Burnside's forces and the enemy, who were strongly posted in a favorable position on the oppo site side. It was necessary to cross the creek, and dislodge the enemy. The stream is spanned by a stone bridge, which joins the turnpike. It was well defended by the rebel infantry and artillery, and after two bloody and unsuccessful attempts to cross it, which cost us many lives, a third and successful one was made, and the enemy driven from his position on the other side. This, the crowning feat of the day's victory, was soon followed by simultaneous shelling along our line, and our troops driving the enemy before them from all their strongholds. The enemy were now, under cover of a heavy artillery fire, endeavoring to push forward on the left a large body of their skirmishers, followed by three columns, but our batteries in front kept them back. At this time, several farm-houses were set on fire by the shells, and added to the exciting scene. Burnside's corps, assisted by the batteries on the hills, was successful; and the rebels, driven on the right centre and left by our advancing columns, plainly told that the battle of Antietam was won by the Union arms, under the able direction of General McClellan, who, during the entire day, with indefatigable energy, personally guided the various movements, riding to and fro, now rallying this point, then another, and leaving nothing to chance. He inspired, by his presence and sagacity, his brave men, who, in turn, stood by him, in this, their bloodiest battle, and added the name of Antietam to the long list of victories to which he had led them. Next morning the battlefield presented a scene of carnage and struggle that baffles description. During the whole night the wounded were being searched for, and continued to arrive at the temporary hospitals. To-day the burying of the dead will be attended to.

CHAPTER XXVI.

THE REBELS RECROSS THE POTOMAC.

The rebel army has succeeded in making its escape from Maryland. They commenced to leave about dusk, on the 18th of September, and by daylight, yesterday morning, were all over except a small rear-guard. They saved all their transportation, and carried off all their wounded but about three hundred. General Pleasanton's cavalry, who led the advance of the Union forces, picked up between three and four hundred rebel stragglers. After our forces occupied the whole field, the rebel loss was found to be far greater—particularly in killed—than was at first supposed. Fully two thousand five hundred were found lying on the field, though a larger number had been buried the day before by their friends. This will make their total loss, in killed and wounded, nearly twelve thousand. Large details were made this morning to bury the dead, which have become offensive. General Stark, of the rebel army, is reported killed, and Generals Ripley, Walker, and Hayes were wounded. The rebels, on Thursday night, burned the railroad bridge and several houses at Harper's Ferry. They are still visible on the opposite shore, in force. They have posted a large amount of artillery to prevent our troops from crossing the river. Nearly every house in Sharpsburg was struck by our shells. Two were burned, and also a large barn located in the centre of the town. The citizens who remained escaped injury by staying in their cellars. One child was killed. Some of the rebels were also killed while cooking in a kitchen.

Movements of the Army, after the Enemy recrossea the Potomac.

Early this morning some rebel cannon were to be seen on the opposite bank of the Potomac, to the left of Shepherdstown. A few gunners were the only men visible. A reconnoissance was ordered. The 4th Michigan, Colonel Childs, and portions of the 62d and 118th Pennsylvania regiments, were ordered across on a tour of observation, accompanied by Griffin's battery, under command of Lieutenant Naslett. The 4th Michigan took the lead, and right gallantly they led the way, in the face of the enemy's frowning guns belching grape and canister. Unflinchingly they plunged into the stream, and forded its dangerous waters, not unlike as they forded the Chickahominy, near New Market bridge, in face of Semmes' whole rebel brigade. During the passage over, one private was killed, and Lieutenant Gordon, company I, and eight privates, wounded. Our men poured a terrific volley of musketry into the rebels, which made them run, leaving their dead and guns on the field. They took possession of the four guns, and recrossed the stream. No rebels were now discernible, and the coast seemed clear. Forthwith, General Martindale's Brigade, Colonel Barnes commanding, consisting of the 18th Massachusetts, 2d Maine, 25th and 13th New York, and 118th Pennsylvania regiments, with the 5th and 10th New York, of Sykes' division, were thrown across the river. As these men were allowed to land undisturbed, it increased the conviction that the enemy was making a hasty retreat into the interior of Virginia. The 3d Indiana cavalry, of General Pleasanton's Brigade, was the only cavalry that succeeded in crossing,—the enemy having suddenly opened a cannonade of shot and shel' upon the remaining regiments, that proved tòo warm a reception, and obliged them to return to the Maryland shore. The principal portion of the day's work now commenced—a brief but spirited battle, in which a small force of our men fought valiantly against a superior number. The enemy began to show himself in unexpected strength, and could now be seen in line of battle as far as the eye, aided with a glass, could extend, on the left of Shepherdstown. It was the duty of our men to stand their ground until beaten or ordered to retreat, and they stood most nobly. The enemy came down on them like an avalanche. The sharp crack of musketry, and the rising smoke, betokened that a battle had begun. Seeing the perilous position of our men, Robertson's, Gibson's, Benson's, and Tidball's United States artillery, took positions on this side, and poured shell and solid shot at a furious rate into the enemy's ranks. But few shots were received in exchange. Our men remained on the other side several hours, although actual firing was kept up but little over half an hour. When the order to recross to the Maryland side was given, our men came back in excellent order, notwithstanding the enemy kept up a continuous fire. Our muskets and artillery had played fearful havoc among the enemy, and our troops had the consolation of knowing that they have left more rebel dead and wounded on the field than of our own. A number of our men were taken prisoners. They belong principally to the 118th Pennsylvania, now in the field. Through some mistake, they took the wrong road on the retreat. They fought with great bravery, and received the commendations of their commanders. Colonel Provost received a severe but not dangerous wound in the side, while carrying the colors of the regiment. The men of all the regiments engaged behaved splendidly. They have suffered heavily. While the battle raged, a woman crossed the river, and imparted to General Morrell information as to the position of the enemy, and stated that they were marching towards our army with the intention of entrapping us.

There has come a lull, in which the contending armies are lying quietly, with the Potomac between them, awaiting developments which will probably ere long bring them into collision; but neither will unadvisedly renew the contest, without exhausting all the precaution which their leaders' skill can suggest.

The battle-field of Wednesday is daily explored by an army of relic-hunters from all parts of the country, who have nearly cleared off all material evidence of the fight. The dead have all been buried, except some poor fellows who in their last hours of agony crawled to a secluded spot or shady corner, and whose bodies escaped the burial parties. Their whereabouts is now easily detected by the intolerable effluvia from their fast-decomposing remains.

I mentioned, in a former chapter, the marked improvement in the surgeons attached to the army in contrast with their inefficiency at the commencement of the rebellion. I cannot with justice avoid alluding to it again. After the battle of Antietam the wounded were more promptly and properly cared for than ever before, notwithstanding the large number to be provided for. This is owing, in a great measure, to the beneficial change in the ambulance service, which, under the efficient management of Lieutenant Dunkelberger, of the 1st United States cavalry, has become more prompt in the discovery and conveyance of the wounded. The surgeons also are more energetic and capable, and the hospital supplies are obtained with less delay and circumlocution than before. These changes, which have been so long and hitherto fruitlessly urged on the surgeon-general, have been produced by the co-operation of the surgeons with the medical inspectors—Drs. Cuyler and Cooledge materially aiding the good work. The Sanitary Commission has also borne a large share of the expense and labor. Its assistants, and the liberal distribution of its clothing and supplies, have again alleviated the sufferings of hundreds. Too much praise cannot be bestowed on this great and good institution. In it the people have a safe and efficient channel for the dispensation of its contributions. The untiring and faithful exertions of the secretary, general agent, and volunteers of the Commission, are a sure guaranty that no wasteful or improper use will be made of the means placed at their disposal. The wounded have been all recovered. Those who were able to bear the journey have been sent to Hagerstown, Chambersburg, Harrisburg, and other places. The worst cases we have placed in the houses and barns in the vicinity of the battle-field, which have been fitted up as temporary hospitals.

Dr. Muir, Medical Inspector-general of the British army, was here on the field. He has witnessed some of our operations and the preparations made for the wounded. Their extent and completeness has called forth his praise. His opinion, in such matters, is entitled to the highest respect from his large and varied experience in the Crimea and East Indies, and the thoroughly organized and well-known efficiency of the surgical department of the British army. Dr. Muir made many valuable suggestions, prominent among which he advised the organizing, under a competent head, of the female nurses, who should be selected between the ages of thirty and forty-five. This suggestion, which coincided with the opinions of many of the surgeons, has been since acted on; and Miss Dix, whose name has for many years been identified with the most philanthropic exertions in behalf of suffering humanity, has consented to take the supervision and management of that department, which has hitherto been a source of annoyance to all the surgeons of the army. Women from New York and other cities, of doubtful age and reputation, had succeeded in getting employed as nurses, and had abused the privileges of their ill-assumed position to plunder the poor wounded soldiers and embezzle the clothing and luxuries generously contributed by individuals and the Sanitary Commission. I can recall to mind more than one of these female harpies who, under the garb of religion and philanthropy, have robbed the dying sufferer of his hard-earned pay, sacredly hoarded and intended for his suffering family. Some of these miserable counterfeits of noble women, have been detected and exposed; but others, I regret to say, have carried on their nefarious practices with such artful and methodical secresy, as to elude detection. The day, I trust, is not far distant, when the generous and self-sacrificing attendance and almost divine sympathy, evinced by the efficient and kind anticipations of the wants of the patients, of that inestimable class of ladies—"The Sisters of Charity," will be sufficient for the wants of the hospitals; their presence in which lends a sanctity to the place, and restrains any disposition to profanity or impropriety that may exist.

The wisdom of the rebels in bringing their famished army to the beautiful Cumberland valley, and on to Harrisburg and Hagerstown, is fully proven by the rich and luxurious landscape it presents; teeming, as it is, with every production of husbandry, and its numerous and well-stocked farm-houses giving unmistakable evidence of the superabundant plenty that abounds. This also suggests the great importance of that repulse which, under the able generalship of McClellan, promptly aided by his gallant officers and men, they have sustained. Had they been permitted to remain this side of the river but a week, they would have found sufficient supplies to feed their half-starved legions for months, and would, undoubtedly, have carried out their threats of capturing Baltimore and Washington.

The head-quarters of General McClellan were moved yesterday three miles nearer to Harper's Ferry. This movement is interesting, as it is supposed to be the percursor of an advance of the army into Virginia. Harper's Ferry is is now held by a large force of our troops, as it is regarded as an important point in the position of the army. The great distance from the centre to the right wing of the army gives one an idea of the immense number of men and the amount of material that has been collected here—for 13 miles the eye never loses sight of the camps. The Virginia side of the river continues to be picketed by the enemy; while our troops do the same on this side. The pickets of both armies, by mutual consent, have abandoned the useless and murderous practice of firing on each other. A few days since a Dr. McLaughlan, of the rebel General Bradley Johnson's staff, crossed the river and gave himself up to the 8th Maryland pickets, stating that he was tired of the rebel service, and preferred being sent to Fort McHenry to serving longer in the Virginia army. Early this morning a large force of our cavalry crossed the river at Blackburn's ford. At Shepherdstown and at Shepherdstown Ferry, there are between three and four hundred wounded rebels. The former place is neutral ground; and not being occupied by either side, is visited alternately by our men and the rebel cavalry. The rebel wounded prisoners at Shepherdstown are guarded by the 91st Pennsylvania regiment. They are under the care of three rebel surgeons, and have been liberally supplied. We have done every thing in our power to make the poor fellows comfortable. Most of them are badly wounded, the greater number of them having lost a leg or arm.

I reached Harper's Ferry this noon, from Sharpsburg, and found important movements going on. Already a pontoon bridge crosses the river, and the railroad bridge—destroyed by the rebels—is being reconstructed by the railroad company, who have a large force employed upon it. Its completion at an early day is of great importance to the movements of the army,—should they advance into Virginia,—it being the only means of supplying the army, should it be necessary to make rapid marches against the enemy in its direction. Our advance is four or five miles out from the river, on the Virginia side; and in our front are two rebel brigades of Louisiana and North Carolina troops, who seem prepared to contest our further progress. A skirmish took place this morning. Our cavalry and artillery drove the enemy some distance, and captured an officer and a squad of their cavalry, who were brought to the Ferry. Preparations are now making to protect Cumberland against an attack, as it is expected the rebels will make a dash on it.

General McClellan's report to General Halleck of the battles of South Mountain and Antietam was made known to-day in the camps along the river. He estimates our loss at South Mountain, as killed, four hundred and forty-three; wounded, one thousand eight hundred and six; missing, seventy-six; making a total loss of two thousand three hundred and twenty-five. The loss at Antietam, it will be seen by the following numbers, is heavier that of any battle since the commencement of the war, though less, by considerable, than the losses in the retreat from the Chickahominy to the James river, or the Seven Days' fight. It amounts to twelve thousand four hundred and sixty-nine, divided as follows: killed, two thousand and ten; wounded, nine thousand four hundred and sixteen; missing, one thousand and forty-three. The total loss, in both battles, is fourteen thousand seven hundred and ninety-four. The immense number of wounded to be cared for—over ten thousand—nearly one half of whom required surgical operations, and all requiring care and hospital accommodation, will give the reader some idea of the amount of duty and responsibility devolving on the medical department of the army, and will show the necessity of placing at its head a man of unquestioned ability, and incorruptible integrity, who cannot be approached by parties interested in obtaining contracts for supplying the hospital stores, medicines, instruments, and appliances, the cost of which, for the last year, has exceeded twelve millions of dollars. The sinful waste of supplies at some places, and the impossibility of obtaining what has been most urgently needed for the sick and wounded at others, together with the guilty sacrifice of human life caused by the incompetency and negligence of men claiming to be surgeons, is justly charged to the governing head of the department, who from either favoritism, ignorance, or imbecility, has permitted such persons to be employed in the government service at a rate of compensation much larger than they merited; though it was, by far, too little for the competent surgeons, whose services were constantly needed. In agreeable contrast to this, I will state, that many eminent surgeons have relinquished a lucrative practice to join the army, since the commencement of the rebellion; and many surgeons justly distinguished in their several communities, volunteered after each of the great battles, and at a great sacrifice of personal convenience and pecuniary gain, rendered valuable aid to the army surgeons in the treatment of the wounded, at a time when overpowered with the overwhelming numbers requiring their aid.

October 1st, 1862.—This morning General Pleasanton crossed the river at Shepherdstown with a force of cavalry and artillery, for the purpose of making a reconnoissance in the enemy's rear, information having reached General McClellan that they were falling back from the river. He came up with their pickets beyond Shepherdstown, and drove them to Martinsburg, from which place they were soon after driven by his artillery. The greater part of the rebels are encamped between Martinsburg and Winchester. General McClellan, with General Marcy, and their staffs, visited Harper's Ferry, Bolivar, and Sandy Hook to-day, and inspected the railroad bridge across the river, which will be completed to-morrow. General Rodman, who was wounded at the battle of Antietam, died yesterday, and will be sent to Baltimore for burial.

Review of the Army by the President.

To-day the whole army are preparing for a grand review. President Lincoln has arrived, and, in company with General McClellan, is now reviewing General Burnside's corps, near the mouth of the Antietam. He will next review the corps of General Franklin, at Bakersville, and then those of Generals Porter and Reynolds. There are crowds of spectators, and the cheering of the soldiers for McClellan can be heard at a great distance. The President has also been well received, but by no means so enthusiastically as General McClellan. His proclamation, issued last month, has caused considerable discontent among the regiments or

Maryland, Virginia, Pennsylvania, New York, and the West. The President came by railroad from Washington to Harper's Ferry, where he was met by General McClellan, at General Sumner's head-quarters. After General Sumner's corps had been inspected, he rode with General McClellan, his staff, and a large number of officers, over the battle-field of Antietam. He will remain to-night at General McClellan's head-quarters, and return to Washington to-morrow, by way of Frederick. Our hospitals at Keedysville and Sharpsburg have to-day been cleared of all our wounded, but the rebel wounded still remain. We are having the vacant houses in Sharpsburg prepared for use as hospitals, as they may possibly be again required, though General Pleasanton, who has just returned from his reconnoissance, says the rebels will not again invade Maryland.

For several days there has been nothing of importance transpiring along our lines. On Saturday, October 4th, a company of the 54th Pennsylvania regiment, guarding the railroad bridge between Hancock and Cumberland, were taken prisoners by a rebel cavalry force; but while they were thus engaged, Colonel McReynold's 1st regiment of New York cavalry captured their camp, and took two pieces of artillery and several wagons and mules. Colonel Egan, of the 40th New York, and his regiment, have returned from a reconnoissance to Leesburg, where they captured a rebel wagon-train, containing supplies, tents, and the personal baggage of General Longstreet. Commanders of corps, divisions, and brigades, are to-day having read to their regiments a congratulatory order from General McClellan, for the victories of South Mountain and Antietam.—Exciting news reached us to-day, October 12th, that General Stuart, with one thousand rebel cavalry, has crossed the river above here, at Hancock, and has marched to Cham bersburg, Pennsylvania, which surrendered to him, there being no troops there. The rebels seized all the government property, carrying off clothing, etc.; they destroyed the machine shop of the Cumberland Valley railroad, and government storehouses, and took away over five hundred horses. Cavalry and infantry are being sent out to intercept the rebels, and if possible to cut them off.—A report received here to-day, October 13th, says that the rebels under Stuart are recrossing the Potomac, at Noland's ford, with over one thousand horses and other property they have captured. Their force which has thus escaped our army, it is said, numbers two thousand five hundred cavalry and four pieces of artillery. General Pleasanton, in his report of the rebel raid of last Sunday, throws the blame on General Stoneman. I learn to-day that the rebels are moving on Centreville in force.—October 16th. Our army are advancing into Virginia to-day. This morning, General Humphrey's division crossed the river at Blackburn's ford, and advanced on Shepherdstown, supported by Gen. Porter's division. They were met by the rebels, who opened a heavy fire on them. Having no artillery they retreated across the river. Part of Sumner's corps, under General Hancock, advanced on Charlestown, met the enemy at Halltown, and, after some artillery fighting, drove the enemy back, and at noon occupied Charlestown. In the afternoon they formed in line of battle near Bunker Hill, and, after some skirmishing, the rebels fell back.

Head-Quarters moved into Virginia.

General McClellan has crossed the river and reached Charlestown in the afternooon. Large reconnoitring parties continue to be sent out daily. Early this morning the cavalry force, under General Pleasanton, with four pieces of artillery, crossed the river, on the new pontoon bridge at Berlin, and proceeded to Lovettsville, in Loudon county. Soon after General Burnside commenced crossing with his corps, which has occupied nearly the whole day. To-day, October 30th, the whole army is now in motion, except Sumner's corps, and are pressing on into Virginia. General McClellan's head-quarters are at Berlin. Yesterday we had a terrible fire at Harper's Ferry, which destroyed fifteen railroad car-loads of hay and a portion of the bridge. The reports to-day represent that the rebels are in strong force between Winchester and the Potomac. General Slocum's division took possession of Leesburg without opposition. Our cavalry have been attacked and driven towards Aldee by fifteen hundred rebels under General Stuart. On Saturday General Pleasanton had an artillery fight with the rebels at Phillimont, which lasted five hours. The rebels retreated to the town of Union, which he took possession of next day. A train of cars, sent to Bull Run, was captured by the rebels, with one hundred men who accompanied it.

Our army is making advances through the gaps of the Blue Ridge mountains, hitherto held by the enemy. Our forces are in front of Ashby's Gap. General Pleasanton, commanding our cavalry, moved on Barbours, near Chester Gap, on the 5th (Nov.). On approaching the town he came up with the rebels, three thousand strong, under General Stuart. They had but one battery, which was posted on a hill, but was driven off. Salem was to-day occupied by our cavalry, under General Bayard. Stonewall Jackson occupies Chester Gap with a large rebel force. General Reynolds' corps took possession of Warrenton to-day at three o'clock. Our men found five rebel cavalry there, the rest having retreated on the arrival of our troops.

CHAPTER XXVII.

GENERAL M'CLELLAN'S REMOVAL FROM THE COMMAND OF THE ARMY OF THE POTOMAC, NOVEMBER 8, 1862.

INTENSE excitement was caused to-day, in all the camps, by the report that McClellan, their beloved commander, was relieved of the command of the Army of the Potomac, and that General Burnside had been appointed to replace him. The order was received at head-quarters last night, and was presented by Assistant adjutant-general Buckingham, in person.

General McClellan at once issued an address to his army notifying them of the change, taking a kind farewell of the men who fought and conquered with him so gallantly through his long and arduous campaign. He will leave for Trenton as soon as he can place General Burnside in full possession of his plans, and turn over to him the command of the army. This will necessarily occupy some time. The excitement in camp is intense, there is nothing else talked of, and many, very many of the best officers express a desire to quit the service; not that they have any dislike to General Burnside, for he is a universal favorite, but they feel and say, that without McClellan, the Army of the Potomac will be powerless. His name alone acts like magic on the men, and the beloved "Little Mac," who is looked upon by every soldier as the father and preserver of the Army of the Potomac, can wield an influence over them that no other general can hope to possess.

Sunday was a sad day in camp, as General McClellan took his leave of the gallant Army of the Potomac, which he loved so well and had done so much to organize; which had shared with him so many perils, and had bestowed on him so much of its confidence and esteem. He visited, one by one, the several army corps he had so often led to victory; and as he rode by, in company with General Burnside, the shattered colors of each regiment, bearing the unmistakable evidence of many hard-fought battles, were lowered in salute, while the long-continued applause of the men spoke fully their love, confidence, and esteem for McClellan, and their regret at losing him for their commander.

In the evening, the officers attached to General McClellan's head-quarters paid their respects to him in his tent, and seldom has such a scene been witnessed. One and all were stricken with grief of no ordinary kind. The love, honor, and respect entertained for him by the soldiers of his army was, if possible, exceeded by that of the officers, whose daily intercourse with him had endeared him to them. "The Army of the Potomac" was the only sentiment given. It was enough. Those few and simple words bore a meaning that required no eloquent elucidation, no lengthy dissertation to explain.

The reason assigned for the removal of General McClellan from the command of the Army of the Potomac by General Halleck, is, that he has refused to advance into Virginia. This, every one who has accompanied the army knows is false. Not a day has passed since the battle of Antietam was won, but some important movement has been made by the Union army. But General McClellan wisely allowed his weary troops to recruit their wasted energies, and, with the skill of a superior general, hesitated to lead his forces, with insufficient supplies and inadequate means of transportation, into the interior of Virginia, every foot of which had been prepared by the enemy, and on which our army had been twice before beaten. Political influence alone, or his hesitation to sacrifice his beloved army to the ignorance of the War Department, has been the cause of his removal.

And now, having accompanied my readers through the trying scenes of battle, with its varied fortunes of defeat and victory, and admonished that I have exceeded the allotted space to these imperfect, though unbiased descriptions of my campaign, I must bid them a reluctant farewell:—shall I say forever? The reply must come from my readers; for, if these pages sufficiently interest them, I will renew our relations of writer and reader, and continue the history of the Virginia campaign; in which it is my intention to give a correct list of the killed and wounded during the several battles described, from the commencement of my connection with the Army of the Potomac.

www.ingramcontent.com/pod-product-compliance
Lightning Source LLC
LaVergne TN
LVHW020233110826
845151LV00003B/911

* 9 7 8 1 4 2 5 5 3 0 3 1 0 *